MANUAL OF SEAMANSHIP

FOR

BOYS' TRAINING SHIPS

OF THE

ROYAL NAVY.

1883.

BY AUTHORITY OF THE LORDS COMMISSIONERS OF THE ADMIRALTY.

LONDON:

Printed under the Superintendence of Her Majesty's Stationery Office,

AND SOLD BY

W. CLOWES & SONS, LIMITED, 13, Charing Cross; HARRISON & SONS, 59, Pall Mall;
W. H. ALLEN & Co., 13, Waterloo Place; W. MITCHELL, 39, Charing Cross;
LONGMANS & Co., Paternoster Row; TRÜBNER & Co., 57 & 59, Ludgate Hill;
STANFORD, Charing Cross; KEGAN PAUL, TRENCH, & Co., 1, Paternoster Square;
and POTTER, 31, Poultry:
Also by GRIFFIN & Co., The Hard, Portsea; A. & C. BLACK, Edinburgh;
A. THOM & Co., Abbey Street, and E. PONSONBY, Grafton Street, Dublin.

1883.

Price Two Shillings.

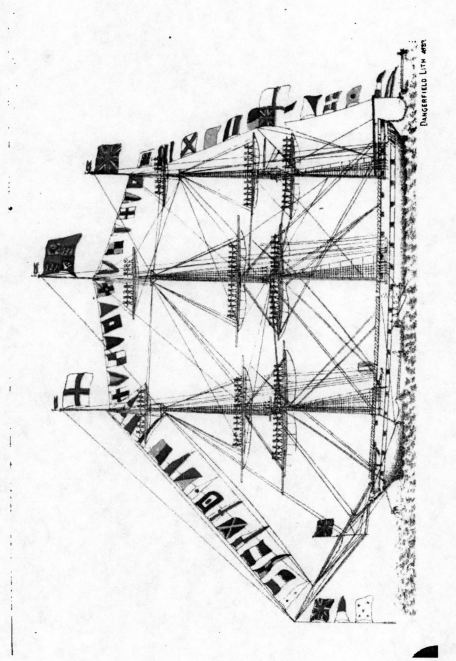

DANGERFIELD LITH

INTRODUCTORY.

DIFFERENT RIGS OF SHIPS USUALLY MET AT SEA.

SHIP.

BARQUE.

TOPSAIL SCHOONER.

FORE AND AFT SCHOONER

BRIG.

BRIGANTINE.

HERMAPHRODITE BRIG.

R 3498.   Wt. 4889.

TWO TOPSAIL SCHOONER.

A

Q. NAME the decks of a three-decked ship?

A. Ships termed in the Navy three-deckers, are so named from having three batteries or gun decks under the upper deck, but they actually have five decks, viz., upper, main, middle, lower, and orlop deck, such as the "Impregnable" and "St. Vincent" training ships for boys; the "Britannia," training ship for Naval Cadets; the "Excellent," gunnery ship at Portsmouth; and the "Duke of Wellington," receiving ship at Portsmouth.

Q. Name the decks of a two-decked ship?

A. So named from having two gun decks below the upper deck, but in reality, a ship termed a two-decker in the Navy has four decks, viz., upper, main, lower, and orlop decks, such as the "Boscawen," "Implacable," and "Ganges," training ships for boys.

Q. Name the decks of a frigate?

A. Upper, main, and lower decks; a frigate has only one gun deck below the upper deck, the main deck.

Q. Name the decks of a corvette or smaller vessel?

A. Upper and lower decks; the upper deck is the gun deck.

REGULATIONS.—TRAINING SERVICE.

SALUTES.

Touching the Hat.   Taking off the Hat.   Standing at attention.

SALUTES.

(1.) The naval salute is made by touching the hat or cap, or by taking it off, always looking the person saluted in the face. By touching the hat is meant holding the edge with forefinger and thumb, as if about to take it off, as taught in 2nd section of First Gunnery Instruction, Art. 47 (3).

(2.) In what follows the phrase "superior officers" refers to admirals, captains, commanders, and officers of similar rank, also the officer commanding the ship to which a boy belongs.

Salutes on Board Ship.

(1.) The starboard side in harbour, and the weather side at sea, is the officers' side, and the ship's company should use the opposite side, except when ordered otherwise.

(2.) When coming on the quarter deck or over the gangway, the hat is to be touched.

(3.) In addressing or being spoken to by an officer, the hat is to be taken off or touched, according to the officer's rank.

When passing an officer between decks, the hat is to be touched, using the off hand.

If standing about or sitting in his mess, a boy is to stand up, and salute if his hat is on, or stand at attention, if it is off; fronting the officer saluted until ordered to sit down.

Officers, passing a ship in a boat, should be saluted from the poop or forecastle, or other positions from which they can be seen.

Salutes on Shore.

(1.) All officers, both naval and military, in uniform, and those in plain clothes who are known to be officers, are to be saluted.

Boys, while under training, are also to salute the schoolmasters and instructors belonging to their own ship.

(2.) The salute is to be made with the off hand, looking the officer straight in the face; it should commence just before meeting the officer, and the hand should be kept to the hat till well past him.

A 2

If a boy, who is standing about, is passed by an officer, he is to front, stand at attention, and salute. The same should be done whenever addressed by an officer.

(3.) Should an officer be at a distance, so long as a boy can make out that he is an officer, he is to be saluted. It must be remembered that there is no excuse for not seeing.

(4.) When marching, or in any military formation, the salutes are given by word of command; and no movement is to be made until this is given. These salutes are laid down in the Gunnery Instructions for the Fleet.

Distinctions.

Q. How are the two watches distinguished from each other?

A. By a piece of bright red tape, sewn on the sleeve of the blue serge and a piece of blue dungaree on the sleeve of the white frock worn on the right arm by the starboard watch, and on the left arm by the port watch.

Q. Are there any other marks of distinction?

A. Yes; all above the rating of A.B. wear a badge of distinction on their left arm—viz.:

A chief petty officer: anchor and crown and wreath of oak leaf.

First-class petty officer: cross anchors and crown.

Second-class petty officer: anchor and crown.

Leading seamen: anchors.

Mark of Distinction worn by Seamen Gunners.

Gunnery instructors: a crown over cross-guns, rifle, and sword.

First-class seamen gunners: a crown over a gun.

Second-class seamen gunners: a gun.

These distinctive badges are now worn on the right arm.

All seamen of good character are now entitled to good conduct badges, of the following colours:—

On cloth	- - -	in gold.
On blue serge	- - -	in red (bright).
On white duck or drill -	-	in blue.

The distance between badges is to be three eighths of an inch.

Each watch is divided into two parts, and in large ships' companies, where there are a great number of men, it is found necessary to again divide the parts into subdivisions.

Q. In working ship, with the hands on deck, how are the watches divided?

A. The starboard watch work the starboard side of the deck, and the port watch the port side of the deck.

Q. Working ship with the watch only, how is the watch divided?

A. The first part, the starboard side of the deck, and the second part, the port side of the deck.

Q. How is the day and night divided into watches?

A. The twenty-four hours is divided into seven watches —viz., afternoon watch, from noon to 4 o'clock; first dog watch, from 4 p.m. to 6 p.m.; second dog watch, from 6 p.m. to 8 p.m.; first watch, from 8 p.m. to midnight; middle watch, from midnight to 4 a.m.; morning watch, from 4 a.m. to 8 a.m.; forenoon watch, from 8 a.m. to noon.

The dog watches, being of only two hours each, and all the other watches four hours each, is the cause of the watches changing every twenty-four hours: thus the watch that had the first watch last night, would have the middle watch to-night; by this plan, each watch has in turns eight hours on deck every other night at sea, and eight hours in their hammocks likewise, every other night.

Q. How is the time denoted on board ship?

A. By striking a bell in the following way :—

Noon or midnight, eight o'clock and four o'clock, 8 strokes of the bell.

Half-past twelve, four, or eight o'clock -	1 bell.
Half-past six in the last dog watch - -	1 bell.
One, five, and nine o'clock - -	2 bells.
Half-past one, five, and nine o'clock -	3 bells.
Half-past seven in the last dog watch -	3 bells.
Two, six, and ten o'clock - -	4 bells.
Half-past two, six, and ten o'clock -	5 bells.
Three, seven, and eleven o'clock -	6 bells.
Half-past three, seven, and eleven o'clock -	7 bells.

Thus it will be found, that the number of bells denoting the time from six to eight o'clock in the last dog watch, differs from the number of bells denoting the same hours in the morning watch, on account of commencing them again with the last dog watch.

FIRST INSTRUCTION.

SECTION I.

(1.) *Bag and Hammock.*

To be able to sling a hammock, plaiting up the ends of the nettles.

To hang a hammock up, and secure the lanyard properly.

To lash a hammock up and know the number of turns to take with the lashing ; except for night quarters, or if the fire-bell should ring.

To stop a hammock or piece of clothes on a gantline or clothesline.

To fold up each piece of clothes for stowing in a bag, and to lay out a whole kit for inspection.

To put in clothes' stops.

To fold up bed, blanket, and bed cover for inspection.

To hold a clean hammock for inspection.

To scrub a hammock and wash clothes.

To mark clothes and bedding.

To use a needle and thimble, and sew on a button.

Boys are allowed ten working days in this preliminary portion of the first section, during which time they do not attend school or other instructions. A tailor is to assist at this instruction.

To be able to sling a Hammock, plaiting up the Ends of the Nettles.

A hammock is slung by clews, which are made of nettle stuff, 24 nettles to each clew ; the nettles are middled and served in the centre to form an eye, which is secured by a seizing. In slinging a hammock care must be taken to give the centre nettles more scope than the side ones.

To hang a Hammock up, and secure the Lanyard properly.

The end of the lanyard is placed over the hammock hook, then through the eye of the clew, again over the hook, through the eye, triced up to the height required, and the end secured by two half hitches.

To lash a Hammock up and know the Number of Turns to take with the Lashing.

The number of turns taken is seven, they are passed at equal distance with a marline hitch. Before lashing a hammock up care must be taken to see that the bedding is fairly distributed over the whole length of the hammock to prevent it appearing more bulky in one part than another.

To lash a Hammock up for Night quarters, or in case of Fire.

The number of turns taken is three only, and the hammock triced up to the beams, or stowed in the nettings as ordered.

To stop a Hammock or piece of Clothes on a Gantline or Clothesline.

The hammocks are stopped to the gantline by a rolling hitch, and clothes' stops are fitted on the bight, the ends crossed above and below the clotheslines, and secured with a reef knot.

To fold up each piece of Clothes for stowing in a Bag, and to lay out a whole Kit for Inspection.

For stowing in a bag, clothes are folded up neatly, for inspection, in neat rolls of uniform size as near as possible, and secured with two stops.

To put in Clothes' Stops.

The stops are passed through the eyelet holes in the hammock, or clothes, and secured by one end being passed under the strand of the other part of the stop near the eyelet hole.

To fold up a Bed, Blanket, and Bed Cover for Inspection.

The bed is laid out flat on the deck, the blanket and bed cover folded in two, showing the name on each.

To hold a clean Hammock up for Inspection.

It is held by the two corners of one end, in front of the body in line with the chin, number uppermost.

To scrub a Hammock and wash Clothes.

Every boy should possess a good scrubbing brush, and secure, if possible, a space on deck large enough to lay the hammock flat; after scrubbing the rough of the dirt off, rinse it well in clean water, give it the final scrub and again rinse. When obtainable a hammock ought to be scrubbed with fresh water and soap.

In washing clothes, the great object is to secure a good tub and plenty of water, more especially in a training ship where there is no limit.

To mark Clothes and Bedding.

See that the type is clean, and the paint not too thick. White paint is used for marking dark clothing and black for white clothing. All frocks are marked under the collar, and trousers on the waist band.

To use a Needle and Thimble, and sew on a Button.

All boys in rotation are taught to mend their clothing under the instructions of a tailor ; boys should never forget that a stitch in time saves nine. The character of a boy can easily be told by the state of his kit.

(2.) Parts of the Ship.

To know the names of, and be able to point out, the following :—

Upper deck.	Amidships.	Forefoot.
Main deck.	Gangways.	Heel.
Middle deck.	Bow.	Rudder post.
Lower deck.	Stem.	Rudder.
Orlop deck.	Stern.	Billboard.
Quarter deck.	Quarter.	Gripe.
Forecastle.	Quarter badges.	Bends.
Waist.	Cutwater.	Counter.
Poop.	Knight heads.	Bulwarks.
Hold.	Figure head.	Waterways.
Under the half deck.	Cat heads.	Hammock nettings.
Davits.	False keel.	Bilges.
Starboard side.	Main keel.	Stern walk.
Port side.	Keelson.	Quarter gallery.

Q. Which is the upper deck ?
A. The highest deck.
Q. Which is the main deck ?
A. The next below upper deck.
Q. Which is the middle deck ?
A. The next below main deck in three-decked ships.

Q. Which is the lower deck?

A. The next below middle deck of a three-decked ship, next below main deck of a line of battle ship or frigate, and next below the upper deck of a corvette or smaller vessel.

Q. Which is the orlop deck?

A. The lowest deck in a line of battle ship formerly called the over-lop, consisting of a platform laid over the beams in the holds.

Q. Which is the quarter deck?

A. That part of the upper deck which is abaft the mainmast.

Q. Which is the forecastle?

A. A short deck raised on the fore part of the upper deck; in flush-deck ships the foremost part of the upper deck forward of the after fore-shroud or main tack block.

Q. Which is the waist?

A. That portion of the upper deck contained between the fore and main hatchways.

Q. Which is the poop?

A. A raised deck on the after part of the upper deck; a vessel is said to be pooped when a wave strikes the stern and washes on board.

Q. Which is the hold?

A. The whole interior cavity of a ship between the floors and the orlop or lower deck. The after hold lies abaft the mainmast; the fore hold is situated about the fore hatchway, and the main hold is just before the main mast.

Q. Which is the half deck?

A. After part of main deck abaft the gangway.

Q. What are davits?

A. Davits are made of wood, or iron curved at the heads, with sheaves or blocks at their upper ends, and are fitted over a vessel's stern, or on the quarter, for hoisting up and suspending boats.

Q. Which is the starboard side?

A. The right side of the ship when looking forward.

Q. Which is the port side?

A. The left side of the ship when looking forward.

Q. Which is amidships?

A. The middle of a ship whether in regard to her length between stem and stern, or in breadth between the two sides.

Q. Which are the gangways?

A. The entrances into a ship generally before the main mast.

Q. Which is the bow ?

A. The fore end of a ship.

Q. Which is the stem ?

A. The foremost piece of timber uniting the bows of a ship ; its lower end scarphs into the keel, the bowsprit resting upon its upper end. The outside of the stem is usually marked with a scale of feet and inches answering to a perpendicular from the keel, in order to ascertain the ship's draught of water forward.

Q. Which is the stern ?

A. The after part of a ship, ending in the taffrail above and the counters below.

Q. Which is the quarter ?

A. 45° abaft the beam.

Q. What are quarter badges ?

A. Carved ornaments near the stern.

Q. Which is the cutwater ?

A. The foremost part of a vessel's prow. It cuts or divides the water before reaching the bow, which would otherwise retard progress.

Q. What are knight heads ?

A. Two large oak timbers, one on each side of the stem, rising up sufficiently above it to support the bowsprit, which is fixed between them.

Q. What is a figure head ?

A. A carved bust or full length figure over the cutwater of a ship.

Q. What are cat heads ?

A. A sort of davit fitted with sheaves for reeving the cat fall, shipped on either side of the bows in a convenient place for lifting the anchor from the water's edge to the cat head in order to pass the cat head stopper.

Q. What is a false keel ?

A. An additional keel secured under the main one, to protect it should the ship happen to strike the ground.

Q. What is a main keel ?

A. The principal keel, as distinguished from the false keel, and the keelson.

Q. What is a keelson ?

A. An internal keel laid upon the middle of the floor timbers, immediately over the keel, and serving to bind altogether by means of long bolts driven from without, and clinched on the upper side of the keelson. The main keelson, in order to fit with more security upon the floor timbers, is notched opposite to each of them, and there secured by spike nails. The pieces of which it is formed are usually less in breadth and thickness than those of the keel.

Q. What is the forefoot?

A. The foremost piece of the keel, or a timber which terminates the keel at the forward extremity, and forms a rest for the lower end of the stern into which it is scarped.

Q. What is the heel?

A. The after end of a ship's keel, and the lower end of the stern post to which it is connected.

Q. What is a rudder post?

A. The aftermost perpendicular timber of a ship for suspending the rudder to, the lower end is scarphed into the keel, and the upper end into the stern frame.

Q. What is a rudder?

A. The appendage secured by pintles and braces to the rudder post, by which a vessel is steered.

Q. What is a billboard?

A. A sloping ledge on the ship's side, covered with iron, to support the fluke of the anchor.

Q. What is a gripe?

A. A gripe is generally formed by the scarph of the stem and keel. This is shaved away according to the object of making the vessel hold a better wind or have greater facility in wearing.

Q. What are bends?

A. The thickest and strongest planks on the outward part of a ship's side, between the plank streaks on which men set their feet in climbing up. They are more properly called wails. They are reckoned from the water, and are distinguished by the titles of first, second, or third bend. They are the chief strength of a ship's sides, and have the beams, knees, and foot hooks bolted to them.

Q. Where is the counter?

A. The counter is the after seat of a ship upon the water, and extends from the lower gun ports to the water line; the lower counter is arched below that line and constitutes the hollow run.

Q. What are bulwarks?

A. The planking or woodwork round a vessel above her deck, and fastened externally to the stanchions and timber ends.

Q. What are waterways?

A. Thick planking, extending all round the sides of a

ship to the deck; also forming a gutter or channel to carry the water away by means of scuppers.

Q. What are hammock nettings?

A. A place on the rail wherein the hammocks are stowed during the day.

Q. What are bilges?

A. That part of a ship near the keel that rests on the ground, if a ship's bottom is stove in, she is said to be bilged.

Q. Which is the stern walk?

A. The galleries attached to the outside part of the stern of line of battle ships and sometimes frigates.

Q. What are quarter galleries?

A. A sort of balcony with windows on the quarters of large ships.

(3.) *Ship's Fittings.*

To know the names of, and be able to point out, the following :—

Hawse holes.	Goose neck.	Cant pieces.
Chain pipes.	Fife rail.	Bulkhead.
Bitts.	Belaying pins.	Ring bolt.
Compressor.	Cleats.	Eye bolt.
Capstan.	Cavils.	Port sill.
Hatchways.	Fish davit.	Hammock cloth.
Gratings.	Bumpkin.	Companion ladder.
Combings.	Chains or channels.	Accommodation ladder.
Scuttles.	Monkey chains.	
Scuppers.	Chain plates.	Man ropes.
Manger.	Stanchions.	Wheel.
Bucklers.	Shelf piece.	Wheel ropes.
Bollards.	Knees.	Yoke or tiller.
Spider hoop.	Carlings.	

Ship's Fittings.

Q. What are hawse holes?

A. Holes cut through the bows of a ship on either side of the stem, fitted with pipes or iron linings called hawse pipes, through which the chain cables work in anchoring or weighing anchor.

Q. What are chain pipes?

A. Apertures through which chain cables pass from the chain lockers to the deck above.

Q. What are bitts?

A. A strong framework of timber round the different masts, secured by being bolted to the beams, fitted with sheaves, for topsail sheets and other ropes to lead through and belay to.

Q. What is a compressor?

A. An iron lever, one end being attached to the beams close to the chain pipes by a large iron bolt, on which it revolves, the other end being worked by a tackle, so as to stop or let the cable run out at pleasure.

Q. What is a capstan?

A. A mechanical arrangement of several pieces of timber and iron, and so constructed as to possess great power; it is used for all heavy purchases, such as weighing an anchor, or sending topmasts up, &c.

Parts of a Capstan, &c.

A Capstan

Is a mechanical arrangement of several pieces of timber and iron, and so constructed as to possess great power; it is used for all heavy purchases, such as weighing an anchor, or sending topmasts up.

Q. Name the parts of a capstan?

A. Barrel-whelps, bed, paul rim, sprocket wheel, spindle, drum-head, chocks.

Barrel

Is the principal piece of the capstan, and has a hole through its centre, in which the spindle ships.

Whelps

Are strengthing pieces of hard wood bolted to the barrel, rounded off for hawsers or any purchase to work smoothly on.

Chocks

Are pieces of wood let in at the top and bottom of the barrel to keep the whelps in place.

Bed.

The part of the deck prepared for the capstan to stand on by placing additional pieces of oak.

Pauls

Are square pieces of iron, bolted to a metal band round the lower part of the barrel, below the whelps, and are easily let down and taken up as required in working the capstan.

Paul Rim.

An iron fitment, fitted with cogs, on the deck, bolted with partners at the foot of the barrel. When the pauls are down in place, they keep the capstan from moving.

Sprocket Wheel

Is an iron band fitted with teeth round the lower part of the barrel, which enters the long links of the chain messenger in weighing anchor.

Spindle

Is an iron bar pivoted in a socket on the deck below that on which the capstan stands, passes through a metal bushed hole in the partners, up through the centre of the barrel. It is to the barrel what an axle is to a cart-wheel.

Drum Head.

A round wooden fitment on the top of the barrel, with a number of square holes at regular intervals for shipping the capstan bars in, by which means the capstan is worked. It is strengthened by two metal bands round it on top and below the holes.

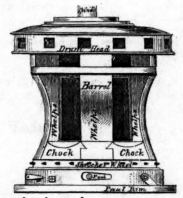

Q. What are hatchways?

A. Openings of various sizes, forming a communication, by means of ladders, from one deck to another. The top coverings to holds of ships are called hatches.

Q. What are gratings?

A. Gratings are formed by pieces of wood being nailed across a framework at right angles, leaving open apertures of certain sizes to admit light and ventilation down the hatchways. In stormy weather, tarpaulins are nailed over them, which is called battening down.

Q. What are combings?

A. A framework of timber, raised round the openings forming the hatchways, to prevent the water from running below; a rabbet is worked in their inside upper edge to receive gratings, hatches, &c.

Q. What are scuttles?

A. Holes in a ship's side to admit light and give ventilation. Circular glass illuminators in iron or brass frames are fitted, and can be screwed in or removed at pleasure.

Q. What are scuppers?

A. Holes in the waterways cut through the ship's side and lined with lead or iron, to free the deck of water.

Q. What is a manger?

A. A portion of the deck, within the manger board in the bows of a ship, extending athwart from side to side.

Q. What are bucklers?

A. Two pieces of wood, fitted together in the shape of a shutter, to keep the hawse plugs in their places, and prevent their being washed out at sea.

Q. What are bollards?

A. Are timber heads, for securing the anchor, hawsers, &c., &c. to; they are also on wharves and piers, for securing vessels alongside.

Bollard.

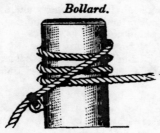

Q. What is a spider hoop?

A. A hoop round the mast to secure the shackles to which the futtock shrouds are attached, also an encircling hoop fitted with belaying pins round the mast for securing ropes.

Q. What is a goose neck?

A. A piece of iron projecting out at the yard arms of the lower and topsail yards.

Q. What is a fife rail?

A. A piece of timber with a number of sheaves and belaying pins, bolted to the ship's side or elsewhere, forming leads and securities for the running gear.

Q. What are belaying pins?

A. Pieces of hard wood, iron, or brass, fitted in the fife rails for belaying ropes.

Q. What are cleats ?

A. Cleats are made of hard wood, and bolted to the ship's side, used for belaying ropes.

Q. What are cavils ?

A. Large cleats for belaying the fore and main tacks, &c., &c.

Q. What is a fish davit ?

A. A large piece of timber, fitted with a double block over the head, for reeving the fish fall through. It tends to keep the flukes of the anchor clear of the ship's side in fishing the anchor, the lower end rests in a shoe in the fore chains, the upper end is supported by topping lift and guys.

Q. What are bumpkins ?

A. Spars, projecting from the bows for hauling the fore-tack down to.

Q. What are chains or channels ?

A. They are platforms bolted to the outside of a ship, near the upper deck, to receive the dead eyes for setting up lower rigging.

Q. What are monkey chains ?

A. Small chains abaft the ordinary chains, on which are secured the topgallant and royal backstays.

Q. What are chain plates ?

A. They are plates of iron bolted to the ship's side underneath the channels. Long links attached to them are led up through the channels ; to these links the dead eyes are secured.

Q. What are stanchions ?

A. Fixed pieces of wood or iron used for strength and support in a variety of ways, in different parts of the ship.

Q. What are the shelf pieces ?

A. Strakes of plank running in a line with the decks inside a ship, for receiving the ends of the beams. They are also called stringers.

Q. What are knees ?

A. There are various kinds of knees ; beam knees are those which secure the shelf pieces to the ship's side ; standard knees have one arm bolted to the deck, the other in an upright position to the ship's side ; they are made of iron.

Q. What are carlings ?

A. Pieces of timber lying fore and aft, to connect the beams together, to which they are let in. They are about 6 ins. square, and are so placed as to prevent the strain of the different fitments on the deck coming more on one beam than another.

Q. What are cant pieces ?

A. They are pieces of timber canted from the keel. The upper ends of those on the bow are inclined to the stem, while those in the after part incline to the stern post above.

Q. What are bulkheads ?

A. Partitions, both movable and fixed, built up in various parts of a ship to form cabins, &c., or to separate one portion of the deck from another.

Q. What are ringbolts ?

A. An eye bolt driven into the deck, or elsewhere, with a ring through the eye.

Q. What are eye bolts ?

A. Bolts which have an eye in one end, driven into ship's side and elsewhere, to hook tackles, &c., &c.

Q. What is a port sill ?

A. Pieces of timber between the framing forming the top and bottom of a port.

Q. What are hammock cloths ?

A. Painted canvas covers secured to the outside of the nettings, and laced inboard to protect the hammocks from getting wet when stowed.

Q. What is a companion ladder ?

A. The ladder by which officers ascend to, and descend from, the quarter deck.

Q. What is an accommodation ladder ?

A. A ladder with rails and stanchions fitted outside the gangways of a ship, by which officers and visitors enter and depart.

Q. What are man ropes ?

A. Ropes attached to the stanchions of the accommodation ladder, and to the ship's side, to assist persons in getting on board.

Q. What is the wheel ?

A. A general name for the helm, by which the tiller and rudder are worked in steering the ship ; it has a barrel round which the tiller ropes or chains wind, and a wheel with spokes to assist in moving it.

Q. What are wheel ropes ?

A. Ropes made of hide, rove through a block on each side of the deck, and led round the barrel of the steering wheel. Chains also are used for this purpose.

Q. What is the yoke or tiller ?

A. A large timber beam, or iron bar, fitted on the head of the rudder, by means of which the latter is moved.

R 3498.   B

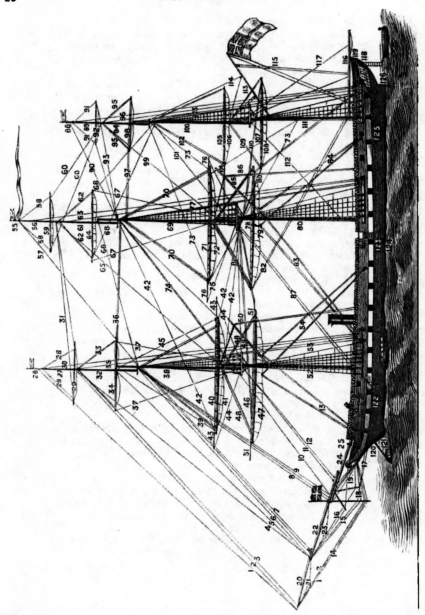

REFERENCES.

1. Fore royal stay.
2. Flying jib stay.
3.   "   halyards.
4. Fore topgallant stay.
5. Jib stay.   "   bowline.
6. " halyards.
7. " halyards.
8. Fore topmast stays.
9. Staysail halyards.
10. Fore top bowline.
11.   " stays.
12.   " bowline.
13.   " tacks.
14. Flying martingale.
15. Martingale stay.
16. Jib guys.
17. Jumper guys.
18. Back ropes.
19. Bobstays.
20. Flying jib boom.
21.   " foot ropes.
22. Jib boom.
23.   " foot ropes.
24. Bowsprit.
25.   " gammoning.
26. Fore royal truck.
27.   " mast.
28.   " lifts.
29.   " yard.
30.   " backstays.
31.   " braces.
32. Fore topgallant mast and rigging.
33. Fore topgallant lifts.
34.   " yard.

35. Fore topgallant backstays.
36.   " braces.
37.   " studding-sail halyards.
38. Fore topmast and rigging.
39. Fore topsail lift.
40.   " yard.
41.   " foot ropes.
42.   " braces.
43. Fore topgallant studding-sail boom.
44. Fore topgallant studding sail tacks.
45. Fore topsail studdingsail halyards.
46. Fore yard.
47.   " foot ropes.
48.   " lifts.
49.   " gaff.
50.   " vangs.
51. Fore topmast studding booms.
52. Fore mast and rigging.
53. Fore topmast backstays.
54. Fore sheets.
55. Main truck and pennant.
56.   " royal mast and backstay.
57.   " royal stay.
58.   " lifts.
59.   " yard.
60.   " braces.
61. Main topgallant mast and rigging.
62. Main topgallant lifts.

63. Main topgallant backstays.
64.   " yard.
65.   " stay.
66.   " bowline.
67. Main topgallant studding-sail halyards.
68. Main topgallant braces.
69. Main topmast and rigging.
70. Topsail lifts.
71.   " yard.
72.   " foot ropes.
73.   " braces.
74. Topmast stays.
75. Main topgallant studsail tacks.
76. Main topgallant studsail booms.
77. Main topmast backstay.
78.   " yard.
79.   " foot ropes.
80.   " mast and rigging.
81.   " lifts.
82.   " braces.
83.   " tacks.
84.   " sheets.
85.   " gaff.
86.   " vangs.
87.   " stays.
88. Mizen royal truck.
89. Royal mast and rigging.
90.   " stay.
91.   " lifts.
92.   " yard.
93.   " braces.

94. Mizen topgallant mast and rigging.
95.   " lifts.
96.   " backstays.
97.   " braces.
98.   " yard.
99.   " stay.
100. Mizen topmast and rigging.
101.   " stay.
102.   " lifts.
103.   " backstays.
104.   " braces.
105.   " yard.
106.   " foot ropes.
107. Crossjack yard.
108.   " foot ropes.
109.   " lifts.
110.   " braces.
111. Mizen mast and rigging.
112.   " stay.
113. Spanker gaff.
114. Peak halyards.
115.   " vangs.
116.   " boom.
117.   " topping lift.
118. Jacob's or stern ladder.
119. Spanker boom sheet.
120. Head knee.
121. Cut water.
122. Port bow.
123. Port beam.
124. Water line.
125. Port quarter.
126. Rudder.

Section II.

(1.) *Masts and Yards.*

To know the names of, and be able to point out, the following:—

Spars.	Top.	Truck.
Lower masts.	Lubber's hole.	Lightning conductor.
Top masts.	Toprim.	Heel of mast.
Topgallant and royal masts.	Toprail.	Head of mast.
	Sleepers.	Fid hole.
Trysail masts.	Bolsters.	Sheeve hole.
Bowsprit.	Rubbing paunch.	Fid.
Jib-boom.	Cap.	Preventer fid.
Flying jib-boom.	Capshore.	Lower yards.
Dolphin-striker.	Wedges.	Topsail yards.
Spritsail gaff, or whisker.	Mast coat.	Topgallant yards.
	Mast head battens.	Royal yards.
Spanker gaff.	Step of mast.	Studdingsail yards.
Trysail gaff.	Bed of the bowsprit.	Slings of a yard.
Studdingsail boom.	Bees of the bowsprit.	Quarters.
Spanker boom.	Saddle of the jib-boom.	Yardarms.
Housing.		Boom iron.
Mast head.	Saddle of the spanker boom.	Clamping, or inner boom irons.
Cheeks.		
Hounds.	Jaws (of a boom gaff).	Snatches for topgallant sheet.
Trestletrees.		
Fishes.	Spindle.	Tyebands.
Crosstrees.		

Q. What are the names of yards, masts, and spars in a full-rigged ship.

A. All spars take their names from the mast to which they belong, viz., foremast, mainmast, mizenmast, fore topmast, main topmast, mizen topmast, fore topgallant and royal mast, main topgallant and royal mast, mizen topgallant and royal mast ; the topgallant and royal mast are in one. Bowsprit, jib-boom, and flying jib-boom are the spars projecting from the bows. The lower yards are named fore and main yards, and the lower yard on the mizenmast is called the cross-jack-yard, on which no sail is set. The topsails, topgallant, and royal yards are named fore, main, or mizen, according to which mast they are attached, dolphin-striker, and spritsail-gaff on bowsprit. Topmast, studding-sail booms on fore-yard ; topgallant studding-sail booms on fore and main topsail yards ; they are seldom carried on a mizen topsail yard. Trysail masts are small masts placed abaft the lower mast to which they are attached, for the purpose of setting the spanker and fore and main trysail on. The spanker, or main boom, is the spar projecting over the taffrail, the inner part is fitted to the mizenmast in a ship, and to the mainmast in a brig, by two cleats or chocks of wood called jaws, forming a semicircle round the masts to keep them in place.

Q. What are spars ?

A. The general term for any mast, yard, boom, gaff, &c.

Q. Which are the lower masts ?

A. The fore, main, and mizenmasts.

Q. Which are the topmasts ?

A. Those directly above the lower masts. .

Q. Which are the topgallant and royal masts ?

A. Those directly above the topmasts.

Q. Which are the trysail masts ?

A. Small spars abaft the fore and mainmasts, for hoisting the trysail.

Bowsprits.

Q. Which is the bowsprit ?

A. The spar projecting over the stem.

Q. Name the parts of a bowsprit, and the furniture attached to it.

A. Tenon, housing, bed, gammoning fish, saddle, bees-block, beeseating or head, and bowsprit cap are the principal parts of the spar.

Like lower masts, bowsprits, when possible, are made out of a single spar ; when built they are composed of four principal pieces, viz. :—Upper and lower main pieces ; the side pieces are called fishes, which are dowelled and bolted together, and finally secured with iron hoops.

A bowsprit, made out of a single spar, has only two hoops on it, one on the heel just before the tenon, and one on the head about 4 ins. abaft the tenon or bowsprit-cap, and three rings or stops for the clothing, instead of cleats, are worked out in making the bowsprit.

N.B.—This is not done in all the yards. The bowsprits are all made round in Portsmouth yard, and pieces of oak are fitted in the wake of the fore-stay collar to give spread to the working of the jib-boom.

The Tenons

Of the bowsprit are the tongues in the outer and inner ends, outer one for the cap to ship on, and the inner one shipped in the bitts.

The Housing

Is that part from the bed or wedges to the tenon in the heel.

The Bed

Is that part which rests on the stem or bowsprit-hole, which is also the given diameter or largest part of the spar. The proportions of a bowsprit are, the outer end two-thirds, and the inner end five-sixths to the given diameter. The length of a bowsprit is reckoned from the outer part of the tenon at the cap, to the after part of the tenon in the bitts.

Gammoning Fish, or Paunch Piece,

Are pieces of stout wood, rounded off at outer end, and nailed on the upper part of the bowsprit, in the wake of the chain gammoning, to protect it from being cut by the chain; it is scored out to receive the chain in a line with the gammoning holes in the stem.

Saddle

Is secured on the upper part of the bowsprit, at one-third the length of the jib-boom in from the bowsprit cap. The upper part of the saddle is eight-square, so as the jib-boom will lie on it parallel with the course of the bowsprit, and the hole in the bowsprit cap. It is in length one-half the diameter of the bowsprit, in width one-half the diameter of the jib-boom, and in thickness one-sixth the given diameter of the jib-boom.

Bees Blocks

Are made out of hard wood; they are large chocks, bolted on either side of the outer end of the bowsprit, just inside the cap, and stand rather in an angular direction to the upper side of the bowsprit, the surface of which is, as far as the bee-blocks extend, flat. In the bee-blocks there are two sheaves for the topmast stays, and in the bees for the fore-top bowline. A cheek with a sheave in it is secured on the top side of the bees, on each side, to form a lead for the fore guys. Facing pieces, which overhang the bee-blocks, are nailed to their top sides, through which sheave-holes, to correspond with those in the bee-blocks for the topmast stays, are cut.

Beeseating or Head

Extends one-ninth the whole length of bowsprit, in from the outer end. The top part of the bowsprit here is worked flat, and the bee-blocks are bolted to it.

Jib-boom Shoe or Conductor

Is a chock of wood, wedge-fashion, fitted inside the bowsprit cap, the part next the cap is fitted level with the cap hole for the jib-boom, and hollowed out so as to direct the jib-boom end through the cap hole, and prevent it taking the lower part of the cap; the inner end of the shoe slopes gradually off to a thin edge, in some cases it extends along the bowsprit as far as a saddle, it being scored out so as to lie over the clothing of the bowsprit and form a protection to it in shifting jib-booms.

Bowsprit Cap,

Like a lower cap is, when possible, made out of one piece of wood, and is in length five times the diameter, and in thickness 1 in. less than the diameter of the jib-boom. It is strengthened by an iron band in width one-third the depth of the cap, which is secured by bolts, two on either side.

Four eye-bolts on the upper shoulders of the band, two on the fore, and two on the after part on either side, are welded in the band, for the jib-boom foot ropes and manropes to secure to.

Four eye-bolts are driven from aft forward, through the bowsprit-cap and clenched on the fore side, for the heel chain and heel rope of the jib-boom.

The bowsprit-cap is secured by a bolt passing through the lower part from aft to forward, and hove taut with a nut and screw, which bolt is part of a plate which is let in the bowsprit, and the cap bobstay bolt passes through it, the cap bobstay strain being inboard and the tendency to cant inboard.

Jib-booms.

Q. Which is the jib-boom?

A. The spar that extends beyond the bowsprit.

The given diameter or largest part is at the bowsprit-cap, or one-third the length of the boom from the inner end, from the cap to the outer end it is tapered off to three-quarters the given diameter. It is made eight-square at the heel, where a notch is cut on top for the crupper chain. An iron shod is fitted in the heel for the heel-chain, a sheave-hole is cut athwart the heel with a sheave fitted for the heel-rope in it, once and one-sixth the diameter of the boom in length. The outer end of the jib-boom is shouldered in length once and one-sixth the diameter of the boom for the funnel outside, the extreme end is eight-square and an iron hoop driven on to receive the flying iron, so as the flying-boom will stand on the starboard upper quarter of the jib-boom. A sheave is fitted within the funnel or rigging for

the jibstay to reeve through. The outer end of the boom is
scored, or has a half-sheave fitted in it for the topgallant-
stay.

Flying Jib-boom.

Q. Which is the flying jib-boom?

A. The spar that extends beyond the jib-boom.

The given diameter of a flying-boom is at the boom-iron,
at the outer end seven-tenths, and the inner end seven-
tenths of the given diameter. A stop is cut in the cap, in
which the heel of the flying-boom steps. A shoulder for the
eyes of the rigging is formed one diameter of the boom from
the outer end. Within the shoulder a vertical sheave is
fitted for the flying jibstay to reeve down through. A notch
or half-sheave is fitted in the flying-boom end for the royalstay. At the inner end an horizontal sheave or round hole
is cut for the heel rope, according to the size of the boom.

Sometimes the jib and flying jib-boom for small vessels
are made in one, in which case the shoulder on the jib-boom
for the funnel or eyes of the rigging will be the length of
the jib-boom, from which to the outer end will be two-thirds
the given length of the flying-boom. Supposing they were
fitted separately, the diameter at the shoulder on the jib-
boom will be three-quarters and at the extreme of flying-
boom one-third of the given diameter—sheaves, cut for jib
and flying jib and royal-stays, the same as before described ;
also for heel-rope. Crupper and heel chain are fitted the
same way ; an additional sheave is cut outside the jib-boom
funnel for the topgallant stay.

Q. Which is the dolphin striker?

A. A short perpendicular gaff spar under the bowsprit
end, for guying down the jib-boom.

Q. Which are the spritsail gaffs or whiskers?

A. Spars projecting on either side before the catheads ;
they are for spreading the guys of the jib-boom.

Q. Which is the spanker gaff?

A. The spar on the mizenmast for extending the head of
the spanker.

The foremost end is termed the jaws, the outer end the
peak. The jaw forms a semicircle, and is secured in its
position by a jaw rope passing round the mast ; on it are
strung several small wooden balls called trucks, to lessen
the friction on the mast when the sail is being hoisted or
lowered.

Q. What are trysail gaffs?

A. Spars on the fore and mainmast for extending the head of the trysails, and made and fitted the same as the spanker gaff.

Q. What are studdingsail booms?

A. Spars rigged out on the fore yard and fore and main topsail yards for the purpose of setting the studdingsails.

Q. Which is the spanker boom?

A. The spar projecting over the taffrail at the stern.

Spanker or Main Booms.

The given diameter or largest part is at the middle of a spanker boom, and at the sheet of a main boom; their outer ends are seven-tenths, and the inner ends seven-tenths of the given diameter.

The Jaws

Are made of oak or elm, in length about 4 ft. or 5 ft. and formed on the fore-part to a half-circle, 1 in. larger than the diameter of the mast, to allow for leathering, and giving a little play; in depth they are about an inch less than the diameter of the fore end of the boom. The boom is worked to a tongue on the fore part, to which the jaws are scarphed and secured by three or four iron hoops being driven over the jaws; under the third hoop, from forward, a bolt is driven horizontally through the two jaw pieces, and the tongue of the boom, and another bolt about 3 ins. or 4 ins. from the hollow of the jaws, is driven through all parts; the after end of the jaw pieces, which are tapered off to a thin edge, are secured to the boom by nails.

Sheave-Hole.

In the outer end or necking of the boom a sheave-hole is cut for the outhaul.

Eye-bolts,

Welded in hoops, are driven on the boom for topping-lifts and standing part of sheet. The eye-bolts are for the topping lifts, two in each hoop, one on each upper quarter; for the sheet, the eye-bolts are in the side of the hoop. The proper distance to place these hoops on the boom are as follows :—For the topping-lists one-third its length, from outer end; for standing part of sheet on a main boom, cheeks, with sheaves, and eye-bolts, are placed each side of the boom end alternately. The boom is coppered in the wake of the crutch and strop of the sheet-block, also lazy guy. Two eye-bolts are fitted underneath the boom for the reef tackle.

Q. What is housing?

A. All the parts of the masts below decks from the heel to the wedges, between the partners of the upper deck.

Q. What is the masthead?

A. The upper part of a mast above the rigging.

Q. What are cheeks?

A. Pieces of wood nailed to the masthead serving as supports for the trestletrees of large and rigging of small masts to rest upon.

Q. What are hounds?

A. Pieces of timber secured to the lower mastheads serving as supports for the trestletrees.

Trestletrees.

Q. What are trestletrees?

A. Trestletrees are two pieces of hard wood, standing fore and aft, resting on the hounds, they are, in length, differing only 1 in. from largest to smallest in proportion of top, the largest being 3 ins. shorter than the top, and the smallest being 2 ins. shorter than the top; this proportion will also apply to length of crosstrees, in relation to the breadth of top, they are let on and bolted together, there is an iron plate on their upper fore part to take the topmast fid, on their after ends an eye-bolt is driven from the lower side, for attaching the truss blocks to, and cheek-block for truss tricing-line.

Q. What are fishes?

A. Long pieces of hard wood used to strengthen a mast or yard when sprung or carried away, by lashing them around it.

Crosstrees.

Q. What are crosstrees?

A. Crosstrees are two pieces of hard wood, on which the tops rest, they fit into scores cut for them in the trestletrees, and stand athwart-ships, they are in length according to the width of top, in the same proportion as trestletrees bear to the length of top, one abaft the lower masthead, and the other before the lower masthead, allowing sufficient room for the heel of the topmast to work between it and the masthead. They are secured to the trestletrees by saucer-headed bolts, driven down through the trestletrees, the points of the bolts have worms cut in them, and go far enough through the lower part of the trestletrees to be secured by nuts, which are hove taut on so as to keep them firm in place.

Tops.

Q. What is a top?

A. Tops for large ships are made in two, or halves, and for small ships they are in one, or what is called a whole top. They are secured by placing two pieces of wood, called sleepers, or riding crosstrees, on the top directly over the lower crosstrees, through which iron bolts are passed and secured underneath by four nuts and screws, generally about two of these bolts, both on each side of each riding crosstree, are placed, which keeps the top in place. Tops are made of fir, the planking laid in a fore and aft direction, and strengthened by pieces laid again in an angular direction between the sleepers, and between the after rim and after sleeper. The width of a top is over the fore crosstree one third, and over the after crosstree nine-twenty-fifths the whole length of the topmast, which gives the proper proportion for the spread of the topmast rigging.

Q. Where is lubber's hole?

A. It is the vacant space between the eyes of the lower rigging and the inner sides of the top, which can be made larger when required, being fitted with a trap or hatch hung on hinges, which, when opened, lifts up and falls down in the top out of the way.

Q. What is a top rim?

A. The after rim of the top is fitted with iron sockets, in which stanchions are shipped for reeving an iron rod through, called the top rail, the stanchions are secured underneath by nuts. In the fore part of the top, abaft the fore rim, a hole is cut for the slings of the lower yard to pass through, on the after part of which is placed a bolster made of African oak to take the chafe of the chain slings.

The rim on either side, through which the futtock plates are passed, are lined with sheet iron, to strengthen the rim, and prevent the futtock-plates cutting through it. Belaying pins are fitted through a piece of wood, which is secured down in the top, called pin racks, between the hatch of lubber's hole and the side rim, in a fore and aft direction, for the purpose of belaying any of the working gear aloft to; an equal portion of the pin, or iron bolt, projects each side of the piece of wood.

Q. What is a top rail ?

A. A rail supported by stanchions across the after part of each top.

Q. What are sleepers ?

A. Are two pieces of wood, in shape and size corresponding with the width of the lower crosstrees, but not so thick, they lie over the upper part of the top, to secure it to the lower crosstrees.

Bolsters.

Q. What are bolsters ?

A. Bolsters are two chocks, made of English oak, on account of wire rigging being introduced instead of rope, one on each side of the lower masthead, nailed to the trestletrees, filling up the vacant space between the trestletrees and lower masthead, they are rounded on the upper edge, and rather overhang the trestletrees, affording a smooth surface for the eyes of the lower rigging to rest on, and preserving them from being chafed by the sharp edge of the trestletrees.

Q. What is a rubbing paunch ?

A. Is a batten that is secured up and down the fore part of the mast over the hoops to prevent them catching or injuring the lower yards in sending them up or down.

Caps.

Q. What is a cap ?

A. Caps for lower masts are made of African oak, when attainable, small ones in one piece, large ones in two ; they are bolted together, and, in either case, are strengthened by iron bolts driven through them, and clenched on iron washers, also an iron band, in width one third the depth of the cap, is driven on whilst hot, so as to fit taut round the centre of the cap. The size of a cap is in breadth two diameters, and in depth 1 in. less than the diameter of the topmast. Four eye-bolts are driven up through the lower side, and secured with nuts and screws on iron plates on the top side of the cap. The eyes stand athwart-ships, they are for hooking the top blocks to, and making the standing part of the top-tackle pendant fast. The after ones are placed in a line with the middle of the lower mastheads, and the foremost ones in a line with the centre of the hole for the topmast, there are also two lift-plates bolted to the cap, with eyes on each side of lower lift-block to hook to, one third from the after part of round hole.

Q. What is a capshore ?

A. A small spar fitted under the fore part of the lower

caps, before the whole for the topmast, to support the overhanging part of the cap, the heel being secured in a shoe to the foremost crosstrees.

Wedges.

Q. What are wedges?

A. Pieces of yellow pine timber, thick at one end, and sloping gradually to a thin edge at the other end, driven between the masts and the partners of the deck, for the purpose of keeping the lower mast in an upright position.

Q. What is a mast coat?

A. A conically shaped piece of canvas fitted over the wedges round the mast and painted, to prevent water oozing down from the decks and rotting the wedges and mast.

Q. What are masthead battens?

A. Battens placed on the lower masthead to protect the eyes of the lower rigging from being cut by the masthead hoops, but more especially to protect the mast from wire rigging.

Q. What is the step of a mast?

A. The timber on which the heel or bottom of the mast rests. The steps of the fore and mainmasts rest upon the keelson, that of the mizen mast rests sometimes upon the lower deck beams.

Q. What is the bed of bowsprit?

A. Is that part which rests on the stem or bowsprit hole.

Q. What are bees of bowsprit?

A. Pieces of wood bolted to outer edge of bowsprit. (*See* Question " Which is the bowsprit?")

Q. Where is the saddle of jib-boom?

A. On the upper part of the bowsprit, the jib-boom being parallel with the course of the bowsprit and the hole in the bowsprit cap.

Q. Where is the saddle of the spanker-boom?

A. Round the mizenmast, it is a circular piece of wood and is nailed to the mast.

Q. What are the jaws of a boom or gaff?

A. They are pieces of timber made and scarphed to the boom, and secured by iron hoops and bolts.

Q. What is a spindle?

A. A vertical iron pin upon which the capstan moves, also the long pin upon which the vanes at the masthead revolve.

Q. What is a truck ?

A. A round piece of wood fitted to the royal masthead, fitted with brass sheaves to reeve signal halyards and in which the. vane spindle is shipped.

Lightning Conductors.

Q. What are lightning conductors ?

A. Lightning conductors are two strips of copper, 80 ozs. and 40 ozs., let in the mast, flush with the wood on the after side and underneath part of bowsprit and jib-booms, and running in a direct line from the truck down to the keelson, connected with a copper bolt through the keel, or else carried by a connecting strip of copper, along one of the lower deck beams, through the ship's side, to the copper on the bottom.

Q. Which is the heel of a mast ?

A. The lower end, which either fits into the step attached to the keelson, or in topmasts is sustained by the fid upon the trestletrees. Heeling is the square part of the spar through which the fid hole is cut.

Q. Which is the fid hole ?

A. A hole cut in the heel of topmasts and topgallant masts.

Q. What are sheave holes ?

A. Holes in the heel of topmasts, for the top tackle pendants to reef through for housing, striking, or fidding. In the heel of a topgallant-mast for the mast rope to reeve through.

Q. What are fids ?

A. Fids are pieces of wood and iron used for fidding the topmasts and topgallant-masts when swayed up to keep them in place.

Q. What is a preventer fid ?

A. An iron bolt which is always kept aloft secured to the eyes of the topmast rigging by a lanyard, is passed through the hole directly the mast is through the mast hole in the trestletrees, so in the event of the mast rope carrying away, the preventer fid will bring the mast up.

Q. Which are the lower yards ?

A. The yards nearest the deck.

Q. Which are the topsail yards ?

A. Those next above the lower yards.

Q. Which are the topgallant yards ?

A. Those next above the topsail yards.

Q. Which are the royal yards ?

A. Those next above the topgallant yards.

Q. What are studdingsail yards ?

A. Small spars to which the studdingsails are bent.

Q. Where are the slings of a yard ?

A. In the centre.

Q. Where are the quarters of a yard ?

A. A sixth the length of the yard from the yard arm on either side.

Q. What are yard arms ?

A. Ends of the yards, on which are secured the brace blocks, reeftackles, and braces.

Q. What are boom irons ?

A. Irons on the fore yard and fore and main topsail yard arms in which the studdingsail booms travel through.

Q. What are clamping or inner boom irons ?

A. Irons on the fore yard which secures the inner end of the topmast studdingsail booms.

Q. What are snatches for topsail or topgallant sheets ?

A. Cheeks fitted with sheaves at the yard arms of the lower yards on the after side. If chain sheets, iron cheeks ; if rope, wooden cheeks. Cheeks on topsail yards for topgallant sheets are wood.

Q. What are tye bands ?

A. Iron bands round the centre of the topsail yards to which the tye blocks are bolted.

(2.) *Standing Rigging.*

To know the names of, and be able to point out, the following :—

Stays.	Ratlines.	Parrel.
Shrouds.	Back ropes.	Trusses.
Backstays.	Jumpers.	Slings of a yard.
Bobstays.	Jib guys.	Necklace of lower
Bowsprit shrouds.	Martingale.	mast.
Gammoning.	Heel chain.	Necklace of topmast.
Bowsprit collars.	Crupper chain.	Topgallant rigging.
Futtock shrouds.	Jackstays.	Royal rigging.
Lanyards of rigging.	Footrope.	Funnels (rigging).
Deadeyes.	Stirrups.	Sheer pole.
Masthead pendants.	Flemish horse.	After swifter.
		Catch ratline.

Q. What are stays?

A. They are of wire or hemp, and extends from each masthead towards the stem of the ship, supporting the masts forward, and preventing it falling aft.

Q. What are shrouds ?

A. They are of wire or hemp, and support the masts at the sides.

Q. What are backstays ?

A. They are of wire or hemp, and support the masts aft.

Q. What are bobstays ?

A. Ropes or chains used to confine the bowsprit downward to the stem or cutwater.

Q. What are bowsprit shrouds?

A. Ropes or chains leading from the outer end of the bowsprit to the bow giving lateral support to the bowsprit.

Q. What is the gammoning ?

A. Chains used to keep the bowsprit in place ; an iron clamp is frequently used in lieu of gammoning.

Q. What are bowsprit collars ?

A. Strops round the bowsprit with thimbles for bowsprit shrouds, stays, and bobstays.

Q. What are futtock shrouds ?

A. Short pieces of rope or chain which secure the lower dead eyes and futtock plates of topmast rigging to a band round the lower masts.

Q. What are lanyards of rigging?

A. Well stretched rope which secures the shrouds and stays, they are rove through the dead eyes at the end of the shrouds or stays, and down through the dead eyes in the chains.

Q. What are dead eyes ?

A. Solid, round, and flat wooden blocks, bound with iron and secured to the chains by the chain plates, they are pierced with three holes through the flat part in order to reeve the lanyards, corresponding with the dead eyes in the shrouds or stay ends.

Q. What are masthead pendants ?

A. Strops or short pieces of rope, fitted on each side under the shrouds upon the heads of the lower masts, for applying tackles for staying the masts or setting up lower rigging.

Q. What are ratlines?

A. Lines like the bars of a ladder running across the shrouds, used to step upon in going aloft.

Q. What are back ropes ?

A. Rope pendants or small chains used for staying the dolphin striker, also ropes long enough to reach from the cat block to the stem, and up to the forecastle, to haul the cat block forward in hooking the ring of the anchor.

Q. What are jumper guys?

A. Additional guys for supporting the jibboom.

Q. What are jib guys?

A. Stout ropes which act as backstays do to a mast, by supporting the jibboom against the pressure of the sail and the motion of the ship.

Q. What is the martingale?

A. A rope extending downwards from the jibboom end to a kind of short gaff shaped spar, fixed perpendicular under the cap of the bowsprit; its use is to guy or keep the jibboom down in the same manner as the bobstays do the bowsprit.

Q. What is the heel chain?

A. The chain that prevents the jibboom running in.

Q. What is the crupper chain?

A. The chain that secures the heel of the jibboom and prevents it from rising.

Q. What are jackstays?

A. Ropes, battens, or iron bars, on the top of the yards for bending the head of the sail to.

Q. What are footropes?

A. Ropes stretching under the yards and jibboom, for the men to stand on, in laying out on the yards or jibboom.

Q. What are stirrups?

A. Ropes with eyes at their ends, through which the foot ropes are rove and supported.

Q. What is a Flemish horse?

A. The outer short footrope for the man at the earring; the outer end is spliced round a thimble on the gooseneck of the studdingsail boom iron, the inner end is seized within the brace block strop and head earring cleat.

Q. What are parrels?

A. Ropes or strops or sometimes iron collars used to confine the yards to the mast.

Q. What are trusses?

A. Chains used to confine the lower yards to the masts.

Q. What are slings of a yard?

A. Chains used in hanging lower yards from the lower masthead.

Q. What is a lower mast necklace?

A. There are two necklaces attached to each fore and main masts just below the knees or hounds of the mast, leaving sufficient space between toe of knees and necklaces for the working of trusses; they consist of chain strops fitted with

R 3498.

c

lugs or ears on their own part, and hove taut round the mast with screws. The futtock shrouds are shackled to them, half to each necklace on either side, as in the event of one necklace giving way only half the futtock and topmast rigging would be adrift. The lugs or ears are fitted on the fore part of the mast and a clump piece fitted of oak the thickness of the lugs, and the opening covered with leather, so as to be out of the way of the working of the gaff rope. Mizen masts and iron masts are frequently fitted with an iron hoop as a necklace instead of a chain strop.

Q. What is a topmast necklace?

A. A square plate with lugs for long links for hanging blocks is now fitted instead of a chain necklace.

Q. What is top gallant rigging?

A. Stays and backstays.

Q. What is royal rigging?

A. Stays and backstays.

Q. What are funnels?

A. Funnels fit close down on the iron hoop round the top gallant masthead, they are made of copper, and afford a smooth surface for the eyes of the rigging to lie on.

Q. What is a sheer pole?

A. An iron bar or wooden batten stretched horizontally along the shrouds, and seized above each dead eye to prevent them from slewing.

Q. What are after swifters?

A. After shrouds of the lower mast.

Q. What is a catch ratline?

A. Every fifth ratline is termed a catch ratline.

(3.) *Sails.*

To know the names of, and be able to point out, the following:—

Courses.
Topsails.
Topgallant sails.
Royals.
Flying jib.
Jib.
Fore topmast stay-
  sail.
Staysails.
Spanker.
Gaff topsail.
Top lining.
Goring cloth.
Roach.
Mast lining.
Lower studdingsail.
Fore topmast stud-
  dingsail.

Topgallant studding-
  sail.
Cloth.
Roping.
Head.
Leech.
Luff.
Slab.
Bunt becket.
Marline.
Bolt rope.
Foot.
Clue.
Tack.
Sheets.
Bunt.
Cringles.
Robands.
Head earing.

Reef earing.
Reef point.
Reef line.
Fore side of a sail.
After side of a sail.
Port side of a fore
  and aft sail.
Naval line.
Eyelet holes.
Tabling.
Bowline bridle.
Buntline toggles.
Reeftackle patch.
Reeftackle pendant.
Buntline cloth.
Reef bands.
Belly bands.
Starboard side of a
  fore and aft sail.

PART I.

Q. Name the sails of a full-rigged ship?

A. Main and fore courses are set on the main and fore yards; topsails, topgallant sails, and royals, on the yards they are named after. Spanker on the mizenmast. Trysails on the fore and mainmast. Fore topmast staysail jib and flying-jib on the bowsprit, jib, and flying jib-booms. Topgallant-sails, royals, and studdingsails are called small sails, and are only used in fine weather. Main topmast and maintop-gallant staysails are set on the main topmast and topgallant stays, fitted for the purpose. The storm sails are fore and main storm staysails, which set on stays fitted for the purpose. Fore and main storm-trysails, which are set on the fore and main trysail-masts, but on shorter gaffs than are used for the large trysails, and a mizen trysail, but in a similar way to the main and fore trysails. Boat sails, for the use of the boats. Wind sails, to give ventilation below. Smoke sails, to be used when a ship is lying at anchor, head to wind, to protect the galley funnel, and keep the blacks from flying about the deck.

c 2

REFERENCES.

NAMES OF SAILS.

1. Flying jib.
2. Jib.
3. Fore topmast staysail.
4. Fore course.
5. Main course.
6. Fore topsail.
7. Main topsail.
8. Mizen topsail.
9. Fore topgallant sail.
10. Main topgallant sail.
11. Mizen topgallant sail.
12. Fore royal.
13. Main royal.
14. Mizen royal.
15. Fore trysail.
16. Main trysail.
17. Spanker.
18. Lower studdingsail.
19. Fore topmast studdingsail.
20. Fore topgallant studdingsail.
21. Main topgallant studdingsail.

COURSES.

22. Clew Garnets.
23. Tacks.
24. Sheets.
25. Inner slabline.
26. Outer slabline.
27. Buntlines.
28. Bowline bridles.

TOPSAILS, &c.

29. Clewlines.
30. Bowline and bridles.
31. Topgallant clewline.
32. Royal clewline.
33. Flying jib sheets.
34. Jib sheet and pendant.
35. Gaff foresail vangs.
36. Peak pendant.
37. Gaff mainsail vangs.
38. Peak pendant.
39. Spanker vangs.
40. Outer peak brail.
41. Inner peak brail.
42. Throat brail.
43. Middle brail.
44. Foot brail.
45. Lower studdingsail tack.
46. Lower studdingsail sheet.
47. Lower studdingsail tripping line.
48. Outer halyards.
49. Topmast studdingsail tack.
50. Topmast studdingsail downhaul.
51. Topgallant studdingsail tack.
52. Quarter boat.

There are also a number of fancy sails—viz., a ringtail, which is set by halyards being rove at the spanker or boom-mainsail gaff end, the tack being hauled out to a boom, fitted on the spanker-boom end, similar to a stundingsail-boom on a yard. A watersail sets under the spanker-boom end. A spritsail, which sets under the bowsprit. Skysails are set over royals.

Merchant ships frequently carry sails above these.

Sails and how Fitted.

Q. What are courses?

A. The names given to the sails hanging from the lower yards of a ship, viz., the foresail and mainsail, and are fitted with two reef bands composed of a single part of canvas, one-third the width of the canvas in breadth, each placed at one-sixth the depth of the sail from the head. A belly band, also single part of canvas, half the width of the canvas in breadth, is placed half way between the lower reef and foot ; and a foot band, extending from clew to clew, also a single part of canvas half the width of the canvas in breadth.

The leeches are lined from clew to earring with whole breadth, and the buntline patches, four in number, are placed at equal distances apart along the foot, extending from foot to middle or belly band.

Holes are worked two in a cloth in the head and reefs, and also for sticking the cringles in the leeches, at the foot in each centre of the buntline patches, and at the clews for the seizings.

Marline holes are worked along the foot, and the foot and clew ropes wormed, &c., similar to topsails.

The largest ropes are the clew ropes, which are spliced with the foot rope, about a foot or 18 ins. outside the outer buntline patches, and with the leech ropes a short distance from the clew, the foot and leech ropes being of one size. The ends of the head rope are spliced into the earrings of the leech ropes. A metal thimble is placed in each bunt-line, similar to topsails, and iron thimbles in the cringles in the leeches, except the bowline cringles, which are three in number in main courses, and two in fore courses. Courses and topsails are seized at each clew with 1 in. or ¾ in. bolt rope, according to the size of the sail.

Course.

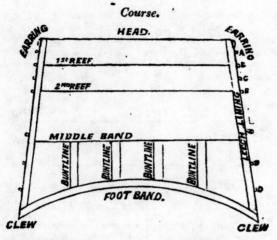

A. Bending cringle.
B. Reef cringle.

C. Reef-tackle cringle.
D. Bowline cringle.

Q. What are topsails?

A. The second sails above the deck. The head of a topsail is secured to the topsail yard by earrings and robands, and the foot is spread by sheets leading to the lower yard arms.

They are tabled all round the edges, and have four reef bands, of half breadth (24 in. canvas), doubled, the lower close reef being generally at half the depth of the sail, and the others at nearly equal distances apart, between that and the head. A middle or belly band, of half breadth, single, half way between the lower reef and the foot, and a foot band also, of half breadth, single, extending from the top lining, on each side, to the clew. The width of the top lining is usually about one-fifth the length of the foot, and the depth from foot to middle band, with a mast lining of about two cloths, extending from the upper part of the top lining to the third reef.

The leeches are lined from clew to earring, the lining being half-cloth wide at the head, and one-and-a-half cloths wide at the foot.

The reef-tackle patches in large sails are of whole breadth, and in small sails two-thirds wide at the outer part and one-third wide at the inner part; they are from two to

three yards long, and placed diagonally to the opposite
clew. The centre of the buntline cloths, which are of
whole breadth, is placed at one-third the length of the foot
from the clew, and the inner edge of the upper part of the
buntline cloths brought to the outer edge of the top lining
at the middle band.

Topsail.

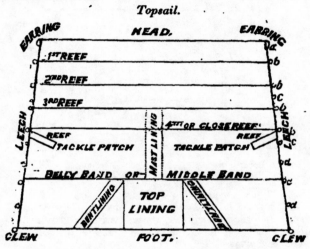

A. Heading rear cringle. C. Reef tackle cringle.
B. Reef cringle. D. Bowline cringle.

Holes are worked two and one in a cloth alternately, in
the head and two upper reefs, and two in a cloth in the
other two reefs; holes are also worked in the leech of the
sail, for sticking the reef and bowline cringles in, also in
the centre of the lower part of the buntlines, and at the
clews, for the seizings. Marline holes are worked along the
foot and a short distance up the leeches, for the purpose of
lacing the foot of the sail with white line to the foot rope,
which is first wormed, tarred, parcelled with canvas, and
served with spunyarn.

Topsails have head, foot, and leech ropes; the ends of
the head rope are spliced into the earring of the leech ropes,
and the foot rope carried round the clews of the sail and
spliced with the leech ropes, from 3 ft. to 6 ft. from the
clew, according to the size of the sail. Thimbles, made of
mixed metal, are placed in the buntline holes, and iron

thimbles in the clews and in the reef and reef-tackle cringles.

Topsails are fitted with four, three, or two bowline cringles, according to the depth of the sail.

Q. What are topgallantsails.

A. The third sails above the deck; they are set above the topsail yards in the same manner as the topsails are above the lower yards.

Two holes are worked in each cloth in the head, each corner of the sail is lined, and two or three bowline cringles, according to the depth of the sail, are worked in the leech ropes.

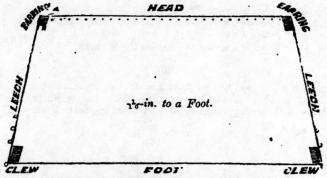

$\frac{1}{16}$-*in. to a Foot.*

The ropes are generally of three different sizes, the head rope extending from earring to earring, the leech ropes, from the head earring, to between the second and third bowline cringles, when fitted with three, and between the two bowline cringles, when fitted with two, and the foot rope through the foot and up the leeches, splicing with each leech rope. The upper bowline is placed at half the depth of the sail, and the others at equal distances between it and the clew. The clews are served with spunyarn and marled with small line, one foot each way.

Q. What are royals.

A. The name of the light sails spread above the topgallantsails in the same manner as the topgallantsails are spread above the topsails.

Two holes are worked in each cloth in the head, and corner pieces fitted, same as topgallantsails. The ropes are of two sizes only—viz., head rope, from earring to earring, and a body rope on the foot and leeches. No thimbles are used in either of these sails, or topgallantsails.

Q. What is a flying jib.
A. A light sail set before the jib on the flying jib stay.
Q. What is a jib.
A. A large triangular sail set on the jib stay.

Jibs.

The edges are turned over and tabled or hemmed down, to make the sail strong enough to bear the strain of the holes and roping stiches ; the width of the tabling varying

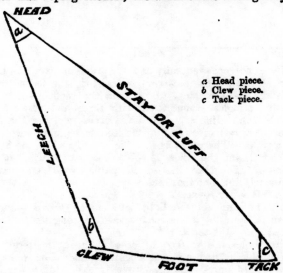

a Head piece.
b Clew piece.
c Tack piece.

according to the size of the sail. Lining, head, clew, and tack pieces, as *a*, *b*, *c* (*see* sketch). Holes, 3 ft. apart, are worked (grommets) in the stay, for the lacing.

Roping.

The largest size rope is sewn on, commencing at the top of the clew piece, and continued through the foot to about 3 ft. or 4 ft. up the stay, where it is spliced into the stay rope, which is sewn on up the stay, continued round the head, and spliced with the leech rope at the lower part of the peak piece, the leech rope being in its turn spliced with the clew rope.

Q. What is a fore topmast staysail.

A. A triangular sail set on the fore topmast stay.

Q. What are staysails.

A. Triangular sails hoisted upon the lower and topmast stays.

Staysails (*Lower*)

Are lined as follows :—A clew piece about two yards long, and peak and tack pieces about one yard long, a foot band of one-third breadth, and two bands also of one-third

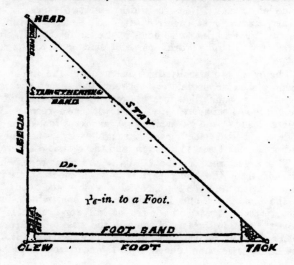

breadth, sewn across the sail at equal distances between the head and clew. Holes for the stay lacing or hanks are worked three-quarters of a yard apart in the stay of the sail, and they are roped similar to jibs.

Staysails, topgallant, and royal are similar in every respect to jibs.

Q. What is a spanker?

A. The aftermost sail in the ship, it is set on the spanker boom and gaff.

Boom, Mainsails, Spankers, &c.

These sails are lined with a clew piece of whole breadth, from the clew to about four or five feet above the upper reef cringle ; a peak piece, also of whole breadth, from the peak to about four or five feet down the leech, according to, the size of the sails, a mast lining one foot wide, from throat to tack ; also a piece about one foot wide, under the clew piece, extending from about 1 ft. 6 in. above the upper reef to the clew ; the corners, and clew as peak, are likewise strengthened by small patches, called clinker pieces.

Head holes are worked, two per cloth, in sails made of canvas 24 ins. wide, and two and one alternately in sails made of canvas 18 ins. in width, and two holes at each corner, and two at each reef, in both leech and luff, for sticking the cringles ; also holes in the luff of the sail, about three-quarters of a yard apart, for seizing it to the mast hoops.

The reefs are usually three in number, the upper one being placed about midway between the throat and tack, the others at equal distances between the upper one and the tack. Small sails are only fitted with two reefs. Reef points, made of stout white line, are crowfooted in the middle, a hole is then made through every seam, and one end of the point passed through, and the crowfoot securely.

The largest rope on these sails is the clew rope, which extends from the upper part of the clew piece, where it is spliced with the leech rope, round the clew, and about 3 ft. in the foot, then spliced with the foot rope, which, in its turn, is spliced with the mast or luff rope, about 2 ft. from the tack in the foot of the sail, the mast or luff rope is then carried round the tack, up the luff, and about 2 ft. into the head; it is then spliced with the head rope; the head

Mainsail.

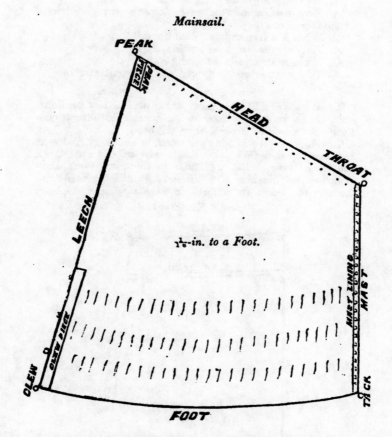

rope terminates about 2 ft. from the peak, where the peak rope is spliced on, which is spliced with the leech rope about 4 ft. or 5 ft. below the head.

Cringles, with iron thimbles, are stuck at each corner, at each reef, both in leech and luff, and likewise midway between the lower reef and tack.

Q. What is a gaff topsail ?

A. A light sail set over the spanker.

Q. What are lower studdingsails ?

A. Fine weather sails set on the lower or swinging booms outside the foresail.

Q. What is a fore topmast studdingsail ?

A. Fine weather sails set outside the topsails.

Q. What is a topgallant studdingsail ?

A. Fine weather sails set outside the topgallantsails.

Lower and Topmast Studdingsails.

These sails are lined at each corner similar to topgallantsails, and have a reef band of one-quarter breadth at one-eighth the depth of the sail, from the head.

Two holes are worked in each cloth, in both head and reef, and are roped as follows :—The largest or body rope, down one leech through the foot, and up the other leech, commencing and finishing with an earring ; and the head rope, the ends of which are spliced into the earring of the body

Topmast Studdingsails.

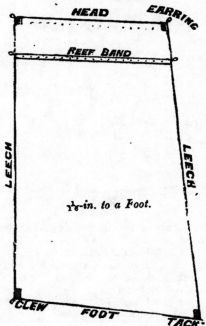

HEAD · EARRING

REEF BAND

LEECH · LEECH

$\frac{1}{16}$-in. to a Foot.

CLEW · FOOT · TACK

rope. A cringle is stuck and an iron thimble inserted, in each leech, at the extremity of the reef band.

Lower Studdingsail.

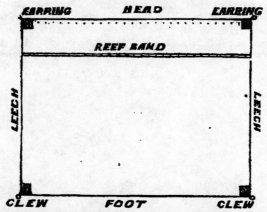

Are similar to the lower and topmast studdingsails, with the exception of not being fitted with a reef.

NOTE.—The lower studdingsail is on a smaller scale than the other sails.

Topgallant Studdingsail.

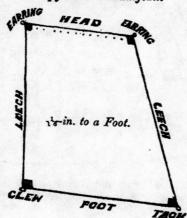

Q. What are storm trysails?

A. Bad weather sails, and are fitted similar to other gaff sails, with the addition of having reef bands of one-quarter breadth and strengthening bands of one-third breadth, the former to take the reef hanks, and the latter at equal distances between the upper reef and the throat of the sail, with the exception of having cringles stuck in the mast or luff rope about 3 ins. apart, for lacing, instead of the grommets worked in the sail to seize it to the mast-hoops, and

Storm Trysail.

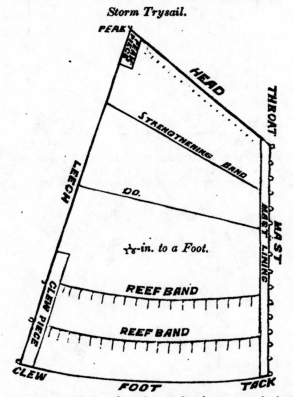

are fitted with two reefs only, each about one-sixth the depth of the mast. In small sails, one reef about one-fifth the depth of the mast.

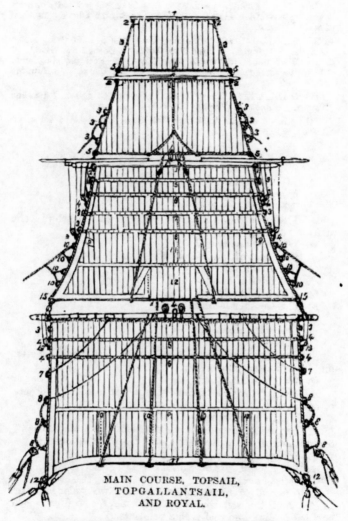

**MAIN COURSE, TOPSAIL,
TOPGALLANTSAIL,
AND ROYAL.**

MAIN COURSE.—1 Head. 2 Earring Cringles. 3 Bending
Cringles. 4 Reef Cringles. 5 First Reef Band. 6 Second Reef Band.

7 Outer Leech Line Toggles. 8 Bowline Cringles. 9 Middle or Belly
Band. 10 Buntline Linings. 11 Foot Band. 12 Clews. 13 Reef
Tackle Cringles.

TOPSAIL.—1 Head. 2 Earring Cringles. 3 Reef Cringles. 4
Reef Tackle Cringles. 5 First Reef Band. 6 Second Reef Band. 7
Third Reef Band. 8 Fourth Reef Band. 9 Reef Tackle Patch.
10 Bowline Cringles. 11 Mast Lining. 12 Top Lining. 13 Buntline
Patch. 14 Foot. 15 Clews.

TOPGALLANTSAIL.—1 Head. 2 Earring Cringles. 3 Bowline
Cringles. 4 Foot. 5 Clews.

ROYAL.—1 Head. 2 Earring Cringles. 3 Leech. 4 Foot. 5
Clews.

Parts of a Sail, &c.

Q. What is a cloth?

A. A breadth of canvas in its whole width.

Q. What is the roping?

A. The bolt rope round the edges of the sail to prevent
it from rending.

Q. Which is the head?

A. That part of the sail which is bent to the yard.

Q. Which is the leech?

A. The sides of a sail.

Q. Which is the luff?

A. The weather leech of a sail.

Q. Which is the foot?

A. The bottom of a sail.

Q. Which is the clew?

A. The lower corners of a sail to which the tacks, sheets,
and clewlines are made fast.

Q. Which is the tack?

A. The rope which hauls down the weather lower corners
of courses.

Q. Which is the sheet?

A. The ropes or chains which haul down the clews of
topsails and upper sails, or hauls aft the clew of a course.

Q. Which is the bunt?

A. The middle part of the sail.

Q. What are cringles?

A. A strand of rope worked through two eyelet holes in
the leech of the sail round the bolt rope, for reef earrings,
bowline bridles, and reef-tackle pendants.

NOTE.—Head earring cringles are spliced in the leech
rope.

Q. Are all the cringles fitted alike?

A. No, the reef-earring and reef-tackle cringles have thimbles in them, to take the chafe of the reef-earrings and reef-tackle pendant, also to prevent the earrings jamming, and insure their rendering easily.

Q. What is a roband?

A. Pieces of sennit plaited round the head rope of a topsail, or any other square sail, for securing it to the jack-stay.

Q. Are all robands alike?

A. No; the midship roband is round rope, so that in shifting topsails the captain of a top will readily distinguish it from the other robands, and as soon as he ascertains the topsail is clear of turns, and on the right slew, he at once secures the midship roband as near the centre of the yard as possible, so, as to prevent the men at the yard-arm from hauling the sail more out to one yard-arm than to the other; midship robands are secured round the tye-block, or blocks; if fitted with a double tye, your sail should be fitted with two midship robands.

Q. What is a head earring?

A. A piece of rope spliced into the head earring cringles, for the purpose of hauling the head of a topsail, or any other square sail out to the head earring strops, and taught along the yard.

Q. What are reef earrings?

A. Reef-earrings are pieces of rope, in size according to the size of the leech-rope, as when a topsail is reefed the reef-earring, when passed is supposed to bear the same amount of strain as the leech-rope.

The first and second reef-earrings are fitted with a running eye round the yard-arm, outside the lifts; they are in length twice and a half the depths of the reefs, *i.e.*, the first reef-earring is twice and a half the depth of the first reef, and the second reef-earring twice and a half the depth of both first and second reefs.

The third and fourth reef-earrings are spliced into the eyelet-hole in the lower part of the third and fourth reef cringles, forming a long eye sufficient to admit of both parts of the eye going round the yard and through the thimble of the reef-cringle again. The two parts of the earrings forming the long-eye are marled together, the bight being seized to the eyelet-hole. The other end of the earrings hitched

as follows :—The end of the third reef-earring is rove through
the second reef earring-cringle, and bowline knotted to its
own part, and the end of the fourth reef-earring in a similar
way through the third reef-cringle.

Q. What are reef points ?

A. Pieces of soft rope or sennit whose length is nearly
double the circumference of the yard, they secure the sail
close up to the yard in reefing.

Q. What are reef lines?

A. Lines running across each reef-band on fore part of a
topsail, from leech to leech, secured to the upper eyelet-hole
of the reef-cringle.

Q. What are naval lines ?

A. Lines running across the after part of a topsail, from
leech to leech, for the purpose of securing the reef-lines, the
ends of the naval lines are also secured to the upper eyelet-
holes of the reef-cringles.

Q. What are eyelet-holes ?

A. Holes, with small grummets sewn in them, formed in
the tabling and reef-bands, for the cringles, robands, reef-
lines, and buntline toggles.

Q. What is the tabling ?

A. A broad hem on the edges of a sail to strengthen it in
that part which is sewed to the bolt-rope.

Q. What are bowline bridles?

A. Pieces of rope spliced into the bowline cringle, as
follows :—For a fore and mizen-topsail, the upper bridle is
spliced, the upper end to the upper bowline cringle, and the
lower end in the middle bowline cringle.   The lower bridle
the upper end, is spliced round the upper bridle, and the
lower end in the lower bowline cringle.

The bridles are in length (when fitted) once and one third
the drift of the cringles.

The upper one is served two thirds up, and the lower one
two thirds down.

For a main topsail, the upper end of the upper bowline
bridle is spliced in the upper bowline cringle, the lower end
to the second cringle.   The lower bridle the upper end is
spliced into the third, and the lower end into the fourth
cringles.   The middle bridle the upper end is spliced round
the lower part of the upper bridle, and the lower end round
the upper part of the lower bridle.

The upper and middle bridles are served two thirds up; and the lower two thirds down.

The length to cut a bowline bridle is one and two thirds the drift from cringle to cringle.

Q. What are buntline toggles?

A. Toggles at the foot of the sail to which the buntlines are toggled.

Q. What is the reef tackle patch?

A. An extra part of canvas, to take the strain of the reef tackle of a topsail.

Q. What is a reef tackle pendant?

A. The rope to which the reef tackle is secured.

Q. What are buntline cloths?

A. A double part of canvas on the fore part of a topsail to take the chafe of the buntlines extending in an angular direction, from foot to belly-band.

Q. What is a reef-band?

A. Double part of canvas across a topsail or course, for working holes for the reef lines.

Q. What is a belly-band?

A. An extra cloth of canvas across the belly of a topsail or course, below the fourth reef-band of a topsail, and the second reef-band of a course, to strengthen the sail midway between the lower reef and foot.

NOTE.—This applies to either sail.

Q. What is the top lining?

A. Double parts of canvas on the after part of a topsail, to take the chafe of the top, extending from belly-band to foot in length, and in width according to the size of the ship.

Q. What is a goring cloth?

A. A side cloth of a topsail, cut obliquely, or lining of a topsail, called by sailmakers the leech lining.

Q. What is the roach?

A. The hollow curvature of the lower parts of upper square sails, to clear the stays when the yards are braced up.

Q. What is the mast lining?

A. An extra part of canvas on the after past of the topsail, to take the chafe of the topmast and cap, extending from the third reef-band to the belly-band, and about two cloths in width.

Q. What is the slab ?

A. The loose part of a sail which hangs down when the sail is reefed.

Q. What is a bunt becket ?

A. A becket nearly at the head of the sail on the after side, to which the bunt whip is hooked when the sail is furled.

Q. What is marline ?

A. Small line composed of two strands, tarred, and white, the latter is used for bending light sails, and the former for laying between the strands of the bolt-rope on the sails.

Q. What is bolt-rope?

A. The rope secured round the sides of a topsail to the tabling, or any other square sail.

Q. Which is the fore side of a sail?

A. The side the roping is not sewed on.

Q. Which is the after side of a sail ?

A. The roping is sewed on the after part of all square sails.

Q. Which is the port side of a fore and aft sail ?

A. The side on which the roping is sewn.

Q. Which is the starboard side of a fore and aft sail ?

A. The side on which the roping is not sewn.

Extra Questions.

Q. What are gaskets ?

A. All gaskets on lower and topsail yards are made of sword matting, cut to the required length, and fitted with an eye in each end. The upper eye is fitted with a lanyard, it is secured to the head rope of the sail. The proper length to cut a gasket is half the round of the part of the yard the gasket is to go on.

For topgallant and royal yards the harbour-gaskets are made, the upper part of French and the lower part of English sennit, an eye is formed in the upper part in making the gasket and seized to the jackstay of the yard.

Sea-gaskets, are made all through of English sennit : an eye is formed in the outer end, which is seized to the yard-arm, the gaskets being long enough to pass round-about-turns round the sail and yard, from yard-arm to quarter, the inner end being secured to the jack-stay.

Q. What is the difference between a bunt and yard-arm gasket ?

A. All bunt-gaskets are of sword matting, and the lanyards are spliced in the lower instead of the upper eyes. The upper eyes, for a course or topsail, are seized to the head ropes of the sail. For topgallant or royal yards they are seized to the jackstays. Bunt-gaskets always cross in the middle, and are secured to opposite quarters.

Q. What is a clew-hanger ?

A. A piece of 1½ or 2 in. rope, according to the size of the topsail, about two fathoms in length ; they are generally spliced round the upper part of the parrel ; when the sail is furled, they are passed round the clew, and hauld taut back to the parrel again, where they are secured.

The clew-hangers on a lower yard are fitted in a similar way, only spliced into the truss strop instead of the parrel ; sometimes they are spliced in the jackstay in the bunt of the lower yard.

Q. What is a spilling line ?

A. A line up and down the fore part of the topsail, for spilling the sail when reefing.

Q. Name the running gear of a course, and how it is bent to the sail ?

To the Leech.

A. Reef-tackles, bowlines, leechlines, and slablines.

To the Clews.

Tacks, sheets, and clew-garnet.

To the Foot.

Buntlines and slab-buntlines, in the bunt a bunt-whip.

Reef-tackle blocks of courses are fitted with clasp-hooks, and are hooked to the reef-tackle cringles in the leech of the sail.

The leech-lines and slablines are bent to the leech of the sail with a running-eye over the same toggle, which is seized to the upper bowline-cringle ; when there are two leechlines and slablines the upper ones are bent to a toggle seized to the reef-tackle cringles. In brigs the leechline is rove through the leechline cringle, taken up abaft the sail, and hitched to the jackstay abreast of the leechline block. This is termed doubling the leechline, as it serves the double purpose of leech and slabline.

Bowlines.

The fore-bowline goes with a running-eye over a toggle, seized to the bowline brible.

The main is fitted with a light runner and tackle, and attached to the lower bowline-bridle with a slip-toggle.

Tacks, Sheets, and Clew-Garnets

Are shackled to the clew of a sail.

The buntlines are bent with running-eyes over toggles, which are fitted with double strops, *two* each *side* of the foot of the sail ; there are two legs to each buntline, each side of the sail.

Bunt slabline is a single rope clenched to the foot of a course on the after part of the sail.

A bunt-whip is hooked to a becket sewed to a double part of canvas in the bunt of the sail when furling.

Q. What gear do you let go and haul on in setting a course?

A. Let go and overhaul leechlines, slablines, reef-tackles, buntlines, slab-buntlines, and ease down the clew-garnets.

Haul on the weather-tack and lee-sheet.

Q. What gear do you haul on and let go in taking a course in ?

A. Haul on clew-garnets, leechlines, slablines, buntlines, slab-buntlines. Let go the bowlines, and ease away the tack and sheet.

Q. Name the running gear of a topsail, and how it is bent ?

To the Yard.

A. Topsail-tye and halyards.

To the Leech.

Reef-tackles (large ships carrying heavy topsails are fitted with first and second reef-tackles) bowlines.

To the Clew.

Sheets, clewlines.

To the Foot.

Buntlines.

To the Bunt.

Bunt jigger.

The halyards are hooked in the chains. The tye-blocks are secured to a band round the sling of the yard by a bolt.

Reef-Tackles.

The reef-tackle pendant is rove through the thimble in the crown of the strop of the reef-tackle block, through the upper bowline-cringle, hitched, and the end seized. If the second reef-tackle is fitted, it is bent to the second reef-tackle cringle, which is between the second and third reef, with a half-hitch, and the end seized back.

Bowlines go with a running-eye over a toggle to the lower bowline-bridle in a fore or mizen, and the middle bowline-bridle in a main top-sail. The sheets, if chain, are either hooked to the clew with clip-hooks, or shackled.

If rope, a thimble is seized in the strop of the topsail sheet-block, by which they are shackled to the clew.

Clewlines are lashed abaft the clew.

Buntlines are secured with a running-eye over a toggle.

A bunt-jigger is hooked to the bunt-becket, and is used in hauling the bunt up in furling sails.

Q. What gear do you let go and haul on in setting a topsail?

A. Let go clewlines, buntlines, and reef-tackles, haul on topsail-sheets and halyards.

Q. What gear do you let go and haul on in taking a topsail in?

A. Let go the topsail-sheets and halyards, and haul on the clewlines and buntlines.

Q. Name the running gear of a topgallantsail and royal?

A. Of a topgallantsail, halyards, clewlines, buntlines, and bowlines.

Halyards are bent with a studdingsail halyard-bend round the slings of the yard, or to a thimble in a strop; the former is the best plan, as it carries the yard much closer up to the sheave-hole of the mast.

Or topgallant halyards or yard ropes are shackled to a band round the slings of the yard, royal halyards or yard-ropes are bent either with a studding halyard-bend or to a strop at the slings of the yard. This is more general now.

To the Leech.

Bowlines are bent with a running-eye over a toggle.

To the Clew.

Sheets and clewlines. The sheets are bent with a sennit-eye over a spring-toggle, and the clewlines with a sheet-bend through the clew of the sail.

To the Foot.

Buntlines are only fitted to topgallantsails in large ships, and is a single buntline with two legs, which are clenched to the foot of the sail, or fitted with a running-eye over a toggle.

Of a Royal.

Halyards. Sheets and clewlines, which are bent in the same way as topgallant sheets, clewlines, and halyards.

Q. What gear do you let go, and haul on in setting a topgallantsail and royal?

A. Let go clewlines for a royal, and bowlines, buntlines, and clewlines for a topgallantsail. Haul on sheets and halyards.

Q. What gear do you let go and haul on in taking a topgallantsail and royal in?

For a Topgallantsail.

A. Let go bowlines, sheets, and halyards, and haul on the clewlines and buntlines.

For a Royal.

Let go sheet and halyards, and haul on clewlines.

Q. Name the running gear of a jib, flying-jib, or staysail.

A. Halyards, downhaul, jib-pendants, and whips or sheets. Lacing for jibs, hanks for fore topmast-staysails, beckets for storm-staysails, tack-lashing, clew ropes, reeving-lines, foot-lines.

Q. How, and to what part of the sail is the gear bent?

A. The halyards of jibs and staysails are hooked to the head cringle; they are fitted with clip-hooks; when double, the clip-hooks are seized in a thimble in the strop next the crown of the block.

The downhaul is rove through the head-cringle and secured with a sheet-bend.

Jib-pendants, or sheets, are secured to the cringle in the clew of the sail with a toggle and strop. This also applies to staysails.

Luff-tackles are used as sheets for storm-staysails.

The lacings of a jib, flying-jib, main-topmast or topgallant staysails, are rove through the eyelet-hole in the luff of the sail, and round the stay. Sometimes the lacing is stopped to the eyelet-holes, and not rove through them, but it is not so secure.

Fore Topmast Staysails.

The eye-let-holes in the luff are seized to hanks which are on the fore topmast stay.

Storm Staysails,

Fore and main, are fitted with beckets in the eye-let holes in the luff of the sail, with an eye in one end, and a knot on the other end of the beckets, they are passed round the stay, and secured by putting the knot through the eye.

Q. Why are jibs and flying gibs fitted with lacings, and a fore topmast staysail with hanks?

A. Jib or flying-jib stays can be unrove, brought in on the forecastle, and then rove through the lacing, but as a fore topmast staysail is set on one of the fore topmast stays, which cannot be let go in bending or unbending the sail, the sail must be taken out to it, therefore all staysails set on standing stays must go with hanks or beckets.

Tack-Lashings

Are spliced in the tack-cringles of a jib or staysail; they are secured round the bowsprit for a fore topmast staysail, jib-boom, and flying jib-boom, for a jib or flying jib with three round turns, each turn being passed through the cringle in the tack of the sail, and secured to its own part; in some cases, for the sake of smartness, a strop and toggle is used for the purpose.

A Clew Rope

Is merely a rope's end bent to the clew of a jib or staysail when the sheets are not bent.

A Reeving-Line

Is a rope's end bent to the becket in the end of the jib or flying-jibstays, to reeve them through the sheave holes in the jib and flying jib-boom ends in shifting jibs or flying jibs.

Foot Line.

A foot-line is a rope's end bent to an eyelet-hole in the foot of the jib, and led through a block at the bowsprit cap, to haul it taut along the jib-boom for furling at sea.

Q. What gear do you let go and haul on in setting a jib or staysail ?

A. Let go the downhaul, and haul on the halyards and jib-whips or sheets.

Q. What gear do you let go and haul on in taking a jib or staysail in ?

A. Ease off the sheets, let go the halyards, haul on the downhaul.

Foot-Line or Gap Rope

Is a rope's end rove through a block at the bowsprit cap, and bent to an eyelet-hole in the foot of the jib, or to the clew of the jib.

It is useful for hauling the foot of the jib taut along the jib-boom when stowing the sail at sea blowing fresh, as it brings it and steadies it in place on the boom while the men are gathering it up.

It is also useful for flattening it in fine weather.

When rove through a block at the head of a jib, and bent to the clew, it is very useful in lightening the crew over the stays in shifting the sheets over.

Q. Name the running gear of a boom-mainsail, spanker, and trysail ?

Boom Mainsail.

A. Throat and peak halyards, vangs, and downhaul. Tack tricing-line, tack-tackle, lacing, boom-sheets, and topping-lifts.

Q. How, and to what part is the gear bent?

A. Peak and throat-halyards are hooked to the gaff. Vangs and down hauls spliced or hooked to the outer part of the gaff.

Tack Tricing-Line.

The tail in the lower block is passed through the thimble in the tack of the sail, and hitched to its own part.

Tack-Tackle

Is hooked to the tack of the sail.

Lacing

Is a piece of soft greasy rope, spliced in an eyelet-hole in the luff of the sail above the reefs.

Boom Sheets

Are rove through a block on the outer part of the boom.

Topping-Lifts

Hooked to an iron band fitted with two eyes on the boom.

N.B.—This applies also to a spanker.

Q. What gear do you let go and haul on in setting a boom-mainsail?

A. Let go vangs and downhalls, tack tricing-line, and ease the boom-sheets.

Haul on the topping lifts, peak and throat-halyards.

Q. What gear do you haul on and let go in taking a boom-mainsail in?

A. Haul on the weather sheet, vangs and downhaul, and lower the peak and throat-halyards, when the boom is amidship, lower the topping lifts, crutch the boom.

N.B.—This applies to a spanker also.

Q. What is the use of a tack tricing-line?

A. To trice the tack of the sail up when required.

Q. What is the use of a tack-tackle?

A. To haul the tack of the sail close down when on a wind.

Q. Name the running gear of a spanker?

A. In addition to the gear attached to a boom-mainsail, as already explained, a spanker is fitted with an outhaul and brails, the gaff being kept always swayed up in place; the peak or throat halyards are not used in setting or taking the sail in.

Outhauls.

A foot-outhaul is hooked to a thimble in the clew of the spanker.

A head-outhaul to a thimble in the peak.

Brails.

The bights are seized to the after-leech.

Q. What is the difference in securing the after-clew of a boom-mainsail and a spanker?

A. The clew of a boom-mainsail is secured to the boom-end by an earring passed round the outer end of the boom, or shackled.

The clew of the spanker is fitted with an outhaul.

Q. What gear do you let go and haul on in taking a spanker in?

A. Haul on the brails, always manning the lee-brails best, so as to spill the sail; let go the outhaul, haul in the sheet; when the boom is over the crutch, lower the topping-lift.

Q. What gear do you haul on and let go in setting a spanker?

A. Let go the brails, and haul on the outhaul, ease off the weather vangs, downhauls, and sheets, and top on the topping-lifts.

Let go the outhaul, haul in the sheet; when the boom is over the crutch, lower the topping lifts.

When the head of a spanker is fitted to run on an iron rod under the gaff, it is fitted with an outhaul at the head as well as the foot, also an inhaul.

Q. Name the running gear of a trysail?

A. The same as a spanker, with the exception of no boom.

The gaffs are usually kept swayed up in place, but are sometimes lowered and swayed up each time the sail is taken in or set, similar to a boom mainsail.

Brails are fitted to a trysail in the same manner as they are to a spanker, the sheet which answers the purpose of an out-haul is generally a luff-tackle hooked to the clew of the sail.

A piece of rope, called a lazy-sheet, is spliced in the clew thimble.

Q. What is the difference in securing the tack of a trysail to that of a spanker?

A. A piece of rope, called a tack-lashing, is spliced in the tack-thimble by which the tack is secured; it does not trice up like a spanker, therefore is not fitted with a tricing-line or tack-tackle.

Q. What gear do you let go and haul on in setting a fore or main trysail?

A. Let go the brails and vangs, and haul on the sheet.

Q. What gear do you haul on and let go in taking a trysail in?

A. Ease away the sheets, haul on the brails (the lee-brails best), so as to spill the sail, steady taut the vangs.

Q. What is the use of a lazy-sheet?

A. To secure the clew of the sail while you hook or unhook the double sheet.

Q. Name the running gear of a gaff-topsail?

A. Halyards, sheet, clewline, tack, and lacing.

Q. How, and to what part of the sail is the gear bent?

A. The halyards are bent to the yard with a studding-sail halyard-bent, about one-third from the inner yard-arm.

The sheet is fitted in various ways—viz., sometimes with clip-hook, or a common hook and mousing, or a screw hook;

in either case it is hooked to the clew of the sail; it is also, in some cases, fitted with a toggle and strop.

The Clewline

Is rove through the clew of the sail, and secured with a sheet-bend when single; when double, a tail is fitted to the lower block, and bent to the sail in a similar way. The upper clew-block is seized to the slings of the yard, and acts as a down-haul as well as a clewline.

The Tack

Is fitted with a hook, which is hooked to the thimble in the tack of the sail.

The Lacing

Is a piece of rope, one end of which is spliced in one of the upper eyelet-holes, in the luff of the sail, the other end being passed through each of the lower eyelet-holes, and rove round the mast as the sail is hoisted.

Q. How is the yard secured to the mast?

A. By a parrel.

Q. What gear do you let go and haul on in setting a gaff-topsail?

A. Hoist on the halyards, pass the parrel and lacing, let go the clewline, haul down the tack, and haul out the sheet.

Q. What gear do you haul on and let go in taking a gaff-topsail in?

A. Ease off the sheet, haul up the clewline, cast off the lacing and parrel, lower the halyards, and haul down on the tack, which acts as a downhaul.

Studdingsails.

Q. Name the running gear of a lower, topmast, and top-gallant studdingsail.

A. Lower studdingsail, inner and outer halyards, tack, long and short sheets, tripping-line.

Inner Halyards

Are either hooked, or a tail is fitted to the block, which is bowline knotted to the inner corner of the head of the sail.

Outer Halyards

Are bent to the yard with a studdingsail halyard-bend half-way or one-third out on the yard.

Tack

Is bent to the outer lower corner or clew of the sail, with a sheet-bend or running-eye over a cross-toggle.

N.B.—This applies to all studdingsails.

The Long and Short Sheets

Are formed out of one piece of rope, rove through the thimble in the inner lower corner or clew of the sail, and seized together.

Tripping-Line

Is bent with a sheet-bend to the tack, or outer lower corner of the sail.

Topmast and Topgallant Studdingsail.

Halyards, downhaul, tack, and sheets.

Halyards

Are bent with a studdingsail halyard-bend to the yard one-third out.

Downhaul

Goes with a running-eye over the outer yard-arm for a topmast, and the inner yard-arm for a topgallant studdingsail.

Tack

Is bent with a sheet-bend to the outer clew of the sail.

Sheets.

There are two to a topmast studdingsail, a long and a short one, formed out of one piece of rope by being rove through the clew of the sail and seized. A topgallant studdingsail has only one sheet.

Q. What gear do you haul on in setting a lower, topmast, or topgallant studdingsail ?

A. Halyards, tacks, and sheets.

Q. What gear do you let go and haul on in taking lower, topmast, or topgallant studdingsails in ?

A. Haul on the tripping-line and sheet for a lower, and the downhauls and sheets for a topmast or topgallant studdingsail, ease away the tacks, and halyards, and short sheets.

Monkey Topsail.

A monkey topsail yard is fitted to each training ship. The newly-raised boys are to be taught to lay out on the yard to loose and furl the sail, to pass an earring, to reef, and shake out a reef. They are to have explained to them the name and use of every part, and how to bend and unbend the sail and the gear. The name of each part of the.topsail is to be painted on it in black letters.

Monkey Topsail Yard.

Loosing Sails.

The lower and topsail yards are generally marked with a white band of paint round them, at a certain distance outside the quarter, called laying-out marks. After the pipe goes, loose and furl sails, and the order is given "away aloft," the hands get on the yards as quickly as possible, keeping between the laying-out marks and bunt, until the order, "trice up, lay out" is given.

Sail loosers on the lower and topsail yards, at the order "lay out," should clear away the gaskets and second reef-earrings as quickly as possible, and see the other reef-earrings clear, that is if the topsails and courses have no reefs in, but the bunt should never be let fall before the quarter and yard-arm gaskets are clear. Very aften, at the order "let fall," the men in the bunt, without ascertaining if the outer gaskets are clear, let fall the bunt, and should one of the quarter or yard-arm gaskets be fast, the whole weight of the sail comes on it, and, in all probability, the lanyard of the gasket has to be cut; the captain of tops, &c. should always see the stops of the top-bowline gone, and the bunt-jigger of the topsail unhooked, also the bunt-whip of the courses; this, at times, has been neglected, and the bunt-becket has been torn out of the sail. Topgallant and royal yard loosers should be very careful to commence loosing at the yard-arms first, and lay in as they cast the gaskets off, more particularly at sea, and never let the bunt fall first, as it might be attended with serious consequences; for instance, it is blowing fresh, the bunt of the sail is let fall before the yard-arms are loosened, the sails fill with wind like a bladder, rises above the yard, the hand at the yard-arm, not expecting it, is knocked backward, and most likely falls on deck.

In loosing jibs, care should be taken by the hand taking the cover of the jib or flying-jib off to cut the stop of the jib-halyards, and see the jib-pendants clear of the eyebolts in the bowsprit cap, and foot-line let go.

N.B.—In stowing jibs, before the covers are put on, the jib-halyards are always stopped to the lower part of the jib-stay, and the clew of the jib and cross-in jib-pendants are always stowed between the eyebolts in the foremost part of the bowsprit-cap.

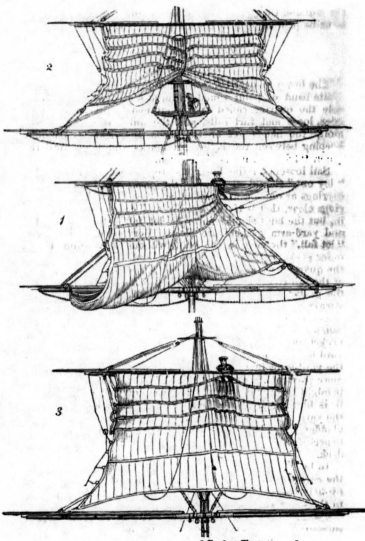

The consequence of having a { Gasket Fast - 1.
Bunt Whip Fast 2.
Reef-Becket Fast 3.

To Furl.

A. As soon as the yards are lowered on the cap, the clews are hauled close up, and the buntlines carry the foot of the sail to a certain distance above the yard, for which purpose they are marked, both buntlines being kept square.

It is a general practice in the Navy to haul the second reef-earring out in furling, this is done to give sufficient skin to stow the sail in (hence the order which is usually given " the second reef-earring in a furl ").

In furling sails it is the duty of the captain of tops to be in the bunt, as everything depends how the sail is stowed there, whether it will be a sightly furl or not. A bulky, mis-shaped bunt to a sail denotes a slovenly set of topmen.

As soon as the order ": trice up, lay out second reef earring and furl," is given, the men at the yard-arms should at once get hold of the second reef-earring and haul it out, bringing the second reef-cringle out square with the head-earring cringle, and the leech-rope of the second reef inside the leech-rope between the first reef-earring and head earring : it is not supposed to be secured, only steadied taught and kept in place by hand, or by the man at the yard-arm putting his foot on it, the second reef-cringle is gathered in towards the bunt; when the second reef-earring is stowed inside the skin thus formed, care should always be taken that this is really done, for some hands, with a mistaken idea of smartness, neglect hauling the earring out at all, but commence to pass the leech in at once, the consequence is, all the sail is gathered into the bunt, the buntlines are let go, the foot of the sail comes down on the already over-filled bunt ; the bunt jigger for a topsail, and the bunt-whip for a course is hauled on, and the men in the bunt of the yard endeavour to foot the sail in the skin without success, in all probability, during this time the officer carrying on is hurrying them, the consequence is, the bunt-gaskets are passed, and the boom lowered on a badly furled sail, which, in nine cases out of ten, ends in extra drill ; whereas, if the second reef-earring had really been hauled out, and the leech of the sail passed in from the second reef, it would equalise the sail and give ample room for properly stowing the bunt ; therefore, it should be borne in mind by young beginner, that the cause of badly-furled topsails commences at the yard-arm, and is generally the cause of a badly-formed bunt.

As soon as the second reef-earrings are out, the man next the yard-arm man should get hold of the leech of the sail

under the second reef-earring. and hand it in towards the
bunt, then commence to gather all the slack sail into the
skin, formed by the. second reef, the hands in towards the
bunt gathering the foot and all the slack sail up in their
hands, in between the clews and the yard towards the bunt
on both sides, making it as light as possible at the yard-
arms; when all the slack sail has been gathered in, and the
bunt-jigger is hooked, pull up on the bunt-jigger, and lower
the buntlines, footing the sail well into the bunt as it comes
down, and taking care there is an equal quantity of sail on
each quarter. All hands look towards the bunt, and give
one good final heave up together; as soon as the sail is fairly
in the skin, pass the gaskets and clew-hangers, and lay in as
quickly as possible; no hand should linger on the yard after
his work is done.

To unbend and to bend the Gear and Sail.

Supposing the topsails to be already made up, furled
for bending, the bending strop seized in place, they are laid
athwartships, abreast their respective yards, the roping of
the head next the deck, and the sails clear of turns.

NOTE.—A double whip, kept rove at the topmast head, will be found
most useful in unbending and shifting sails, shifting topsail yards, &c.
This tackle is named the centre burton.

The sail-tackle is overhauled down, and hooked to the after
part of the bending strop. When the sail-tackle is worked
on the main deck, a bowline, bent to the strop of the sail-
tackle block, will keep the sail in going up clear of the top
rim. Man the sail-tackles, and walk it up until the clews of
the sail are above the top.

Bend the reef-tackles, and second reef-tackles, if fitted,
buntlines and topsail-clewlines, so as to have command of the
sail in case the lanyards of the gaskets should get loose, and
the sail blow adrift.

NOTE.—Second reef-tackles are only bent to heavy topsails.

As soon as the topsail is up, the captain of the top, who is
in the bunt of the topsail yards, sees it is clear of turns, and
secures the midship roband as quick as possible, and hooks
the bunt-jigger, the reef-tackles being bent, the yard-arm
men get hold of the head-earrings, and lay out with them in
hand, the hands on deck clapping on the reef-tackles at the
same time, which lights the sail out to the yard-arms, assisted
by the men on the yard; the outer turns of the head-earrings
are passed as quickly as possible, the hands on each side of

the yard facing towards the bunt, and lighting the head of the sail taut along the yard-arms; the midship roband having been previously well secured prevents the head of the sail being hauled more out to one yard-arm than the other; as soon as the two outer turns of the head-earrings are passed, the four inner turns are passed, and the robands secured round the jackstay. The sheets, if chain, are either hooked with clip-hooks or shackled; if rope, the topsail sheet block is fitted with a thimble and shackled, and the clewline-block is lashed abaft the clew. Bowlines are bent. The seizing of the bending-strop is cut as soon as the bunt-jigger is hooked, and hauled well taut. When all the gear is bent, the hands on the yards cast off the lanyards of the gaskets, which are secured to the sail, toss the sail well up, taking care to have a good skin, and pass the lanyards of the gaskets round the jackstays, always remembering to reeve the first and second reef-earrings, and tuck them into the sail. It should ever be borne in mind the longer the clews are the easier it will be to bend the sheets and clewlines. In shifting courses and topsails for exercise, it is a common practice to send the sails down by the buntlines, but now it is the custom to keep the bending-strop in place, and shift the sails furled, they are sent down equally as quick by the tackle; it is, however, a wise precaution, in shifting heavy topsails, to use the topsail buntlines as well as the sail-tackle, as if anything happens to the sail-tackles or bending-strop, the buntlines will save the sail from falling on deck.

Q. How is a topsail bent, made up, not furled?

A. The sail-tackle is hooked to the bending-strop, in the same way as it is when being bent or shifted furled. If the sail is secured with ropeyarn stops, they are cut as the sail is swayed about the top; if secured with gaskets, the lanyards are cast off by the men in the top. When the clews are above the top, and it is ascertained the topsail is clear of turns, and on the right slue, the head of the sail is lowered level with the yard, and the midship robands secured. The gear is bent as before explained. When the men at the yard-arms have the outer turns of the head-earring passed, and the hands on the yard have hold of the head of the sail ready for passing the robands, and the fore part of the top is clear of men, cut the seizing of the bending-strop, and let the sail fall.

In shifting topsails, as soon as the men are at their respective stations aloft, the lanyards of the bunt-gaskets are cast off from abaft the mast, and well secured round the bunt of

the sail; great care should be taken in doing this well, so as
to keep the bunt together as the sail goes down; nothing
looks worse than a sail blown adrift and falling on the deck
in an unshapely lump; equal care should be taken in casting
the lanyards of the other gaskets off the jackstay and securing them taut round the sail. When the sail is landed on
deck it ought to be ready to stow away; this will not be the
case if care is not taken in securing all the lanyards of the
gaskets taut round the sail. The clew-hangers, robands,
and inner turns of the head-earrings are cast off, all the
gear is unbent with the exception of the buntlines, the
bights of which are hitched round each side of the bending
strop. In shifting topsails for exercise, they are generally
sent down by the buntlines. The outer turns of the head-
earrings are let go at the order to "ease in." In sending the
other topsail up, proceed as explained in bending topsails.

To Reef.

If on a wind, the weather braces are rounded-in, so as to
spill the sail; if running free the yards are braced forward
for the same purpose; the topsails are then lowered on the
cap, and the reef-tackle hauled out, so as to leave a slack
leech for the men at the yard-arms to haul the earrings out.

In taking the third or fourth reef in, the clews of the topsails are raised, and the buntlines steadied well taut.

The yards are always laid with the braces well taut, and
the reef-tackles hauled out, before the order is given to the
men to lay out. The second reef-tackle, in large ships, is
generally used in taking the first and second reefs in.

Q. In reefing topsails, after the word "lay out" is given,
what ought the men on the yard to do?

A. Get hold of the spilling-lines and gather up, and get
hold of the reef-line as quickly as possible, the men at the
yard-arms see their earring clear, and ready for passing,
when the hands have hold of the reef-line, all face to leeward, and light the sail out to windward, so as to assist the
man at the weather yard-arm in hauling the weather earring-
out. When out to windward, all face to windward, and
light the sail over to leeward, when the lee-earring is out,
toggle away*; when the earrings are out, the men at the
yard-arms will make a signal by holding up (the man at the
starboard yard-arm his right hand, and the man at the port
yard-arm his left hand) as a signal, so as to prevent any

---

* Slab reef should be hauled up before the men lay in, slab lines are
fitted to all topsails for that purpose.

singing out, which should always be avoided, more especially aloft. At night, when the signal cannot be seen, the man at the weather yard-arm, when the weather-earring is out, will give the order "haul out to leeward," and when out to leeward, the man at the lee yard-arm will give the order " toggle away."

No other man should speak on the yard.

Q. How many turns would you take with the first reef-earring?

A. One outer, and two inner.

Q. How many turns would you take with the second reef-earring?

A. One outer, and three inner.

Q. How many turns would you take with the third reef-earring?

A. Two outer, and three inner.

Q. How many turns would you take with the fourth reef-earring?

A. As many outer turns as I could get.

Q. Explain what you mean by an outer and inner turn?

A. Outside the lift, a reef-cleat is nailed on to the yard-arm, fitted with notches or stops, over which notches the reef-earrings are passed, so as to keep the head of the sail taut out. The first reef-earring over the first notch, and the second over the second, and so on ; these are the outer turns. The inner turns are passed round the yard-arm, in a similar way to a head-earring, each turn passing through the reef-cringle, the ends of the earrings are secured round the topsail-lift with a clove-hitch.

Q. What gear ought to be hauled well taut before the hands lay out on the topsails and lower yards?

A. Braces, lifts, trusses, and rolling-tackles ; as the courses are never reefed but in bad weather, there is certain to be considerable motion on ; therefore, for the safety of the hands going aloft, the yard should be well secured and kept as steady as possible.

To shake out Reefs.

Round in the weather braces, haul taut both reef-tackles ; settle the halyards roundly until the leeches of the sail are well slackened, steady the yards by hauling well taut the braces before giving the order to " lay out," and see that the reef-beckets are clear before easing down the earrings, being careful to ease down the lee earring first. Time is saved by properly laying the yards and well checking the halyards.

To pass an Earring.

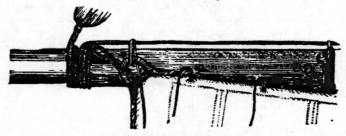

PASSING A HEAD EARRING.

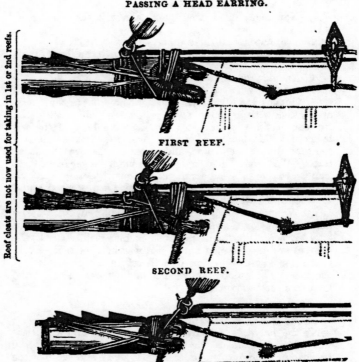

FIRST REEF.

SECOND REEF.

THIRD REEF.

Reef cleats are not now used for taking in 1st or 2nd reefs.

Section III.

(1.) *Boat Pulling*.

To get out oars.
To give way by numbers.
To lay on oars.
To toss oars as a salute.

To toss oars coming alongside.
To lay in oars, coming alongside at sea.
To get out bow oars.

To lay in bow oars.
To use the boat hook.
To shove off.
To get fenders in and out properly.
To back and hold water.

Instructions for Boats' Crews.

For the Training Service.

When a boat is called away, the crew will man their boat, sit down on their thwarts, and wait for orders from the Coxswain.

The outer-bowman will cast off and coil down the painter, the inner-bowman holding on with the boat-hook.

The stroke-oarsman nearest the ship uses the stern boat-hook, and the remainder of the crew see their oars clear and in order by their numbers, the stroke-oars being nearest the boat's side, and, unless ordered to the contrary, unship their poppets.

Note.—The inner-bowman always holds on or attends the boat rope; the outer bowman fends off. Stroke-oar nearest ship's side attends boat-hook or stern-fast.

"*Up Oars.*"

The crew get hold of their oars, and, watching the stroke-oarsmen, will toss them up together, placing the looms on the bottom boards between their feet, every oar upright, blades "Fore and Aft," dressed by the after-oar each side, with the hand nearest boat's side just below the leather, midship hand as low as possible, body upright.

Note.—This is the position of "Tossing Oars."

"*Shove Off.*"

The bowmen shove the bow of the boat off, toss their boat-hooks upright, wait a pause, boat them together, sit down on their thwarts, haul their fenders in, unship their poppets, and then toss their oars up together.

The remainder of the crew haul their fenders in at the order " Shove Off."

The stroke-oarsmen nearest ship keeps stern clear, then places his boat-hook amidships, with head aft, sits down, and tosses his oar.

" *Down.*"

At the order " Down," lift the oar about a foot, and let it fall quietly into the rowlock.   All oars to be horizontal, and blades feathered.

NOTE.—This is the position of " Laying on Oars."

" *Give Way Together.*"   (*By numbers.*)

" *One.*"—Lean aft, straighten the arms, turning the knuckles down as the blade goes forward, bringing the blade square.   All the oars to be parallel with the stroke-oar, the blade just clear of the water.

" *Two.*"—Place the blade in the water, and pull the loom towards you, dropping the elbows and wrist as you arrive at the end of the stroke, taking the oar out of the water, and come to the position of " Laying on Oars."

" *One,*" " *Two,*" &c., &c.

Note.—A pause of about three seconds is to be made between each order, until all the crew thoroughly understand feathering their oars ; as they improve, the interval to be lessened.

Stand by to " *Lay on your Oars.*"   (*A caution.*)

" *Oars.*"—At the order " Oars," which will follow the caution, complete the stroke, and come to the position of " Laying on Oars."

Stand by to " *Toss Oars.*"   (*A caution.*)

" *Oars.*"—At the order " Oars," the starboard stroke-oarsman looks over his shoulder, and, at the completion of the stroke, gives the word " Up," when all the oars are to be tossed together, placed and held in the position of " Tossing Oars."

INSTRUCTIONS FOR BOATS' CREWS BY NUMBERS.

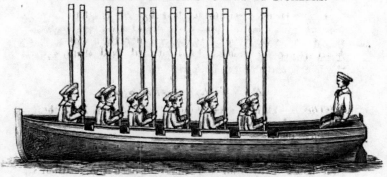

Tossing Oars. *See Instructions.*

At the word "One,"—lean aft, straighten the arms, &c. *See* Instructions.

At the word "Two,"—pull the loom of the oar towards you, throwing your body back, &c. *See* Instructions.

Laying on Oars. *See* Instructions.

Note.—If oars are to be laid in, the caution will be "Stand by to lay in your Oars," and after the oars are tossed "Boat your Oars," at which order they will be laid down quietly in rotation from forward, boat them, square the looms, and ship the poppets.

" *Back of All.*" (*By numbers.*)

" *One.*"—At the word " One," lean back a little, bring the loom close to the chest, blade clear of the water, and perpendicular.

" *Two.*"—Place the blade in the water and push from you, bringing body upright, feathering the oar by turning your hands away from you, and return to the position of " Laying on Oars."

Stand by to " *Hold Water.*" (*A caution.*)

" HOLD WATER."—Oars to be held perfectly steady, all the blades the same depth in the water.

" *Stand by Bows.*" (*A caution.*)

" Bows."—The bowmen will look towards each other and toss their oars together, wait a pause, boat their oars, ship poppets, out fenders, stand up on head sheets, and then toss their boat-hooks up ; remainder of the crew out fenders.

" *Way Enough.*"

At the order " Way Enough," give one stroke after the order. Oars to be tossed together by the word " Oars " from the starboard stroke-oarsman, as in " Tossing Oars."

Stroke-oarsman nearest ship will boat his oar and attend stern boat-hook.

SPECIAL DUTIES FOR LIFEBOAT'S CREW.

25 feet, 10-Oared Cutter, fitted with Kynaston's hooks. Jackstays from davits to water-line, &c.

First hands up slip gripes. Each man on entering the boat will put his cork jacket on, and take his place on his respective thwart as quickly as possible.

STROKE-OARSMEN see plug, in, safety-pins out of after-hook, and attend after-lizard.

BOWMAN.—Out safety-pins of foremost-hook, attend boat-rope, and see it ready for slipping, boat-hooks ready for use.
Second thwart attend lizard.

COXSWAIN.—Have whip clear for slipping, and ship "Tiller." The rest of boat's crew sit down and hold on to "Life-lines."

Salutes in Boats.

(1.) To superior officers, boats fitted with crutches "lay on oars," boats fitted with rowlocks "toss oars," the coxswain standing up and taking his hat off. To other officers "lay on oars," the coxswain standing and touching his hat. Boats towing or laden with stores do not "toss" or "lay on oars," the coxswain only stands up and salutes.

(2.) Should a boat be laying on her oars, superior officers will be saluted by the oars being tossed, if the boat is fitted with rowlocks, the coxswain and bowmen standing up and taking their hats off; if the boat is fitted with crutches, the coxswain and bowman only salute. Other officers are saluted by the coxswain and bowmen standing up and touching their hats.

(3.) Should a boat, manned but having her oars laid in, be passed by superior officers, the crew stand up and take their hats off; to other officers they stand up and touch their hats.

(4.) Boat-keepers will stand up and take their hats off to superior officers, or stand up and touch them to others; and on boats coming alongside or leaving the ship, they are to go to the bows of their boats, ready to haul out of the way.

(5.) When under sail, superior officers are saluted by easing the sheets, if on a wind, or lowering the sail, if running; the coxswain taking his hat off, sitting. For other officers the coxswain only salutes.

(6.) Officers and others, in charge of, or taking a passage in, boats, are to be guided by the general rules of the service.

Remarks.

Silence is at all times to be kept in boats, and the crew properly dressed. Strict attention must be paid to this rule, as nothing shows a bad state of discipline more than a noisy and slovenly boat's crew. When a boat is required to be manned to leave the ship, the pipe will be—

"AWAY GALLEYS," or whatever boat is required, "AWAY (name of boat)," always means that the boat is going to leave the ship.

If the boat is to hook on or moor, the pipe will be as follows—

"FIRST CUTTERS HOOK ON."

"Second Launches Moor your Boat."

Never stand or sit on the gunwale, or stand on thwarts.

As a rule, masts to be got down before going alongside in harbour, at sea it should always be down. Oars are not to be tossed going alongside a ship at sea, but thrown out of the rowlock, blade forward, and boated at once; and on leaving, blades to be lifted clear of gunwale, and the oar brought aft into its rowlock at the order "Out Oars."

If a sail does not set properly, shifting the strop two or three inches in or out on the yard will often correct it. If carrying too much weather-helm, shift the weights further aft; if lee-helm, further forward. Never belay a sheet, and always keep halliards clear. Luff to the wind, and ease the fore-sheet in a squall; and, in lowering the sail, always hauling down on the luff.

Boat's crews learning to pull are to have their thwarts changed, so that they may pull as well on either the starboard or the port side, also that their acquaintance with the duties of stroke and bow-oars may be ensured; and they are to be taught the names of parts of boat and oars.

No boy to be stationed in a boat until he has passed through these pulling instructions.

To ensure working together, the orders, with the previous caution, are always to be given as laid down hereafter—

CAUTION.	ORDER.
Stand by to "Toss Oars" - -	"Oars."
„ „ - -	"Down."
„ "Lay on Oars" -	"Oars."
„ in "Bows" - -	"Bows."
„ "Back" (Starboard or Port Oars) -	"Back."
„ "Back of All" -	"Back of All."
„ "Give Way" Starboard (or Port), "Back" Port (or Starboard) Oars -	"Give Way" Starboard (or Port), "Back" Port (or Starboard) Oars.
„ "Hold-Water" -	"Hold Water."
„ "Ease Sheets" -	"Ease Off."
„ "Lower Sails" -	"Lower Away."

EXTRA QUESTIONS.

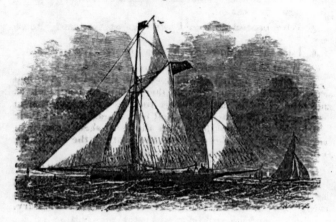

YAWL.

BOAT EXERCISE.

PART I.

Q. You have been taught to pull an oar, and you are now stationed in a boat. What is the first thing you would attend to on your boat being ordered to be manned alongside?

A. Take my place on the thwart I am stationed on, and see I have the right oar corresponding to the number of my thwart, put the fender next me out, and see my oar ready for tossing.

Q. What precaution is necessary in manning a boat at sea, or when a ship is rolling much?

A. Not to toss the oars, or ship the mast until clear of the ship, for fear they should catch under the ports, or any other part of the ship's side, and go through the bottom of the boat.

Q. What is to be done at the order " shove off " ?

A. In fenders, the off bowmen haul in, and coil the painter down if out, the bowmen nearest the ship or landing place bear the boat off.

Q. What precaution would you take at the word " down oars " ?

A. Ease the oar down by the hand nearest the gunwale.

Q. What is to be done at the word " bow " ?

A. The men pulling on the foremost thwart to give one stroke after the word bow, if a double-banked boat, look at each other, lift the hand nearest the gunwale as a signal to toss together, toss their oars, and boat them, take up their boat-hooks and stand firmly on the head-sheets, the man nearest the ship or shore to fend the boat off, the outer man to hook on, all fenders to be put out.

Q. What is to be done at the order " way enough " ?

A. Give one stroke after the order, lift the hand nearest the gunwale, as a signal, toss the oars together, always waiting for the order to boat them ; when it is necessary, the short boat-hook will be used by the man sitting on the after-thwart nearest the ship or landing place, who will boat his oar for that purpose.

Q. When the boat you belong to is ordered to be lowered, what are the necessary things you should attend to ?

A. See the plug in, rudder shipped, oars and boat-hooks properly secured, the falls clear for running, and a proper turn taken for lowering, life-lines clear, and the lanyards of the gripes gone.

Q. What is a boat's fall ?

A. A tackle by which a boat is hoisted up to the davits.

Q. You say you would see the life-lines clear, and lanyards of gripes gone ; explain what they are, and their use ?

A. Gripes are made of sword matting, made fast to the davit-heads, usually crossed outside the boat, and passed under her, and secured by lanyards in-board, to keep the boat steady when at sea, or when the ship is rolling ; life-lines are also secured to the davit-heads, and are used for steadying the boat when being hoisted, also to keep her from sending fore and aft, which is done by crossing the life-lines ; that is, the man in the stern taking the foremost,

and the man in the bow taking the after life-line ; when
the boat is high enough to take a turn with the falls, the
bight of the life-lines is rove through the slings, and over
the davit-heads, then two or three round turns round all
parts.

Q. What is to be done when a boat is ordered to be
hoisted up ?

A. The coxswain and one of the bowmen generally go
into the boat, hook the slings in their proper places, haul
taut the steadying lines, and make them fast, see that the
oars and boat-hooks are properly secured, and before hooking
on the boat's tackles, look over their heads to see they are
clear of turns ; the foremost tackle should always be hooked
first when a ship is lying in tide way, or moving ahead at
sea, the danger of the after tackle being hooked first, and
the boat having no boat-rope in from forward is, she may
swing broadside to the tide, and cause some accident ; when
the order is given to " haul taut and hoist away," the men
in the boat should take hold of the life-lines, and light
themselves up, taking their weight off the boat until high
enough ; the man tending the foremost tackle should stand
before, and the man tending the after-tackles abaft the
boat's-tackles. When the boat's-tackles are belayed, it is
the coxswain's duty, or the man tending the after-tackle, to
see the plug out, so as to prevent the boat holding water in
the event of rain ; life-lines, if not required, to be properly
coiled down in the boat, rudder unshipped, rowlock plates
shipped, fenders in, gripes properly passed and secured, and
the falls clear for lowering; the bowmen, after assisting in
those things, if at sea, will see a boat-rope passed forward
ready for lowering.

Q. What is a steadying line, and its use ?

A. Slings are hooked to the bottom of a boat, steadying
lines are secured to the boat's gunwale, from a hook in the
upper part of the slings, so as to prevent a boat capsizing
when a strain is brought on the tackles; boat's tackles
should always be fitted with a thimble (instead of a hook)
to take the hook in the slings; hooks in boat-tackles are
very dangerous when a ship is rolling much, as if not
rounded up out of the way smartly they may catch some
part of the boat, or even hook a man out of the boat, and
cause some serious accident.

R 3498.   F

Rig of Boats used in the Navy.

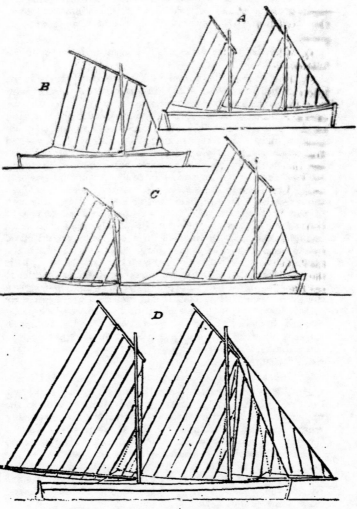

A. 28-feet Cutter Life-Boat, Standing Lug, Fine Weather Rig.
B. 28-feet Gig, Dipping Lug.   C. 30-ft. Cutter, Dipping Lug.
D. 42-ft. Launch, Standing Lug.   SCALE ⅛-inch to a foot.

(2.) *Parts and Fittings of a Boat.*

Gunwale.	Rudder.	Painter.
Thwarts.	Rudder lanyard.	Lazy painter.
Stern sheets.	Tiller.	Grapnel.
Poppets.	Yoke.	Stretchers.
Piggin.	Yoke lines.	Clamps.
Breaker.	Head sheets.	Step of mast.
Rowlocks.	Back-board.	Tabernacle.
Slings.	Bottom-board.	Crutches.
Steadying lines.		

Q. What is the gunwale?

A. A piece of timber going round the upper part of the boat as a binder for the topwork.

Q. What are thwarts?

A. The seats athwart a boat whereon the rowers sit to manage their oars.

Q. What are stern sheets?

A. That part of a boat between the stern and the aftermost thwart, furnished with seats for passengers.

Q What are poppets?

A. Pieces of wood shipped in the space which form the rowlocks when the oars are not in use or the boat is under sail.

Q. What is a piggin?

A. A little pail having a long stave for a handle, used to bale water out of a boat.

Q. What is a breaker?

A. A small barrel, carried in a boat, for containing water.

Q. What are rowlocks?

A. Spaces in the gunwales of a boat's side, wherein the oars work in, in the act of rowing.

Q. What are slings?

A. Chains with hooks and rings, hooked in the stern, bow, and bottom of a boat, to which the boat's tackles are hooked in order to hoist the boats up to the davits or inboard.

Q. What are steadying lines?

A. Slings are hooked to the bottom of a boat, steadying lines are secured to the boat's gunwale, from a hook in the upper part of the slings, so as to prevent a boat capsizing when a strain is brought on the tackles; boat's tackles should always be fitted with a thimble (instead of a hook) to take the hook in the slings; hooks in boat-tackles are very dangerous when a ship is rolling much, as if not rounded up out of the way smartly they may catch some part of the boat, or even hook a man out of the boat, and cause some serious accident.

Q. What is a rudder?

A. The rudder is a piece of wood attached to the stern-post of a boat by pintles and braces, and guides her in any required direction.

Q. What is the rudder lanyard?

A. A piece of rope knotted and rove through the rudder, the other end being fastened to the ring in the stern-post inboard to prevent the rudder going adrift, should it become unshipped.

Q. What is a tiller?

A. A piece of wood fitted in the rudder head to steer by.

Q. What is a yoke?

A. A substitute for the tiller, made of wood or metal, and ships on the rudder head.

Q. What are yoke lines.

A. Lines which are attached to the yoke to steer the boat.

Q. What are head sheets?

A. A small platform in the bow of the boat, whereon the bowman stands to fend off with the boat hook.

Q. What is a backboard?

A. A piece of wood generally ornamented, shipped in the stern of a boat, at the termination of the stern sheets.

Q. What are bottom boards?

A. Long pieces of wood nailed together, which lay from the stern sheets to the bow, and to which small cleats are attached wherein the stretchers are shipped.

Q. What is a painter?

A. A rope fastened to the ring in the stem inboard, and used for making the boat fast to the booms, &c.

Q. What is a lazy painter?

A. A small light rope used for the same purpose.

Q. What is a grapnel?

A. A kind of small anchor with four claws at one end, and a ring at the other, used for securing boats, or creeping for anything on the bottom.

Q. What are stretchers?

A. Pieces of wood against which the rowers place their feet in rowing.

Q. What are clamps?

A. A piece of shaped iron fitted to the sailing thawt to secure the mast when shipped.

Q. What is the step of mast?

A. A wood socket secured to the keel-board in which the mast is stepped.

Q. What is a tabernacle?

A. A wooden frame extending from the socket secured to the keel-board, and sailing thawt through which the heel of the mast is shipped.

Q. What are crutches?

A. Crutches are made of iron or metal, and are shipped in crutch plates let in on the gunwale, wherein the oars are worked when rowing.

SECOND INSTRUCTION.

Section I.

Bends and Hitches.

To know the names of, the use of, and to be able to make the following :—

Half hitch.
Timber hitch.
Clove hitch.
Roband hitch.
Rolling hitch.
Round turn and half hitch.
Marling spike hitch.
Blackwall hitch.
Fisherman's bend.
Studdingsail halliard bend.
Catspaw.
Swab hitch.
To pass a stopper.
To mouse a hook.

To put a strop on a rope.
To put a strop on a spar.
To know the use of a parbuckle.
To sling a cask.
Bowline.
Running bowline.
Bowline on a bight.
Sheet bend.
Reef knot.
Sheepshank.
Clinch.
Figure of eight knot.
Overhand knot.

Carrick bend.
Two hawsers half-hitched and seized.
Ropeyarn knot.
To sling a cask on end.
To sling a grating.
To lower a man down from aloft.
To take a turn round a cleat.
To put on a topgallant and royal purchase.

Q. How do you make a half-hitch ?

A. Pass the end of your rope round the standing part, bringing it up through the bight.

Q. What is a timber-hitch used for, and how is it made ?

A. For securing the end of a rope to a spar ; in towing a spar, always use a half-hitch in addition to a timber-hitch.

To make the Knot.

Take the end of a rope round a spar, pass it under and over the standing part, then pass three turns round its own part, and haul it taut.

Q. What is a clove-hitch used for, and how is it made ?

A. It is used for rattling down the rigging. It is made by passing the end of a rope round another rope or spar, over, and bringing it under and round behind its standing part, over the rope or spar again, and up through its own part. It can be stopped or hitched to its own part as required, the only difference between two half-hitches and a clove-hitch is, one is hitched round its own standing part, and the other is hitched round a spar or another rope.

Q. How is a roband-hitch made?

A. For a topsail or course, by taking the end over the jackstay and under, then through the eyelet hole in the head of the sail and clove hitched to the jackstay, thus securing the head of the sail to it. For a topgallant sail or royal, it is passed the same way, but not clove-hitched, the two nearest robands being reef-knotted together.

Q. What is a rolling-hitch used for, and how is it made?

A. Bending a small rope to a large one, putting a tail jigger on a backstay. Make the hitch by taking a half-hitch round the standing part with the end of a rope, and another through the same bight, hauling it well taut in place above the first hitch and the upper part of the bight, and dog the end above the hitch round the standing part, and stop it back with spunyarn or a ropeyarn.

Q. How is a round turn and half-hitch made?

A. It is made by passing the end of a rope once round the spar, or ring, &c., then round the standing part, and bringing the end up through its own bight, and seizing it back to the standing part.

A Marline-Spike Hitch (also called a Midshipman's or Admiralty Hitch)*

Is made by placing the marline-spike upon top of the end of the seizing you are going to heave taut, the end part is then brought over the marline-spike, forming a round turn ; the marline-spike is then brought back under the standing part of the seizing, and up between it, and the other part of the round turn thus formed ; the greater strain you bring on the seizing, the more the end jambs and prevents it from slipping.

If used for the hook of a tackle, the hook is passed down between the round turns.

Q. What is a Blackwall hitch used for, and how is it made?

A. For hooking a tackle to a rope, such as setting up lower rigging instead of a cat's-paw, where the end of the lanyard is not long enough to form a cat's-paw, but a strop and toggle is preferable.

---

* Used for heaving the turns of a seizing taut with a marline-spike or hooking the hook of a tackle to any rope where a smart pull is required ; it is preferable to a cat's-paw, as it never jambs.

To make the Hitch.

You form a bight or a kink with the end of the lanyard, keeping the end part underneath, and the standing part on the top, put the hook through the bight, taking care to keep the bight well up on the back of the hook, until there is a strain on the tackle.

A Fisherman's Bend.

Take two round turns with the end of a rope round a spar, or through the ring of an anchor, take one half-hitch round the standing parts, and under all parts of the turns, then one half-hitch round the standing parts above all, stop the end to the standing part, instead of taking the last half-hitch, tuck the end under one of the round turns, and it becomes a studding-sail halyard bend.

Q. What is the use of a studdingsail halyard-bend, and how is it made?

A. It is used in bending studdingsail, topgallant, and royal halyards; it allows the yards to go closer to the blocks or sheaves than any other bend.

To make the Bend.

Take two round turns round the yard; pass the end from right to left under both turns, then from left to right over one, and under the other turn.

Q. What is a cat's-paw used for, and how is it made?

A. It is used for setting up lower rigging. To form it, you first lay the end part of the lanyard across the standing part, which will form a bight; then lay hold of the bight with one hand on each side of it, breaking it down and turning it over from you two or three times; clap both bights together and hook on to both parts. A boatswain's toggle and strop should always be used in preference to a cat's-paw, as it is almost certain to burst the outer yarns of the lanyards.

Q. How is a swab-hitch made?

A. It is simply a single sheet bend used for bending a rope's end to swabs when washing them overboard.

Q. What use is a bowline knot, and how is it made?

A. A bowline knot is used for sending a man aloft, or one down from aloft, for riding down stays, backstays, making a pair of slings, and many other purposes. Take the end of your rope in your right hand, and the standing part in your left, lay the end over the standing part, then with your left hand turn the bight of the standing part over the end part, so as to form a cuckold's neck on the standing part; then lead the end through the standing part above, and stick it down through the cuckold's neck, and so the knot is completed.

Q. What is a running bowline used for, and how is it made?

A. It is used for throwing over anything out of reach, or anything under water.

How to make the Knot.

You take the end of the rope round the standing part, through the bight, and make a single bowline upon the running part.

Q. What use is a bowline on the bight, and how is it made?

A. A bowline on the bight is used when both ends are occupied, or to send a man down from aloft when he is hurt, as it is much easier to sit in.

To make the Knot.

With the bight of a rope in your right hand, and the standing part in your left, throw a cuckold's neck over the bight with the standing parts, then haul enough of the bight up through the cuckold's neck to go under and over all parts, haul all taut, and the knot is completed.

Q. What is the use of a sheet bend, and how is it made?

A. Making a rope's-end fast to anything, such as a becket of a swab or block.

How to make the Bend.

Pass the end of a rope through the bight of another rope, or through the becket of a block, or a clew of a sail; then round both parts of the bight or becket, and take the end under its own part; it is sometimes put under twice, and the end stopped back to the standing part; also for bending topgallant and royal clewlines, jib and staysail down-hauls.

Knot Yarns.

Reef Knot.

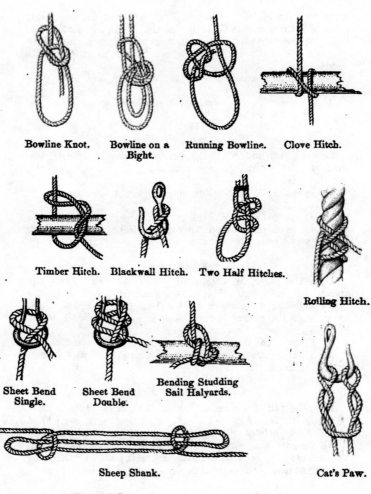

Bowline Knot.   Bowline on a   Running Bowline.   Clove Hitch.
                    Bight.

Timber Hitch.   Blackwall Hitch.   Two Half Hitches.

Rolling Hitch.

Sheet Bend   Sheet Bend   Bending Studding
Single.   Double.   Sail Halyards.

Sheep Shank.   Cat's Paw.

Carrick Bend.   Bend Hawsers.

Q. How do you make a reef-knot, and what is its use?

A. It is used for reefing sails, fitted with reef points, such as trysails, spankers, and boat sails. First make an over-handed knot round the foot of the sail, then bring the end which is next to you over the left hand and through the bight; haul both ends taut, and it is made.

Q. What is the use of a sheep-shank, and how is it made?

A. For shortening in a rope, which requires to be lengthened again, such as topgallant and royal backstays, the rope is doubled in three parts, and a hitch taken over each bight with the standing part of the backstays, and hauled taut.

Q. What is the use of an inside clinch, and how is it made?

A. For securing the standing part of a reef-tackle round the goose-neck or any other rope that you wish to jamb.

To make the Clinch.

Take the end over and under its own part, and inside, put two seizings on opposite each other, they are called the throat and quarter seizings; exactly the same as are used for turning-in lower rigging.

Q. What is the use of an outside clinch, and how is it made?

A. For securing the standing part of a rope topsail sheet, or any rope you wish to let go smartly.

To make the Clinch.

Take the end over and under its own part and outside, put the two seizings on exactly the same as for inside clinch.

FIGURE OF EIGHT KNOT.

To make the Knot.—Pass the end of a rope over and round the standing part, up over its own part, and down through the bight. It is used for the end of running rigging, or any rope rove through a block or sheave to prevent it unreeving.

OVER-HAND KNOT.

To make the Knot.—Pass the end of a rope over the standing part and through the bight. It is used for the end of running rigging, or any rope rove through a block or sheave to prevent it unreeving.

A CARRICK BEND.
To Bend two Hawsers with a Carrick Bend.

Take the end of a hawser and lay it across the top of standing part forming a bight, reeve the end of the second hawser down through the bight thus formed, up and over the cross, and down through the bight again on the opposite side, from the other end; one end will then be on top, and the other underneath, one each side of the standing part; if both ends come out on top, it will form a granny's knot.

To Bend two Hawsers with two Half-Hitches and seizing the ends back.

Make a half-hitch in the end of the first hawser, leaving a bight at least a fathom long, reeve the end of the second hawser through the bight of the first hawser, haul end enough through on both hawsers to have at least four feet end, put a seizing on about two feet from the half-hitch, on each hawser, and stop the ends to the standing part.

Q. How do you knot yarns?

A. Take the ends of two yarns, split them in halves about 2 ins. down, marry them together and form a reef-knot, with the opposite ends as nearly as you can; yarns are knotted for the use of the ropemaker, for making spunyarn, nettle-stuff, or any small rope.

Q. How do you pass a stopper?

A. By taking a half-hitch round and against the lay of the rope, and lashing the end of the stopper in the lay.

Q. How do you mouse a hook?

A. Middle a yarn and pass several turns round the neck and the bill of the hook, expend the end round all parts and secure it. It is used to prevent the hook of a tackle or sheet coming unhooked.

Q. How do you put a strop on a rope?

A. By taking round turns with one bight round the rope, bringing the upper bight round the strop and rope and hook the tackle to the two bights.

Q. How do you put a strop on a spar?

A. By passing a round turn round the spar, and reeving one bight through the other.

The use of a parbuckle.

It is used for hauling up or lowering down a cask, or any cylindrical object where there is no crane or tackle. Middle the rope to be used for the parbuckle, place the bight over a post or pin as most convenient, the two ends are then passed under the two quarters of the cask, bring the ends back again over it, and they being both hauled taut or slackened together, either raise or lower the cask as may be required. Care must be taken to keep an equal strain on both parts to prevent the cask slipping out.

Q. How do you sling a cask ?

A. There are several methods of slinging a cask, either with a pair of butt slings, bale slings, or a bowline knot. A cask should always be slung, bung up, or on its head; should one of the heads be defective or out, a bowline knot is used for this; it is very useful, for the instruction of boys, to have small miniature casks slung in the different ways, and hung up in a conspicuous part of the ship, set apart for seamanship instruction.

Q. How do you sling a grating ?

A. By passing the bight of the rope under the ends of the grating and clove hitching them round the grating at each corner.

Q. How do you lower a man down from aloft ?

A. By a bowline on the bight.

Q. How do you take a turn round a cleat ?

A. By taking a half turn round the cleat then under and over both ends of the cleat, taking care not to jamb the rope.

Q. How do you put on a topgaliant and royal purchase ?

A. By hitching the tails round the yard rope right and left handed, close down to the upper block of the purchase, the ends are expended by dogging turns and seized round the yard rope. The royal purchase is rove-on its own yard rope. Two single blocks are kept rove on the yard rope and stopped in the top to form a purchase when the sail is set.

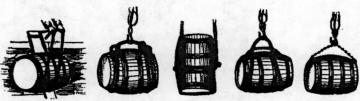

Parbuckle.   Butt Slings.   Head up.   Bale Slings.   Can Hooks.

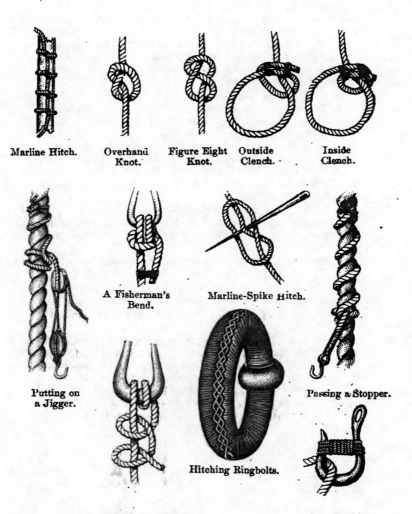

Marline Hitch.

Overhand Knot.

Figure Eight Knot.

Outside Clench.

Inside Clench.

A Fisherman's Bend.

Marline-Spike Hitch.

Putting on a Jigger.

Passing a Stopper.

A Round Turn and Two Half Hitches.

Hitching Ringbolts.

Mouse a hook.

Section II.

Compass.

To know the use of the compass.	To give the names of the half and
To explain the construction of the	quarter points.
compass card.	To know the lubbers' point.
To give the number and names of	To box the compass.
the points.	

COMPASS INSTRUCTION.

Part I.

Q. What is a compass card ?

A. A circular card, by which a ship's course is denoted: it is divided into 32 equal parts, called points ; again divided into 32 equal parts, called half points ; and again divided into 64 equal parts, called quarter-points, each point being distinguished by a letter or letters.

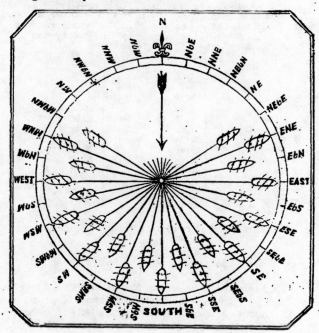

Q. How are the points distinguished or known by letters?

A. N. S. E. and W. stand for North, South, East, and West; these are called the cardinal points; any two or three of these letters, added together, represent the intermediate points, as in the following example :—

REPEAT THE COMPASS.

N. stands for North.	S. by W., South by West.
N. by E., North by East.	S. S. W., South South-West.
N. N. E., North North-East.	S.W. by S., South-West by South.
N. E. by N., North-East by North.	S. W., South-West.
N. E., North-East.	S. W. by W., South-West by West.
N. E. by E., North-East by East.	W. S. W., West South-West.
E. N. E., East North-East.	W. by S., West by South.
E. by N., East by North.	W., West.
E., East.	W. by N., West by North.
E. by S., East by South.	W. N. W., West North-West.
E. S. E., East South-East.	N.W. by W., North-West by West.
S. E. by E., South-East by East.	N. W., North-West.
S. E., South-East.	N. W. by N., North-West by North.
S. E. by S., South-East by South.	N. N. W., North North-West.
S. S. E., South South-East.	N. by W., North by West.
S. by E., South by East.	N., North.
S. South.	

Repeat it the reverse

North.	S. W. by W.	E. S. E.
N. by W.	S. W.	E. by S.
N. N. W.	S. W. by S.	East.
N. W. by N.	S. S. W.	E. by N.
N. W.	S. by W.	E. N. E.
N. W. by W.	South.	N. E. by E.
W. N. W.	S. by E.	N. E.
W. by N.	S. S. E.	N. E. by N.
West.	S. E. by S.	N. N. E.
W. by S.	S. E.	N. by E.
W. S. W.	S. E. by E.	North.

*To answer opposite points, or what is called boxing
the compass.*

Q. What is the opposite point to N.E. ?
A. S.W.

With a very little attention to the question, the young beginner will be able to answer any opposite points most readily, always bearing in mind that the letter N. is opposite to S., and E. to W., and remembering that two or three of these letters added together represent all the points of the compass. For instance—E.N.E. is the opposite point to W.S.W. | S.S.E. to N.N.W. | N.E. by E. to S.W. by W. | N.W. by N. to S.E. by S. | N.E. by N. $\frac{1}{4}$ N. | S.W. by S. $\frac{1}{2}$ S. | W. $\frac{1}{2}$ N. to E. $\frac{1}{2}$ S. | N. $\frac{1}{4}$ E. to S. $\frac{1}{4}$ W., and so on, to any point of the compass.

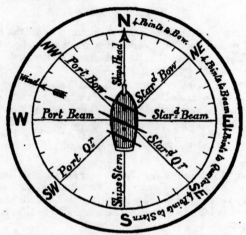

THE COMPASS MADE EASY.

Cardinal Points.

The compass is composed of four letters only—N.S.E. and W., which represent the four cardinal points—viz., North, South, East, and West.

Half-Cardinal Points.

So called because they come halfway between two cardinal points from which they derive their names. Thus, N.E. comes between North and East, and by adding the two letters together, N.E. is produced; in like manner the other half-cardinal points are formed—viz., N.W., S.E., and S.W. There are four half-cardinal points.

False Points.

So called because they borrow their names from the two points between which they come. Thus, N.N.E. comes

R 3498.

G

between North and N.E., and by putting these two points together, taking care to put the letter of the nearest cardinal point first, N.N.E. is produced ; in like manner are all the other false points formed : they are as follows :—E.N.E., E.S.E., S.S.E., S.S.W., W.S.W., W.N.W., and N.N.W. There are eight false points.

The By-Points.

So called because they derive their names from the nearest cardinal or half-cardinal points they are near or by. Thus, N. by E. is by or near North, and taking a direction towards East becomes N. by E.

N.E. by N. is by or near N.E., but being nearer North than East it becomes N.E. by N. ; in like manner all the other by-points derive their name : they are the following :— N.E. by E., E. by N., E. by S., S.E. by E., S.E. by S., S. by E., S. by W., S.W. by S., S.W. by W., W. by S., W. by N., N.W. by W., N.W. by N., and N. by W.—16 in number.

Half-cardinal points are always four points from a cardinal point ; if a ship's head marks a cardinal point, such, for instance, as North, her stern and either beam will also mark a cardinal point ; half-cardinal points marking the two bows and quarters.

For Example.

Ship's head is North, or stern is South, port-beam West, starboard-beam East, port-bow N.W., starboard bow N.E., port-quarter S.W., starboard quarter S.E.

Q. What is lubber's point ?

A. A black line drawn down the centre of the metal bowl in which the compass card is shipped, in a direct line with the ship's head, and as the ship's head moves to the right or the left, the compass card revolves past the line called lubber's point, whatever point of the compass cuts this line, denotes the course the ship is steering.

Section III.

Hand Lead and Line.

To know, and be able to point out, the following :—

Hand lead—
    Lead and line.
    Size of lead line..
    Length of lead line.
    Weight of lead.
    Shape of lead.
    Arming of lead.
    From which end is a lead line marked ?
    Name the marks.
    Name the deeps.
    How are soundings called ?
    Where is the lead hove from ?
    How to hold the line while heaving, right and left.
    How to haul in the line, right and left.
    Explain the use and make of breast ropes.
    Explain the use and make of aprons.
    To be able to heave the lead from the mortar boat.
    To call soundings.
Deep sea lead—
    Explain the use and make of deep sea lead and line.
    How is deep sea line marked ?

Q. What is a lead and line ?

A. A line to which a leaden weight is attached, for the purpose of ascertaining the depth of water a ship is in.

Q. What is the size of lead line ?

A. Generally three-quarter-inch rope made for the purpose.

Q. What is the length of lead line ?

A. A hand line is 20 fathoms in length and divided into 20 equal parts called marks and deeps, there are nine marks and 11 deeps.

Q. What is the weight of lead ?

A. From seven to 14 pounds.

Q. What is the shape of lead ?

A. Various shapes, 6 square, 8 square and round, 7 lbs. lead $7\frac{1}{2}$ inches long, the 14 lb. lead 14 inches long with a hollow in the bottom to contain arming.

Q. What is the arming of lead ?

A. Filling the hollow in the bottom of the lead with tallow.

Q. From which end is a lead line marked ?

A. The end nearest the lead.

G 2

Q. Name the marks?

A. 2, 3, 5, 7, 10, 13, 15, 17, 20, 2, 3, and 10 are distinguished by pieces of leather. 2 has two ends to it; 3 has three ends to it; and 10 has a hole in it. 5 and fifteen fathoms are distinguished by a piece of white bunting; 13 by a piece of blue bunting; and 20 by two knots.

Q. Name the deeps?

A. 1, 4, 6, 8, 9, 11, 12, 14, 16, 18, 19.

Q. Having learned the marks and deeps, how will you call them, supposing, for instance, you have 9 fathoms, or any of the following marks or deeps:—7, 10¼, 11¾, 5½?

A. If I had 9 fathoms, I should call by the deep 9.

If I had 7 fathoms, by the mark 7.

If I had 10¼, and a quarter ten.

If I had 11¾, a quarter less twelve.

If I had 5½, and a half five.

Q. Where is the lead hove from?

A. From the main chains, or most convenient place, such as a quarter boat, where there are no chains.

Q. How do you hold the line when heaving right or left?

A. With a round turn round the hand.

Q. How do you haul in the line right and left?

A. In the starboard chains, you haul the line in with the left hand under and the right hand over. In the port chains, right hand under and left hand over.

Q. Explain the use of breast ropes and their make?

A. The breast rope is made of sword matting and has two eyes, to which ropes are made fast and secured when the lead is being hove.

Q. Explain the use and make of aprons?

A. They are made of canvas and painted, to keep the leadsman dry.

Q. How do you heave a lead from a mortar boat?

A. From the most convenient place, such as the quarter boats.

To call Soundings.

Q. What is the first thing to be done on going into the chains to heave the lead?

A. See the breast ropes properly secured, the line clear, and the end of it fast in the chains; measure the distance from the chains to the water with the lead line.

Q. Supposing it was a dark night, how would you know what sounding you had?

A. If more than 15 fathoms, I should reckon from 20 fathoms or the two knots, the length of line that passes through my hand, also the number of pieces of bunting ; if under 15 fathoms, I should reckon in a similar way from 10 fathoms, which I should readily know by a piece of leather with the hole in it ; if under five fathoms, the piece of leather at 2 and 3 would be my guide ; so I could always determine the real depth of water by reckoning the distance between either of these marks, and the depth obtained. For instance, if I obtained 13, it would be the next piece of bunting to 10, or the leather with the hole in it ; if 17, it would be the piece of bunting nearest 20, or the two knots ; if 5, it would be the nearest bunting to the piece of leather denoting 3 fathoms.

Deep Sea-lead.

Q. When is a deep-sea lead and line used ?

A. On approaching the land, when the true position of the ship is not known for certain, and the depth of water is very great. The bottom of the deep-sea lead is hollowed out ; when used, this hollow is filled with tallow (which is termed arming the lead), so as when it comes in contact with the bottom, any small substance will stick to the bottom of the lead, such as gravel, sand, small shells, &c. ; it will also denote a hard or soft bottom. On approaching the land, deep-sea soundings are taken at regular intervals ; and the depth of water and the nature of the bottom is entered in the ship's log-book, which enables the pilot to judge what coast the ship is on, also to tell how far she is from land.

Q. What is the weight of a deep-sea lead ?

A. 28 pounds.

Q. How is a deep-sea line marked, and what length is it?

A. It is usually 100 fathoms long, and is marked exactly the same as the hand line, up to 20 fathoms. At 25 fathoms 1 knot; at 30, 3 knots ; 35, 1 knot ; 40, 4 knots; so on, up to 100, between every 10 fathoms 1 knot ; and at 50, 60 70, 80, 90, and 100 fathoms, 5, 6, 7, 8, 9, and 10 knots.

Q. How are soundings obtained by the deep-sea lead ?

A. The deep-sea lead line is kept on a reel ready for use. When required, the reel is taken aft, and held by two men ; the end of the line is then passed out on the weather side, and taken forward on the weather bow outside, and clear of all rigging. The quartermaster having ascertained the lead is well armed, it is bent to the line, and a careful hand holds the lead ready for heaving; a number of men are ranged along outside the weather side of the ship at certain intervals, each with a coil of the deep-sea line in hand. All being ready, the officer of the watch gives the order to stand by as a caution to all, and then to heave, when the man on the weather bow throws the lead as far forward as possible, and calls out " watch there, watch," which is repeated by each man as the last fake of the coil goes out of his hand. It then runs off the reel, which is held in a convenient position not to stop it until the lead is on the bottom, or sufficient line is run out to show there is no bottom, with the length of the line ordered. A quartermaster, or an experienced leadsman, always attends aft to ascertain when the lead touches the bottom, which he does by allowing the line to run loosely through his hand. When the lead touches the bottom, the line is checked and brought up and down, to ascertain the correct depth, which is noted by the officer of the watch in the log. The line is then hauled in and reeled up ready for use again. When the lead is inboard the arming is examined, and the nature of the bottom is also noted in the log, and the lead is re-armed ready for use. Before taking a cast of the deep-sea lead, the way of the ship through the water is checked as much as possible.

N.B.—There are two descriptions of deep-sea leads—the patent and common deep-sea lead.

Q. How is the lead bent to the hand or deep-sea line ?

A. In the end of the line there is always a long-eyed spliced. In the upper end or top of the lead there is a hole, through which a becket is worked, the eye in the end of the line is passed through the becket, and over the bottom of the lead, and hauled taut up to the becket again.

Q. How is a deep-sea lead and line hauled in ?

A. A small snatch block, made for the purpose, and fitted with a tail, is attached to one of the quarter davits, or any other convenient place, the line is then placed in the snatch, and walked in by a portion of the watch.

THIRD INSTRUCTION.

(1.) Section I.

To be able to make, pass, worm, parcel, serve, and explain the following :—

Eye splice.	Serving.
Short splice.	Cross seizing.
Long splice.	End seizing.
Grummet.	Quarter or flat seizing.
Wall and crown.	Throat seizing.
Matthew Walker knot.	Rocking.
Selvagee strop.	Rose lashing.
Point and graft a rope.	Common whipping.
Four stranded splice.	Sennett whipping.
Worming.	To strop a block in all ways.
Parcelling.	

AN EYE-SPLICE.

An eye-splice is used in forming an eye for any common purpose, lower lifts, &c., and made by opening the end of a rope, and laying the strands, at any distance upon the standing part of the rope, according to the length of the eye it is intended to make. Divide the strand by putting one strand on the top, and one underneath the standing part, enter the middle strand, having opened the lay with a marline-spike, and stick it under its respective strand, take the next end over the first strand and under the second ; the third and last end is taken through the third strand on the other side. With a four-stranded rope, put the left-hand strand under two strands or two lays of the rope, and cover it with the next strand.

A SHORT-SPLICE.

A short-splice is used for joining standing rigging, or any gear not required to travel through a block, strops of blocks, &c.

To form a Short-Splice.

Unlay the rope to the required length, which is twice the circumference of the rope for the long ends, and once and a half the circumference of the rope for the short ends ; when this is done, whip all the ends with a yarn, then crutch them together, put a stop round the crutch, the long ends are put in twice, and the short ends once, pass the left-hand strand over the first strand next to it, stick it underneath the second strand, and haul it taut in the lay of the rope, then enter the right-hand strand, and lastly the middle strand, in a similar manner to the first or left-hand strand, haul them taut along the lay of the rope, being the long ends, put them in again as before, cut the stop off the·crutch, and put the short ends in once in a similar way, stretch the splice, whip the ends, and cut them off. If it is intended to serve over the splice, put the strands in once and a half each way, take a few of the underneath yarns from each strand to fill up the lay of the rope for worming, scrape the ends, and marl them down ready for serving.

To make a Long-Splice.

Unlay the ends of the two ropes to the length of five and a half times the circumference of the rope, crutch them together in a similar manner to a short-splice, unlay one strand, and fill up the vacant space which it leaves with the opposite strand next to it, then turn the rope round and lay hold of the two next strands that will come opposite their respective lays, unlay one, filling up the vacant space, as before, with the other. Take one-third out of each strand, and knot the opposite strands together, and heave them well in place, stick all six ends once under one strand ; having stretched the splice well, cut the ends off.

Q. How do you make a grommet ?

A. Cut a strand three times the length of the grommet required, allowing end enough also in addition for finishing it off. Middle the strand, lay the right hand end over the left, and lay the strand up again until the rope is re-formed, then tuck the ends and finish off, as in a long-splice.

A SINGLE-WALL CROWNED.

To make the knot.—Make the single-wall as described, and then lay one end over the top of the knot, lay the second end over the first, and the third over the second and through the bight of the first. It is used on the end of a rope, rove through a hole, in a similar way that a single-wall knot is.

To make a Matthew Walker Knot.

Unlay the ends of a rope, and take the first strand round the rope and through its own bight, and the second end round the rope underneath through the bight of the first, and through its own bight, take the third end round the same way underneath, and through the bight of all three, haul the ends well taut.

A Matthew Walker knot is used for the standing part of the lanyards of lower rigging, and any other purposes.

To make a Selvagee Strop.

Drive a couple of bolts or large nails into a piece of plank, or any convenient place, or else seize a couple of hooks which will answer the same purpose; put the nails or hooks at the required distance apart, according to the length of strop you want, take the ends of the ball of ropeyarns and make it fast to one of the spikes or hooks, then take it round the other one, keep passing roundabout-turns, taking care to have every turn well taut until the strop is to the required thickness. If it is to be a very large strop, marl it down with spunyarn, if a small strop two-rope yarn.

Q. How do you point or graft a rope?

A. Put a stop on at once the circumference of the rope from the end or eye, which will leave about the length for pointing or grafting, unlay the rope to the stop, then unlay the strands, split a number of the outside yarns and make a nettle out of each yarn; when the nettles are made, stop them back on the standing part of the rope; then form the point with the rest of the yarns, by scraping them down to a proper size with a knife, and marl them down together with twine; divide the nettles, taking every other one up, and every other one down; pass three turns with a piece of twine which is called the warp very taut round the part where the nettles separate, taking a hitch with the last turn, continue to repeat this process by placing every alternate nettle up and down, passing the warp, or filling, taking a hitch each time until the point is to its required length; you can either form a bight with the last lay by passing the warp through the bights, haul them taut, and cut them off, or work a becket in the end, by taking a small piece of rope one-fourth the size of the rope, form a bight, unlay the ends, and twist the six strands up again by twos, taking some of the inside yarns and lay them up as rope, then short-splice that and the becket together and marl it down.

How do you Long-Splice a Three and Four-Strand Rope together?

To form a long-splice with a piece of three and four-strand rope, such as tailing a royal backstay when used for a fall for the topgallant breast backstays. Unlay the ends of the two ropes to the required distance, and crutch them together, then unlay one strand of the three-strand rope, and fill up the vacancy with a strand of the four-strand rope, turn the rope round, and unlay a strand of the four-strand rope, and fill up the vacancy with a strand of the three-strand rope, as far as required; there will then remain two strands from the four-strand rope, and one from the three; lessen the latter, by taking one-third out of it, and knot it to one of the strands of the four-strand rope; then unlay the other strand, and fill up the vacancy with the reduced strand of the three-strand rope; then knot them together, and tuck them once under one strand with all eight strands; the splice should be well stretched before cutting the ends off.

Another plan is, instead of dividing the strand of the three-strand rope, knot the whole of the strands, and tuck the remaining strand of the four-strand rope under the strands of the rope. This is called sinking a strand.

NOTE.—The first plan is the neatest.

How do you Short-Splice a Three and Four-Strand Rope together?

You unlay the ends of the two ropes to a sufficient distance, make four strands out of the three by dividing one strand in two, and lay the four strands up a sufficient length for the ends of the other rope to be put in once, then crutch them together, and splice them as two four-strand ropes.

Another method for splicing a three and four-stranded rope together for a short-splice is, divide the fourth strand into three parts, and lay one part in with each of the three-strands, and splice it as a three-stranded rope.

For a long-splice, work three strands in in the usual way, and when finished tuck the fourth strand in, as convenient, under the nearest strands to it.

N.B.—This is called sinking a strand.

Q. What do you mean by worming a rope, and what use is it ?

A. To fill up the vacant space between the strands of the rope with spunyarn or small rope to render the surface smooth and round for parcelling and serving, to give it a neat appearance. The strops of gun-tackle blocks are wormed.

Q. What do you mean by parcelling a rope ?

A. Parcelling a rope is laying round it with the lay of the rope strips of old canvas dipped in tar, from two to three inches wide, according to the size of the rope, before serving it ; each turn of the parcelling should overtop the other, in fact, like tiles on the roof of a house.

Q. What do you mean by serving a rope ?

A. The service is of spunyarn, put or hove on by an instrument called a serving mallet, it has a score in the under part, according to the size of the rope, so as to lay on the rope, and a handle about fifteen inches long. Service is always laid on against the lay of the rope ; a man passes the ball of spun-yarn, taking the turns well out of it, at some distance from the man that is serving the rope. When the required length of service is put on, the end is put under the last two turns, hauled taut and cut off. All standing rigging, or any other rope likely to be chafed, is always served.

Worm and parcel with the lay,
And serve the rope the other way.

Short Splice, 1st.   Short Splice, 2nd.

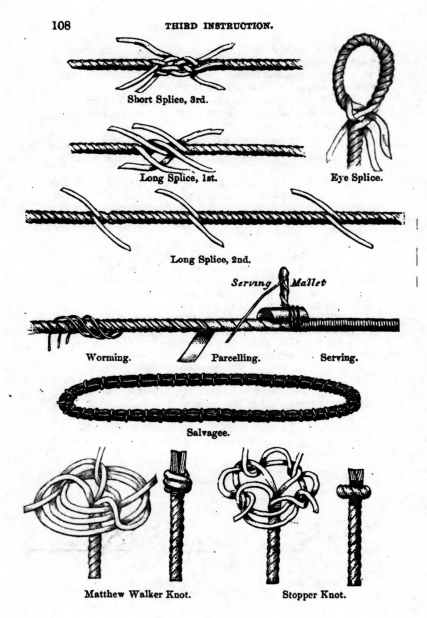

Short Splice, 3rd.

Long Splice, 1st.

Eye Splice.

Long Splice, 2nd.

Serving   Mallet

Worming.   Parcelling.   Serving.

Salvagee.

Matthew Walker Knot.   Stopper Knot.

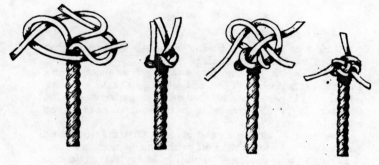

Single Wall Knot.   Single Wall and Crown.

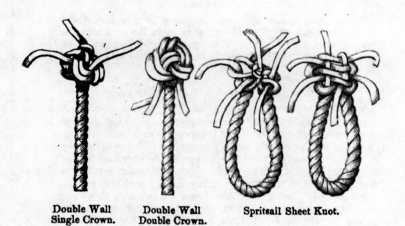

Double Wall   Double Wall   Spritsail Sheet Knot.
Single Crown.   Double Crown.

A Cross Seizing

Is used when the rigging is turned in with the end up; it is simply a round seizing, but instead of being finished off with a round turn round all parts, and a clove-hitch, after the riding turns are passed, the end is merely dipped down between the lower and upper turns, and the end is expended round the standing part of the shroud, and secured with a yarn.

An End Seizing

Is merely a flat seizing.

Q. How do you pass a quarter or flat seizing, and at what distance from the throat-seizing?

A. The width of the throat-seizing, or about 4 ins. from it. It is about half an inch less in size than a throat-seizing. It is passed and finished off in a similar way to the throat-seizing, each turn being hove well taut, but has no riding turns.

The reason of having an end part left after the throat and quarter seizings are finished off with a clove-hitch is in case of having to turn the lower rigging in at any future time, so the same seizing would do again.

A Throat or Round Seizing.

This seizing is used for many purposes, such as inside and outside clenches, strops of blocks, turning in lower or topmast rigging and stays, seizing the eyes of rigging, &c. All small rope to be used for seizings should be well stretched for the purpose.

To Pass a Throat or Round Seizing.

Splice an eye in one end of the seizings, take it round both parts of the shrouds, and pass seven turns, working towards the standing part of the shroud, reeve the end back between the turns of the seizing already passed (which are called the lower turns), and up through the eye of the standing part of the seizing, and it will be in the right position to commence passing the six upper turns, or riding turns, which will exactly come between the parts of the lower turns; care should be taken to heave each lower turn of the seizing well taut by means of a Spanish windlass, and the upper turns well taut by hand. After passing the sixth and last riding turn, pass the end down between the two last turns of the lower turns, and heave it hand taut. Then take a round turn round all parts of the seizings, heave it well taut with a Spanish windlass, and secure with a clove-hitch, one part of the clove-hitch being each side of the round turn, expend the end in round turns round the end of the shroud, and secure the end with a yarn. Any number of lower turns can be taken, the riding turns must always be one less in number; 7 or 9 are the numbers of lower turns generally taken in turning a dead-eye in, or seizing the eyes of rigging.

A Racking

Is used to prevent a rope rendering when hauled taut, such as lanyards of lower rigging, &c. It is made by passing in and out turns with a piece of spun yarn, with the lay of the rope over and under the hauling and standing part of the rope to be secured.

Q. In turning a dead-eye, in wire rigging, what seizings do you use?

A. A racking and end seizing, the racking seizing forming as it were a throat and quarter seizing.

The standing part of the seizing is made fast to the standing part of the shroud with an eye-splice. Thirteen racking turns are then passed from the eye towards the end, leaving sufficient space between each racking turn for a roundabout turn to lie. After the thirteen racking turns are passed, the roundabout turns are passed from the end towards the eye, each roundabout turn being passed between the racking turns; when the last roundabout turn is passed, the end is passed up between both parts of the shroud, that is, between the standing part and end, ready for passing the cross turns, which are passed by taking the end along the seizing and passing it down between the seventh and sixth turns along the seizing, again towards the eye, up between the two parts of the shroud as before, and again drawn between the seventh and sixth turns, then round the other way, over the thirteenth turn, repeating that also twice.

This also applies to wire stays.

A Rose Lashing

Is used for many purposes, such as securing the collars in clothing a bowsprit, and strops in rigging a lower or top-sail-yard. In fact, all collars and block-strops, fitted with lashing-eyes, such as bobstay, and bowsprit shroud-collars, jeer-blocks, truss-strops, topsail sheet-blocks, clew garnet-blocks, quarter-blocks for topsail yards, &c., when not fitted, with tails.

NOTE.—Clew garnet-blocks are fitted at Portsmouth Yard with a pendant spliced in one end, and an eye in the other; the length of pendant is once and a third the round of yard, the pendant is passed from forward aft, under the jackstay, round the yard, and seized to the jackstay, then a small strop is placed over the block, and brought up abaft the yard, and seized to jackstay, for steadying the block.

A rose-lashing can be passed either with one end or two.

To pass a rose-lashing on one end, splice the other end into the eye of the strop or collar you are going to lash, then pass either from right to left, or left to right, passing it over the eye on one side and under on the other, until sufficient number of turns are passed to bear the strain equal to the collar or strop being lashed, which is generally about seven turns; then the end is passed between the crossing turns twice, and dipped up through as near the centre of the seizing as possible, and is finished off by crowning and walling the end close to the crossing turns.

To Pass a Rose Lashing on both Ends of a Lashing.

The lashing is middled in the centre of one of the eyes; the eyes are then passed, one under and one over the eyes; for instance, the end that goes over the right-hand eye goes under the left-hand eye, until sufficient number of turns are passed; the ends are then dipped, in opposite ways, through the crossing, each end twice each way; both ends are finished off, as before, being crowned first, and walled after.

ROSE LASHING.

A Common Whipping.

To whip the end of a rope (twine is generally used for this purpose) lay the end of the whipping in the lay of the rope, in the same direction as the end of the rope, pass a few turns of the whipping over its own end to keep it in place, then lay the other end of the whipping pointing in an opposite direction to the first, and on the top of the turns already passed, and pass the remainder of the turns on the bight round the rope, and the both ends of the whipping, hauling the end through when sufficient number of turns have been passed, to keep it taut in place, and cut it off.

The turns of the whipping are always passed up towards the end of the rope.

RACKING SEIZING,
Forming a Flat Seizing as used for Wire Rigging.

A Sailmaker's Whipping, for Sennit, such as Topgallant and Royal Sea-Gaskets, or Jib-Tyers

Is put on with a needle and twine. The needle is entered where the whipping is to commence, and the twine is drawn through the sennit, leaving about an inch of end, then pass a number of roundabout turns round the sennit, and over the end of the twine, so as to keep it in place; when turns enough are passed, stick the needle through the sennit again, and pass two cross-turns from end to end

R 3498.   H of the whipping, passing the twine through the sennit with a needle at each turn, securing it with two half hitches at the upper end of the whipping.

Stropping Blocks.

Q. How do you strop a block ?

A. There are various ways of stropping a block, depending upon what they are required for.—*First.* There is the common strop, used for all general purposes, which is formed by short-splicing the two ends of a rope together, forming a ring, in which the block and thimble, or hook and thimble, is seized.

For this purpose the rope is got on a stretch. All above 3½ ins. is wormed, parcelled, and served ; below that size is only served with two or three yarns, spunyarn ; cut the rope for the strop off, the length depending on what the strop is required for. If it is intended to put the ends in twice one end, and once the other, put a chalk mark, or a stop, on the piece of rope already cut to length, at twice the round of the rope from one end, and once and a half the round of the rope from the other end ; then unlay the strands to the chalk marks or stops, heave the service back, crutch them together, close up to the chalk marks or stops, and enter your strands, as if making a short-splice, only taking great care to marry your splice slack, so as when you come to stretch the strop the strands will draw down in place and form a neat strop. If it is not intended to serve the strop over, put the chalk mark or stop at twice the round of the rope each end, and put the strands in twice each way. By putting the strands in once and a half each way, you make a neater strop, especially if it is intended to serve over it. After your strands are tucked, and the strop has been well stretched, cut the ends off, work the service up to the splice, and finish it off ; the strop is then ready for placing the block and thimble in place. When the block and thimble are in place, put a temporary seizing on, and with a couple of small wedges made for the purpose, set the block well in place, until the splice of the strop takes well in the score of the ass of the block ; take the temporary seizing off, and heave the strop between the block and thimble well together with a Spanish windlass, then pass the seizing for a full due.

To Strop a Single Block with a lashing Eye.

You proceed exactly the same as if stropping a block with a thimble. The length to cut the strop depends upon what it is required for, the size of the eye is generally once or once and a half the round of the rope.

To strop a block with two lashing eyes is merely putting an eye-splice in each end of the strop after it is cut to length and before the block is seized in place; the length of the eyes are from once to once and a half the round of the rope.

To Strop a Double or Single Block with a Tail.

The strop is sometimes cut long enough to admit of the strop and tail being in one; and it is also fitted separately, the tail being spliced in a thimble seized in the crown of the strop; the latter is by far the better plan, as it can be replaced at pleasure, which is at times most convenient, as the tail invariably fags out before the strop is half worn.

To make a Grommet Strop.

After the rope is cut to length, unlay the strands; each strand will form a strop; thus, one length of rope will make three strops; lay each strand up, as if making a common grommet and worm them, the block and thimble is then seized in place, as in any other strop.

These strops are always used for gun-tackles.

To fit a Salvagee or Warped Strop.

Lash two hooks, or seize two bolts at the length the strop is required apart, then pass roundabout turns sufficient with whatever you intend making your strop, until you have it to the required thickness, then pass marling-turns all round, taking care each part of the strop has equal strain; it is either grafted over or covered with leather, the block and thimble are then seized in place. These strops are frequently used for boom-sheet and reef-tackle blocks for boom-mainsails.

To form a Double-Strop for a Double-Scored Block.

According to the size of the rope, it is got on a stretch and wormed, parcelled, and served or only served; it is then cut to length, and the two ends short-spliced together, the block is placed, and the four parts of the strop seized together, the two bights forming two lashing eyes. These strops are used for quarter-blocks on lower yards for topsail sheets, lower yard brace-block, upper or masthead jeer-blocks.

To fit two Single Strops.

These strops are also used for double-scored blocks, such as lower jeer-blocks, or topsail brace-blocks. After the strops are cut to length, the ends are short-spliced together, each strop is placed on the block separately, and the four parts of the strop seized together. In the case of lower jeer-blocks, one strop is fitted longer than the other.

To make a Jumpsurgee Strop.

After the strop is cut to length, which will be three times the round of the block and once the round of the thimble and rope, put a mark on each end at once the round of the block, unlay the strands on each end to the mark, marry them together, and put a temporary seizing on to keep them in place, then unlay each strand and make them into nettles, divide the nettles when made equally, picking up every alternate nettle and graft both ways from where the strands are married, finishing off on the quarter, then seize the block, or block and thimble, in place. A strop thus made is considered to be three times the strength of a common strop.

To make a Jew Strop.

A jew strop is used when a single-scored block is required to be given a particular stand in the absence of a double-scored block ; for instance, it can be used with efficiency in the event of a lower jeer-block being carried away, and having no double-scored block to replace it. It is merely fitting a single block with a long lashing eye, working a grommet round the eye which rests round the strop between the lower yard and the crown of the block, the eye goes round the yard in a similar way to the long eye of a lower jeer-block, up before all, and is lashed to the grommet.

TABLES FOR FITTING BLOCKS.

DESCRIPTION OF STROP.	How to Measure for		What it is used for.	Remarks.
	Cutting the Strop.	Marrying the Strop.		
Seizing Strop.	Twice the round of block and rope.	Once the round of block and four times the round of rope.	Leech-lines, slab-lines, &c.	
Long Seizing Strop.	Twice the round of block and four times the round of rope.	Once the round of block and six times the round of rope.	Jib-stay, purchase, top-gallant royal halyards, &c.	
Hook and Thimble Strop.	Once the round of block, hook, and thimble, and six times the round of rope.	Once the round of block, hook, thimble, and rope.	Leading blocks, &c.	
Do. with two Seizings, or double Seizing Strop.	Twice the round of block and six times the round of rope.	Twice the round of block and once the round of rope.	Lower blocks of yards and stay-tackles.	
Do.	Three times the round of block and once the round of rope.	Twice the round of block and three times the round of rope.	Lower blocks of burton's.	
Quarter Blocks.	Once the round of block and yard and six times the round of rope.	Once the round of block, yard, and rope.	Quarter blocks for topsail, topgallant, and royal yards.	

TABLES FOR FITTING BLOCKS.

DESCRIPTION OF STROP.	How to Measure for		What it is used for.	Remarks.
	Cutting the Strop.	Marrying the Strop.		
				As a rule, allow in cutting five times the round of rope for splicing, in addition to the measure for marrying.
Quarter Blocks.	Twice the round of yard and rope and three times the round of block.	Twice the round of yard and block and four times the round of rope.	Topsail sheet blocks on lower yards.	
Hanging Jeer-Blocks.	Four times the round of masthead, twice the round of block, and seven times the round of rope.	Four times the round of masthead, twice the round of yard and block.	Upper jeer-blocks.	
Jeer-Blocks on the Yard.	*Long leg,* the same as for marrying, but six times the round of rope. *Short leg* as above.	*Long leg,* once and a third the round of yards, once the round of block and rope. *Short leg,* two-thirds the round of yard, once the round of block and rope.	Jeer-blocks on the yard.	
Brace Block.	Allow in cutting five times the round of rope, in addition to the length given for marrying.	Twice the round of block and thimble, and three times the round of rope. *Dog Strop,* once the round of yard-arm and thimble, and three times the round of rope.	Brace-block on lower yards.	

EXTRA QUESTIONS.

English Shroud-Knot.

Shroud-knots are used when a shroud is shot, or carried away.

To make an English Shroud-Knot.

Unlay the ends of the shroud you are going to splice, and commence in a similar way to a short-splice, then single-wall the ends of one rope round the standing part of the other, and wall the other three ends in the same manner; open the ends of the strands and take out a few yarns from each, and lay them in for worming; taper the remainder down, and serve over them with spunyarn.

French Shroud-Knot.

You place the ends of the two parts of the shroud in a similar way to forming an English shroud-knot, drawing them close together, then lay the first three ends upon their own part, and single-wall the other three ends round the bights of the first three ends and the standing part, taper the ends, marl them down, and serve over them. This knot is much neater than the English shroud-knot.

Q. How do you make a Turk's head, and what is it used for?

A. It is used for the foot ropes of jib and flying jib-booms and spanker-booms, being much neater than overhand knots, also for man ropes and Jacob's ladders; it is generally made of white line or nettle-stuff.

To make it.

Take a round turn round the rope you intend to make the Turk's head on, cross the bights on each side of the round turn, and put one end under the cross on one side, and the other end under the cross on the other side, after which follow the lead until it shows three parts all round, and finish it off.

A Point, its Use, and how it is Made.

For reefing sails: make the point by taking five foxes and middling them, working them down sufficiently to form the eye, viz., 3 ins., place the two parts together, which will give the eye 1½ ins.; after having formed the eye, work down 6 ins., then leave out the short end, and work the point to the length required.

A SINGLE DIAMOND KNOT.

To make the knot.—Unlay the end of a rope to the required distance for making the knot, with the strands, form three bights down the side of the rope, holding them fast with the left hand.

Take the end of one strand, and pass it with the lay of the rope over the strand next to it, and up through the bight of the third. Take the end of the second strand over the third, and up through the bight of the first. Take the end of the third strand over the first, and up through the bight of the second. Haul taut, and lay the ends up together.

This knot is used by men-of-war's men to form the eye in their knife lanyards, for going over their heads.

A DOUBLE DIAMOND KNOT.

To make the knot.—Make a single diamond, as before described, laying the ends up. Follow the lead of the single knot through two single bights, and the ends will come out at the top of the knot. Point the last strand through two double bights, and steady them, and lay the ends up.

This knot is used for lanyards of fire buckets.

A SPRITSAIL-SHEET KNOT.

To make the knot.—Unlay two ends of a rope to a sufficient length to form the knot, and place them together, making a bight with one strand, walling the six strands together, similar to a single-walling made with three strands, by putting the second over the first, and the third over the second, the fourth over the third, the fifth over the fourth, and the sixth over the fifth, and through the bight of the first. Then haul taut. You can crown it by taking two strands, and laying them over the top of the knot, and passing the other strands alternately over and under those two, hauling them taut. You may also double-wall it, by next passing the strands under the wallings on the left of them, and through the small bights, when the ends will come up for the second crowning. This is done by following the lead of the single-crowning, and putting the ends through the single-walling, as with three strands.

It is sometimes used for a stopper-knot, and other purposes.

A SINGLE-WALL KNOT.

To make the knot.—Unlay the end of a rope to a sufficient length for making the knot, then form a bight with one strand, holding its end down to the standing part in your left hand. Pass the end of the next strand round the strand so formed. Pass the remaining strand round the end of the second strand, and up through the bight you formed with the first strand. Haul the ends taut with care, one by one. It is used on the end of a rope, rove through a hole, to prevent it unreeving, such as the standing part of the throat halyards.

A DOUBLE-WALL.

To make the knot.—Make a single-wall slack, and crown it, then take one end, bring it underneath the part of the first walling next to it, and put it through the same bight. Repeat the same with the other strands, putting them up through two bights. When made it forms a double-wall and a single crown. It is used on the end of a rope, rove through a hole, such as throat halyards.

A DOUBLE-WALL, DOUBLE-CROWNED.

To make the knot.—Form a double-wall, single-crowned, then lay the strands by the sides of those in the single-crown, putting them through the same bight in the single-crown, and down through the double-walling.

It is used for man-ropes, stopper-knots, &c., also called a man-rope knot, tack or topsail-sheet-knot.

A BUOY-ROPE KNOT.

To make the knot.—Unlay the three large strands of a cable-laid rope, and then the three small strands forming the large strand, which will be nine in all. Lay the large ones up again, as before, leaving the small ones out.

Single and double-wall the small strands (as for a stopper-knot) round the rope, worm them along the divisions, and stop their ends with spunyarn.

This knot is used for a buoy, to prevent the buoy-rope slipping through the seizing.

Stopper Knot.

Stopper-knot is used in the end of stoppers, it is usually formed by double walling, in some cases crowned; there is,

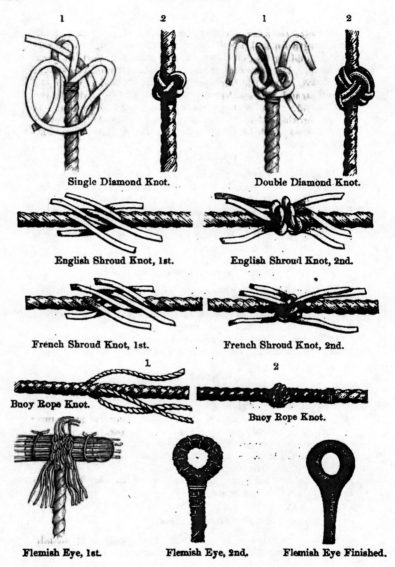

Single Diamond Knot.

Double Diamond Knot.

English Shroud Knot, 1st.

English Shroud Knot, 2nd.

French Shroud Knot, 1st.

French Shroud Knot, 2nd.

Buoy Rope Knot.

Buoy Rope Knot.

Flemish Eye, 1st.

Flemish Eye, 2nd.

Flemish Eye Finished.

however, no necessity for this; heave the ends together, seize and cut them off to within three ins. of the knot. But the best method of making a stopper-knot is to wall and half-wall it, put a good whipping on about two or three inches from the knot, and cut the ends off. A stopper-knot made this way will never capsize. A stopper-knot made with a double wall will capsize when a great strain is brought on it.

A Flemish Eye.

Having put a whipping on at the distance from the end of three and a half times the round of the rope, unlay the end to the whipping, then lash a piece of wood at least twice the size of the eye you are going to make, securely, in a convenient place for working, by some yarns on top of it, so as to stop the eye down after it is formed. With a four-stranded rope, unlay and divide the heart in two, then put the rope underneath the piece of wood with two strands, and halve the heart each side, pass the two part of the heart over and half-knot it on the top, heaving the rope close up to the piece of wood by means of a bolt on each side. The proper width for the eye is one-third the round of the rope. Take from each strand two yarns for every inch the rope is in circumference. Suppose it to be a 12-in. rope, take twenty-four yarns, which twist up and half-knot them on the top of the wood, heaving them taut and passing them down the lay of the rope for worming; clap a seizing of spunyarn over it, close to the toggle, and another 9 ins. below it; make a yarn fast round the ends, to keep them in the lay of the rope, then take two-thirds as many yarns from each strand as you did for worming, haul them taut up from the bosom, and half-knot them on top, haul them taut, and so continue till they are all expended.

Care should be taken to haul the yarns taut up from the bosom, to ensure them bearing an equal strain. Smooth the yarns down, and put a stop round all, close underneath the wood, them half-knot the stops that are laid on the wood, heave them taut with a bolt each side of the eye; from the other half-knot, and heave it taut.

The eye is then marled with two or three-yarn spunyarn, the hitches almost 1 in. apart, commencing at the centre of the eye and working both ways, cut the stops as you come to them; when the marling of the eye is finished, pass a strand round all, close underneath the wood, and heave it taut by means of bolts; take a part of the strand off, and put on a seizing of spunyarn, beating the strand down as you marl the yards down.

If it is for a stay when the collar is spliced and served, the eye is finished by parcelling it, and serving it with spunyarn, when fidded out it is completed.

An Artificial Eye

Is formed by unlaying one strand to the required distance, depending on the size of the eye you are about to form. The eye is formed by placing the two strands along the standing part of the rope, and crossing the odd strand over the standing part, and laying it in the vacant place you first took it from, filling up the vacancy until the strand comes out at the crutch again, and lies under the other two strands. Take a few yards out of each strand for worming, and taper the remainder down.

A Grecian Splice.

Put a whipping at twice the round of the rope from the ends of the two pieces of rope you are going to form the splice with, then unlay the ropes to the whippings, twist the outside yarns up into foxes, the number of yarns in each fox will depend upon the size of the rope being used for the splice, for example, about two yarns to every inch the rope is in circumference, leaving about one-fourth of each strand of the inside yarns to be laid up as rope, long enough to tuck the strands once each way, after which take out of each strand a sufficient number of yarns for laying them in the lay of the rope for worming, and cut the remainder off, then form a cross point with the foxes, by bringing the upper fox down, and the lower fox up, and crossing each other all round the rope; then put the last lower fox under the bight of the first upper one that was brought down; and is thus secured. Commence again by putting the end over one fox, and under the bight of the other, and so on until you have worked close up to the whipping, the foxes are then scraped and marled down, and served over with small spunyarn.

When properly made, the splice will be but very little larger than any other part of the rope, but strong enough to break the rope.

This splice, being much neater than a shroud-knot, is sometimes made in standing rigging instead of a shroud-knot.

There is also another way to make a Grecian splice, by making all the yarns into foxes, leaving no heart, but the first way is the strongest and best.

This splice is also used for tailing a smaller to a larger size rope, when it has to travel through a block such as lower lifts, when the lifts and falls are in one.

A MARINER'S SPLICE (OR TO LONGS-PLICE A CABLE-LAID ROPE).

To form the splice.—Heave the turns out of the two ends of the warps you are going to use for this purpose, stretch it well, then beat it with a mallet to make it supple, unlay the strands of both ends to six times the round of the warp, which will be the required length to form the splice; they are then crutched together in a similar way to forming a short-splice, but married much tauter; put a stop round them, to keep them in place, taking care to leave out the strand to be unlaid; you now commence to form the long-splice, by unlaying one strand, and filling up the space it leaves with the opposite strand next to it, to about three times the round of the rope; these strands being composed of three small strands, which are called readies, they are then unlaid and crutched together, a good stop being put round them, leaving out the ready to be unlaid, then unlay one ready, fill up the space it leaves with the opposite ready the distance of twice the round of the rope, half-knot them together, and stick the end under one strand; or, instead of half-knotting them, lay them across each other, and stick their ends under the next strand to them; then put the end underneath two strands or readies, and the end will come out under the strand, and when cut off will be out of sight. Then take hold of the next two readies that will come opposite their respective lays, unlay the ready, and fill up the space it leaves with the other, the same distance as before, and splice them the same; then the two readies in the place where they were first married, half-knot them, and stick them the same as with the first readies, after which turn the work round, and take the stop off from the place the strands were first crutched together, leave out the two next strands that will come opposite their respective lays, and put the stop on again, to secure the two strands that remain, then repeat the process, by unlaying one strand and filling up the space it leaves with the other, the same distance as before from the place they were married, then

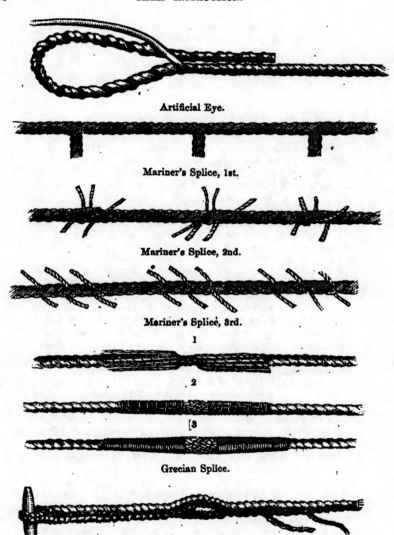

Artificial Eye.

Mariner's Splice, 1st.

Mariner's Splice, 2nd.

Mariner's Splice, 3rd.

1

2

3

Grecian Splice.

Reef Becket.

unlay the strands, marry the readies together, and long-splice them as before, then turn the work round to the two strands where they were first crutched together, and long-splice the six readies the same as before directed. Well stretch the splice, cut the ends off.

To put a Strand in a Rope.

It is frequently done when the part of a strand is chafed, and the other strands are good; cut the strands at the place where it is chafed, unlay it about two feet each way, then take a strand of a rope of the same size, and lay it in the vacancy of the rope, half-knot, and tuck the ends the same as a long-splice.

Snaking a Seizing.

Take the end under and over the outer turns of the seizing alternately, passing over the whole. There should be a marline-hitch at each turn.

A Rope-Maker's Eye

Is generally made in the end of a jibstay when fitted with a slip at the jib-boom end, and has a thimble in it to receive the slip ; it is also used for the collars of topmasts and jib-stays, for forming the lashing eyes, being quicker made, and quite equal in strength to a Flemish eye, it forms a rope-maker's eye, with two strands round the thimble.

To form a Rope-Maker's Eye with a Four-Stranded Rope.

Unlay the rope eight times the round of the rope, from the end which will be the required length ; marl two strands together to the distance of the round of the thimble; form the eye with these strands, to the size of allowing the thimble to go in after it is parcelled; put the thimble in, well tarring the eye first, then unlay the other two strands one at a time, and fill up the vacancy with the opposite strand that formed the eye, about two feet from the thimble ; unlay the other strand one foot from the thimble, and lay in the other strand that formed the eye, then cross, and stick the ends in once, the same as a long-splice ; after which, well stretch the splice, and serve it over with spun-

A Lashing Eye.

Put a whipping on at about twice and a half the round of the rope from the end, then enter the marline-spike at the eleventh lay from the whipping, bend the rope up, and form the eye, thus leaving nine clear lays from the strand ; the marline-spike is under to the first strand to be entered. Enter the strands once and a half and serve them over with spunyarn.

The above will be found the right length for a lashing eye for bowsprit-shroud and bobstay-collars, strops for clew garnet-blocks, topsail clew-line, and topgallant sheet-blocks, the inner ends of foot-ropes, &c.

ELLIOT'S EYE.

To make the Eye.

Put a whipping on, allowing 6 ins. for every inch of the size of the rope, that is, for an 18-in. rope put a whipping on at 9 ft. from the end, unlay all three strands to the whipping, well stretch them, take the lay out, and beat them well with a commander.

1st. Take the first strand round the thimble, and long-splice it to the second strand.

2nd. In the third strand form an eye-splice rather larger in size than the thimble (as shown in plate 1), taking care that the ends of the strand forming the eye-splice come out in the lay of the rope for worming.

3rd. Take the whipping off, put a capstan-bar or hand-spike through the eye-splice and long-splice, and heave all these strands up together to the size of the eye-splice (as shown in plate 2), withdraw the capstan-bar or handspike, and hitch the two parts of the eye together with small rope ; the eye formed by the first and second strands being long-spliced together, and the third strand having an eye-splice in it, the thimble is then put in place, and the seizing put on, which is a common throat or round seizing (as shown in plate 3), the cable is then served, or, as is termed, kackled with 2½-in. rounding, for the distance of 9 ft. from the eye. The eye is now finished and ready to receive the shackles.

Q. How is a reef-becket and toggle fitted ?

A. The becket is a piece of 2-inch rope with a long eye in one end, the other end being well whipped, in the bight of the eye a toggle is seized, the becket is then rove round the jackstay of the yard to which it belongs, and is seized with

the toggle uppermost; in reefing, the other end of the becket
is rove through the reef-line, and hauled up, until the eye is
high enough to go over the toggle. Toggles are fitted to the
jackstay in pairs, one being for the first and third reefs and
the other being for the second and fourth reefs. In taking
in the third and fourth reefs the first reef-beckets must be
untoggled when taking in the third reef, and the second reef-
beckets when taking in the fourth reef. When the first and
second reef-beckets are let go in taking the third or fourth
reefs in, care should be taken to haul the slacksail taut up by
the slab-points. Slab-points are now usually fitted to all
topsails, about four of a side, or more if necessary, according
to the size of a topsail. This precaution is very necessary;
if the slacksail was allowed to hang down abaft the yard in a
gale, and beat about, it would chafe the sail through. A preventer jackstay is generally fitted for the second and fourth
reefs, so as all the strain should not be on one jackstay.

To make a Reef-Becket and Toggle, as done in Portsmouth Dockyard.

Form the eye with five parts of spunyarn, then work down
with nine ends, work 1 ft. 2 ins., then form an eye with five
parts one side, and four parts the other, make the eye 7 ins.,
then marry and work down with the nine ends 1 ft. 2 ins.
more, put on a good whipping at the end and the lower part
of the eye.

N.B.—For small ships form your eye with four parts, and work
down with 7, as above.

Spanish Windlass.

To Rig a Spanish Windlass.

A good strand, well greased in the centre, is generally
used for this purpose; place the strand over the two parts of
the rope that are to be hove together, and bring the ends of

R 3498.   I the strand up again, place a bolt close to the strand, take the ends of the strand and lay them up with their own parts (so as to form a bight), take a round turn with this round the bolt, put a bolt or marline-spike through each bight, and heave round. A bolt is the best, as a marline-spike is apt to slip.

A West County Whipping

Is used for putting a mark on braces, &c., bracing up mark on fore-brace. It is formed by middling the twine round the part of the rope to be marked, and half-knotting it at every half turn, so each half knot will be on opposite sides; when sufficient number of turns are passed, finish it off with a reef knot.

An American Whipping

Is used for the ends of hawsers, as it is not so liable to come undone. It is commenced in the same way as a common whipping, but finished off by having both ends out in the middle of the whipping, and forming a reef knot. This is done by leaving the first end out, when you commence to pass the turns on the bight over the last end.

(2.) Blocks.

To know the names and use of the following :

Parts of a block—	Blocks—	Swivel.
Shell.	Single.	Iron.
Sheave.	Double.	Gin.
Bush.	Treble.	Hanging.
Pin.	Clump.	Fly.
Top.	Brace.	Tye.
Bottom.	Shoulder.	
Swallow.	Fiddle.	Deadeye.
Score.	Long-tackle.	Heart.
	Sister.	Fairlead.
	Snatch.	

Parts of a Block.

Q. What is a shell?

A. The outside case of a block, and is made of ash, elm, or iron.

Q. What is the sheave?

A. The wheel on which the rope travels, and is made of metal, lignum vitæ, or iron.

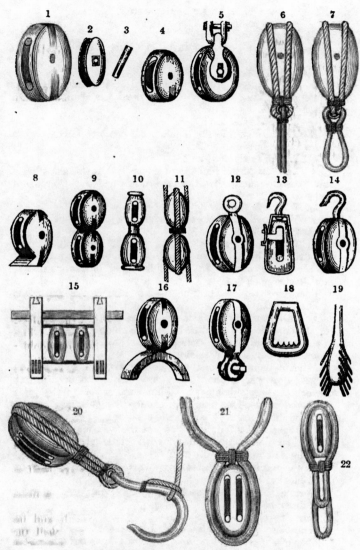

1. Shell.	7. Topsail Brace Block
2. Sheave.	(2 Single Straps).
3. Pin.	8. Shoulder Block.
4. Clump Block.	9. Fiddle Block.
5. Metal Block.	10. Sister Block.
6. Lower Brace Block	11. Shoe Block.
(Double Strap).	12. Hanging Block.

13. Snatch Block.	19. Euphroe.
14. Top Block.	20. Cat Block.
15. Ninepin Blocks.	21. Jeer Block, Upper
16. Monkey Block.	(Double Strap).
17. Tye Block.	22. Jeer Block, Lower
18. Heart (for Lower	(2 Single Straps).
Stays.	

Q. What is the bush?

A. The centre piece of metal or iron, which travels on the pin.

Q. What is the pin?

A. It is made of iron or lignum vitæ, and has a head at one end, it passes through the centre of the shell and bush of the sheave.

Q. Which is the top?

A. The crown of the block, and has not such a deep score as the bottom.

Q. Which is the bottom?

A. The tail of the block, and is easily known, as it has a 'much deeper score than the crown, to receive the splice of the strop.

Q. Which is the swallow?

A. The open part between the sheave and the shell.

Q. Which is the score?

A. The groove in the outside part of the shell to take the strops, either single or double scores, according to what the blocks are required for. Double-scored blocks are always double stropped.

There are two sorts of blocks—morticed blocks, and made or built blocks.

The largest morticed block made is 28 ins., and the smallest for ship use 3 ins.; smaller blocks are made for boats. The 28-in. single blocks are double scored, and used for double-brace blocks in first-class ships.

A made or built block can be constructed to any size; 50 ins., however, is about the size of the largest used in any Government establishment. The number of pieces it is composed of depends upon the number of sheaves; as the partition between each sheave is a separate piece, they are bolted together by four bolts, two at the top, and two at the bottom, and are always fitted with metal sheaves, and a shoulder to one side of the shell.

Large purchase or careening blocks are always built or made blocks.

Morticed blocks are used for all general purposes, as hereafter described.

The size of a block is denoted by the length, and its classification by the flatness or thickness of the shell, the number of sheaves, the number of scores, and the quality of the stropping.

For instance—if a shell of a block is 6 ins. in length, it is called a 6-in. block; if it is 10 ins., 15 ins., or 20 ins., it is called a 10-in., 15-in., or 20-in. block, according to whatever length the shell might be.

A block, if one sheave, is called a single block; two sheaves, a double block; three sheaves, a treble; four sheaves, a four-fold block, and so on, according to the number of sheaves.

If one score, it is termed a single score block; if two scores, a double scored block.

There are rope strops and iron strop-blocks, both double and single. The rope stropping is fitted in various ways: for instance, single strops, double strops, and two single strops, according to the stand the block is required to have to establish a fair lead with any given point.

A block is supposed to carry a rope one-third its length in circumference: that is to say, a 6-in. block a 2-in. rope, an 8-in. block a 2½-in. rope, a 9-in. block a 3-in. rope, and so on.

Blocks, either morticed, made, or built, are composed of several parts, and are named as follows :—

Blocks are distinguished by the following names, viz. :—

Single.	Snatch.
Double.	Swivel.
Treble.	Iron.
Clump.	Gin.
Brace.	Hanging.
Shoulder.	Fly.
Fiddle or long tackle.	Tye.
Sister.	Deadeye.

Heart, Fairlead.

Common Blocks, Single, Double, and Treble,

Are used for nearly all common purposes, reeving purchases, boats' tackles, gun tackles, &c., quarter blocks, span blocks for topmast studsail halyards, and peak brails, jewel blocks at the topsail and topgallant yard-arms for the studsail halyards, in fact, for most of the running gear.

Clump Blocks

Are made shorter and thicker, and have metal sheaves, which are smaller in diameter than those of other blocks, but reeve the same size rope. Tacks and sheets are fitted with clump blocks.

Lower Brace-Blocks

Are single, thin, double-scored blocks. They are fitted with
a double strop with a thimble, and a thimble rove through it,
to take the yard-arm strop, which are called unity thimbles.

Fore and Main Topsail Brace-Blocks

Are single, thin, double-scored blocks, and are fitted with two
strops and union thimbles. The yard-arm strop is fitted
round the thimble that is rove through the thimble of the
brace-block before the block is stropped.

Shoulder Blocks

Are made with a projection left on one side of the top of the
shell, which bearing against the place of connexion prevents
the fall from being jammed, such as purchase and foretack
blocks.

Fiddle or Long Tackle Blocks

Are used for yard-tackle purchases, and reef-tackles of boom
mainsails ; they are long single blocks, made on end in one
piece with two metal sheaves, sometimes one metal, and one
lignum vitæ, one sheave being smaller than the other, but the
same size score. The upper sheave is the smallest in diameter,
which causes a loss in power, for all the parts of rope are kept
more clear of each other in this kind of block, and as they
do not cross, there is less friction.

Sister Blocks

Are tapered, the upper part of the block being smaller than
the lower part, having a deep score, as they are seized between
the foremost pair of shrouds in the topmast rigging ; they
are thus constructed not to interfere with the spread of the
rigging ; they are also two in one on end, the reef-tackle
being rove through the upper, and the topsail lift through
the lower sheave, they are sometimes fitted in separate
pendants, and answer very well.

Snatch Blocks.

The shell abreast the swallow of the block is cut away,
leaving a space according to the size of the block, the iron
stropping over this space is fitted with a clamp on a hinge,
the other end being secured when in use by a pin, so the
clamp can be easily thrown back, and the bight of a rope or
hawser, readily snatched and unsnatched, doing away with
the necessity of reeving the end, these blocks are used as

leading blocks, but should never be used for any heavy purchases.

Swivel Blocks

Are iron bound blocks with a swivel either in the crown or hook. . The blocks in davit heads are generally swivel blocks.

Iron Stropped Blocks,

Hanging blocks, tye blocks, top blocks, çat blocks, fall blocks for top-tackle pendants, double and treble blocks for boats' tackles, snatch blocks, &c., &c., are all iron-bound, and are either fitted with hooks, eyes, or lugs, standing or swivel, according to what they are required for.

Gin Blocks

Are iron blocks with metal sheaves used for various purposes, such as peak halyards in steamships, &c.

Hanging Blocks

Are fitted with a lug for shackling to the long links of the topmast necklace.

Fly Blocks

Are used for topsail halyards, and are the upper purchase blocks.

Tye Blocks

Are fitted with two iron lugs, and are secured to the eye-bolt on the topsail yard by an iron pin, and are swivel blocks.

Dead Eyes

Are round, and made of elm; they have three holes at equal distances to take the lanyards of the rigging, with a deep score, according to their size, round them to take the shroud. The size of a dead eye is denoted by the diameter. Dead eyes, intended for wire rigging, have a smaller score. The largest size dead eyes are 17 ins., the smallest, 3 ins.

Hearts

Are another description of dead eyes, used for setting stays up, are turned in the end of stays, and seized in the fore stay collars on the bowsprit. Lower ones, for main or mizen stays, are iron-bound. Like dead eyes, they are made of elm, something resembling a heart in shape, with one large hole through the centre; in the largest heart there are four scores,

and in the smallest three scores, for the lanyard to lay in.
Round the outside is a rounded groove to take the stay.
The largest size heart made for the Navy is 20 ins., 18 ins.,
however, being the largest in use; the smallest size, 4 ins.,
whether iron bound or for turning into the stay.

Fairleads

Are made of iron, wood, or lead ; and is merely a round shell
hollow in the middle for leading ropes through, or lead
pipes are fitted through the bulwarks in various parts of the
ship.

Strop Bored-Blocks

Are made with a projection on each side of the lower part
of the shell through which the strop passes, and which is intended to keep small gear out of the swallow.   They are used
for reef-tackles, clew garnets, &c., &c.

Shoe Blocks

Consists of two sheaves on end in one piece, but, unlike a
fiddle block, the upper sheave stands in a contrary direction
to the lower one, that is, the sheaves in the block are fitted
swallow to swallow, and as the buntlines are rove up towards
the tops, the whip it rove down on deck ; the sheaves being
fitted in this way, admit of each rope being rove as it should
be in the swallow of each sheave.

The sheaves of a fiddle block are fitted to reeve a rope
leading in the same direction, therefore when used as a buntline block, the lower part or tail of the upper block or sheave
is cut or burnt away to the size of the swallow, to admit of
the rope being rove; it would be a great convenience, when
fiddle blocks are intended to be used as buntline blocks, if
they were made in the sheaves like a shoe block, swallow to
swallow; two single blocks are frequently seized together in
the same strop on end, crown to crown, a good seizing being
passed between them for buntline block, forming a fair lead
for each rope, and are also called shoe blocks.

Top Blocks

Are iron bound, and are fitted with a hook to take the eye-
bolt in the cap for reeving the top-tackle pendant through.

Fall Blocks, for Top-Tackle Pendants,

Are iron-bound swivel-hooked blocks, either double or
treble, according to the size of the ship.

Blocks for Boats' Tackles

Are iron-bound, those in the davit-heads working on a swivel, the lower ones being fitted either with a hook or a thimble.

Ninepin Blocks

Is applied to a rack of nine sheaves, arranged horizontally, or to any given number of sheaves, fitted horizontally between the bitts, abreast of each mast on deck, to form a lead for the running rigging, or any rope to be led along the deck.

Monkey Block

Is a large iron-bound block secured to a wooden chock bolted to the deck.

Cat Blocks

Are either double or treble blocks, according to the size of the ship, fitted with a large open hook so as to take the ring of the anchor readily, and as a swivel block.

On the foremost side of the shell of this block are two small eye-bolts for fitting a rope to, called the cat-back or back-rope bridle, which is used in hooking the cat, as a support to the block; the rope bent to the bridle is called the cat-back, and in large ships is led through a leading block secured to a convenient place on the bow, or in the head.

JEER BLOCKS, UPPER AND LOWER.

Upper Masthead Jeer Block

Is a double block, double-scored, stropped with two single strops, the four parts—or that is, the two parts of each strop —are seized together at the crown of the block, leaving two long bights or eyes, which are passed up through the after hole in the fore part of the top, and lashed on the after part of the masthead.

Lower Jeer Blocks.

These are single thick, double-scored blocks, fitted with two strops, one long and one short, so as the sheave shall stand fore and aft and correspond with the upper or masthead jeer block. The bight of the long strop is passed down abaft the yard, up before all, and lashed to the bight of the short strop with a rose lashing.

A Bull's-Eye

Is a wooden thimble, with a hole in the middle, rounded off at the edges, with a groove round the outside for a strop or seizing to lay in. They are generally seized to the lower shrouds in Merchant ships, to act as fair leader for the running rigging.

A Centipede,

Or, as it is sometimes called, a Euphroe, is a long piece of wood rounded, the largest part near the middle, the upper end sloping gradually off to a point. The lower end resembling in shape a dumb bell, it has a groove for a stropping to lay in, cut in an up and down direction. A number of horizontal holes are pierced through it. Its length depends on the number of holes required. It is used as a crowfoot, fitted with a number of legs, for ridge ropes of awnings.

(3.) Rope.

To know the names and use of the following :—

Yarns.
Strands.
Hawser-laid rope.
Shroud-laid rope.
Cable-laid rope.
Shroud hawser.
Spunyarn.
Nettle stuff.
Sennett.
Fox.
Spanish fox.
Junk.
Rounding.
Oakum.
Rumbo.
Twice-laid.

Six-thread stuff.
Coir rope.
Hide rope.
Length of a coil.
How size of rope is measured.
Standing rigging.
Running rigging.
Gun gear.
Left-handed rope.
Size for different blocks.
Use of hawsers.
Why hawsers are so made.
Use of cables.
To known which end of a new coil should be taken out first.

Yarns or Threads

Are made from hemp laid up right-handed, each yarn or thread is supposed to bear the weight of one hundred pounds.

Strands

Consist of a number of yarns laid up together, the number depending on the size rope the strands form ; those intended for a right-handed rope are laid up left-handed, and for a left-handed rope, they are laid up right-handed.

Hawser-Laid Rope.

There are several descriptions of hawser-laid rope.

Hawser-laid rope for standing rigging is termed shroud-hawser rope. It is a four-stranded and right-handed, made in lengths of 106 fathoms.

The largest size made is 14½ ins., used for forestays of first-class ships.

The smallest size made is 2 ins., used for royal backstays of small ships.

N.B.—All four-stranded ropes have a centre strand, in addition, called the heart, so as to ensure the four strands, when laid up, laying smoothly without a hollow.

Shroud-Laid Rope

Is hawser-laid rope as explained above.

Cable-Laid or Cablet Rope

Is nine-stranded left-handed rope. It is made by first laying up with the sun, or right-handed, the nine strands into three separate ropes, three strands in each, and then laying the three ropes thus made up into one rope, left-handed, or against the sun; when completed, it resembles three small ropes laid up together. It is made from 2 ins. to 26 ins. in circumference.

All above 2¼ in. in coils of 101 fathoms in length; 2 ins. and 2½ ins. are made in lengths of 102 fathoms.

Shroud Hawser

Is supplied in the event of any of the shrouds being carried or shot away.

Spunyarn

Is a number of yarns, twisted up right-handed, varying in number, from three to fifteen yarns.

Nettle Stuff.

It is made of two or three yarns laid up together by a jack; it is also made by hand, by twisting them between the thumb and finger, and laying them up against the twist of the yarn. They are used for clews of hammocks, for making harbour-gaskets, and other purposes.

Sennett

Is made of a number of yarns, plaited up into square, round or flat sennett as required, and used for various purposes.

To make a Fox.

Make two or three yarns fast to a belaying pin, or some other convenient place, stretch them out taut, and twist them together, then rub it down smooth with yarns, or a piece of old canvas; it is used for making gaskets, mats, plaits, and temporary seizings, &c., and many other purposes.

To make a Spanish Fox.

This is made by taking a single rope-yarn, making one end fast to a belaying pin, untwisting and twisting it up again the reverse way, and rubbing it smooth with a few yarns or a piece of canvas. It is generally used for small seizings.

Junk

Consists of lengths of condemned rigging, cut into five-fathom lengths, or pads of outside yarns.

Rounding

Is condemned running rigging, supplied for lashings or other purposes, where good rope is not required, and for making wads, &c.

Oakum

Is old rope unlaid, and the yarns picked into hemp, for caulking the seams in a ship's deck or side, and for many other purposes, cleaning brass-work, &c.

Rumbo

Is made from outside yarns. It is a coarse, soft, pliable rope, and very useful for many purposes, such as stage lashings, &c.

Twice laid.

Hawser-laid right-handed three-stranded rumbowline twice-laid or re-manufactured rope, is hawser-laid, three stranded right-handed. It is made from the best yarn of old rope or rounding.

Six-thread Stuff

Is six yarns made up into hawser-laid rope.

Coir Rope

Is three-stranded right-handed rope, made from the fibres of the cocoa-nut tree.

It is one-third lighter than hemp rope, but not nearly so durable, as it soon rots after being wet, if not well dried before it is stowed away; as it floats so light, it is very useful as warps, and quite equal in strength to hemp rope.

Hide Rope

Is nine-stranded left-handed, made in a similar way to cable-laid or cablet rope. It is used for wheel-ropes, as it is much stronger than hemp; when wet it swells and shrinks; therefore should, if possible, be kept dry, and, in all cases, well greased, which duty is always assigned to the quarter-masters.

Three-stranded rope is used for all common purposes, such as reeving, running, rigging, purchases, &c. It is made from half an inch to 10 ins. in circumference, in coils of 113 fathoms.

Length of a Coil.

113 fathoms.

How size of Rope is measured.

By its circumference.

Standing Rigging

Is made of four-stranded rope.

Running Rigging

Is made of three-stranded hawser-laid rope.

Gun Gear

Is hawser-laid three-stranded left-handed rope, generally termed reverse-laid rope. The yarns and strands being laid up right-handed, and the rope, left-handed, renders it soft and more easy to handle; for all it is not so durable, as it is more apt to admit the wet and cause it to rot.

The large size, which is used for gun-breechings, is most difficult to splice; as the strands are unlaid, each strand has to be marled down separately to keep it together; the yarns and strands being laid up the same way, they are apt to open out as soon as a strand is unlaid.

Left-handed Rope.

Rope laid up reverse to right-handed, principally used for gun tackles.

Size for different Blocks.

A block is three times the size of the rope which is rove through it, for example, a 6-in. block will take a 2-in. rope, and so on.

Use of hawsers.

Are used for warping or towing ships.

Why Hawsers are so made.

Because they are less liable to take kinks in coiling down in boats for warping.

Use of Cablets.

Cablets are used for anchoring and mooring boats.

Which end of a new Coil should be taken out first?

A. The lower inside end.

SECTION II.

Compass and Helm.

To be able to take the wheel at the Model, and explain the following :—

The bearing of an object.
Direction of the ship's head.
The number of points a ship will lie from the wind.
In how many points she will tack.
In how many points she will wear.
Keep away.
Bear up.
Starboard tack.
Port tack.
Weather side.
Lee side.
Tacking.
Going about.
Staying.
Missing stays.
Wearing.
Beating to windward.
Abaft the beam.
Abeam.
On the bow.
To weather.

On a wind.
By the wind.
Close hauled.
Full and by.
Wind abeam.
Wind aft.
Wind on the quarter.
To bear up.
Off the wind.
Luff.
Nothing off
No higher.
Very well " dice."
Starboard.
Port.
Steady.
'Midships.
Keep her away— points.
Bring her up— points.
Going free.
Running.
On the quarter.
Astern.
Boxing off.
Before the wind.

Scudding.
Conning a ship.
Hauling to the wind.
Hove to.
Lying to.
Ships meeting, close hauled, which gives way ?
Ships meeting, one going free, which gives way ?
Rule of the road in boats.
Steering in a tideway.
Making a stern board.
Sternway.
Leeway.
Taken by the lee.
Broaching to.
Weather tide.
Lee tide.
Before the beam.
Aback.
Wake of a ship.

The Bearing of an Object.

How any given object bears by compass from the ship.

Direction of the Ship's Head

Is the point of the compass which is cut by the lubber's point.

The Number of Points a Ship will lie from the Wind.

When the sails are well set, a ship is supposed to lay five points from the wind, but in most cases it is six points.

In how many Points will she Tack.

Q. Supposing a ship to lay five points from the wind, how many will she tack in?

A. Ten points.

In how many Points will she Wear?

A. Twenty-two points.

Keep her away.

To run the ship's head off the wind.

Bear up.

To put the helm up, and run the ship off the wind. To bear up round is to put the ship right before the wind.

Starboard Tack.

A ship is said to be on the starboard tack when she has her starboard tacks on board or the wind is blowing five points on the starboard bow, which is called the weather bow.

Port Tack.

A ship is said to be on the port tack when she has her port tacks on board, or the wind is blowing five points on the port bow, which is called the weather bow.

Weather side.

The weather side is the side on which the wind blows.

Lee side.

The lee side is the side opposite from which the wind blows.

Tacking.

A. Supposing a ship to be sailing close to the wind on the starboard tack, laying S. E. by E., the wind would be South. By manœuvring the helm and sails she is brought head to wind, and paid off on the port tack, until the sails are again full, or her head is S.W. by W. ; she would then lie on the port tack, supposing the wind to be steady, and the ship would work in ten points or lie five points from the wind.

Going about

Is an evolution performed by manœuvring the sails and helm, by which means a ship is made to pass round head to wind from one tack to another.

Staying.

To bring the ship's head to wind and by manœuvring the helm and yard to cause the sails to fill on the opposite tack.

Missing Stays.

A ship is said to miss stays when she fails to go about.

Wearing.

To run a ship off before the wind, and bring her to the wind on the opposite tack.

Beating to Windward.

Sailing against the wind, by alternate tacks in a zig-zag line.

To Weather.

A ship is said to weather another when she sails to windward of her.

On a Wind.   By the Wind.   Close Hauled.

When a ship is as close to the wind as she will lie, with her sails full.   These terms are synonymous.

Full and by.

A ship is said to be full and by when she is as close to the wind as she will lie, without suffering her sails to shake.

Wind Abeam.

A ship sailing with the wind eight points from the bows, or at right angles with the keel.

Wind Aft.

A ship is said to be sailing with the wind aft when her sails are squared and she is running before the wind.

Wind on the Quarter.

A ship is said to be sailing with the wind on the quarter when the wind is four points abaft the beam.

To bear up.

Paying the ship's head off from the wind.

Off the Wind.

Sailing with the wind two points before the beam to seven points abaft the beam.

Luff.

To bring a ship's head nearer the wind.

Nothing off.

Signifies that a ship requires a little lee helm when she is falling off from the wind.

No higher.

Signifies that a ship requires a little weather helm to prevent her sails from getting aback and shaking.

Very well dice.

To steady a ship's head in any given direction.

Starboard.

A man standing the starboard side of the wheel turns the wheel from him; if standing the port side he hauls it towards him, the tiller to starboard, and the rudder to port; it causes a ship's head (supposing her to have headway) to pay off to port.

Port.

If standing the port side of the wheel, turn it from you, if on the starboard side, pull it towards you, the tiller going to port, the rudder to starboard, a ship with headway will pay off to starboard.

A ship having sternway the helm has the opposite effect to headway; therefore her head pays off in the same direction as the tiller, and a contrary direction to that in which the rudder is placed.

R 3498.　　　　　　　　　　K

Steady.

To keep a ship's head on a given point or in a direct line for any particular object.

Midships.

Is an order given when the helm is either to starboard or port, and the rudder is required at once to be placed in a line with the ship's keel.

Keep her away Points.

To run off the wind, the number of points ordered by the officer in command.

Bring her up Points.

To haul closer to the wind.

Going Free.

When a ship is going off the wind.

Running.

When the wind is aft.

Before the Wind.

When the wind is dead aft.

Scudding.

A ship running before the wind with close-reefed sails, or under bare poles, is said to be scudding.

Conning a Ship.

Any person directing the helmsman how to put the helm is said to be conning the ship.

Hauling to the Wind.

Bringing a ship's head as close to the wind as possible, by bracing the yards up, &c., and giving her lee helm.

Hove to.

A ship is said to be hove to when by an arrangement of her sails she is kept close to the wind and makes very little head way through the water.

Lying to.

A ship is said to be lying to when owing to heavy weather she is obliged, by so arranging her sails, to remain nearly in the same position.

Ships meeting, close hauled, which gives way.

A. The vessel on the port tack.

Ships meeting, one going free, which gives way?

A. The vessel going free.

Rules of the Road in Boats.

Boats under oars give way to boats under canvas.

Two boats meeting under canvas on opposite tacks, both on a wind, the boat on the port tack gives way.

Boats under canvas meeting, the one going free gives way to the one on a wind.

Steering in a tide way.

Care should be taken not to give a ship too much helm as it is liable to cause her to break her sheer, which might be attended with very serious consequences.

Making a stern board.

It is effected by throwing the sails aback, and may at times be a manœuvre of great importance.

Stern way.

Going through the water stern foremost.

Lee way.

What a ship loses by dropping to leeward of her course. Under all plain sail, in smooth water, a ship makes no lee way. Under reefed sails, in a sea way, a ship makes lee way in proportion to her power of resistance, by being forced to leeward.

Taken by the Lee.

A ship is said to be taken by the lee, when the wind suddenly shifts and all her sails are thrown aback.

Broaching to.

To fly up in the wind. It generally happens when a ship is carrying a press of canvas, with the wind on the quarter and a good deal of after sail set.

Weather Tide.

That which running contrary to the direction of the wind by setting against a ship's lee side while under sail, forces her up to windward.

Lee Tide.

A tide running in the same direction as the wind, forcing a ship to leeward of the line upon which she appears to sail.

Before the Beam,

The bearing of any object, which is before a right line to the keel, at the midship section of the ship.

Abaft the Beam.

The bearing of any object which is abaft a right line to the keel, at the midship section of the ship.

Abeam.

At right angles to the keel.

On the Bow.

The bearing of an object at any angle on either side of the stem up to 45°, then it is either four points on the bow, or four points before the beam.

On the Quarter.

The bearing of any object, being in that position, with regard to the ship, as to be included in the angles which diverge from right astern, to four points towards either quarter.

Astern.

Any distance behind a vessel.

Boxing off.

Flattening in the head sails, or bracing the head yards round to pay a ship's head off, when she has been brought all in the wind by bad steering, or the wind has suddenly headed her.

Aback.

The position of a ship when by a sudden shift of wind her sails are thrown flat aback, that is, their surface bearing against the mast forces the ship astern.

Wake of a ship.

The marked track of a ship caused by her movement through the water.

SECTION III.

Brig Model.

To know the names, lead, and use of Running Rigging :—

Royal braces.
Topgallant braces.
Topsail braces.
Fore braces.
Preventer main braces.
After main braces.
Crossjack braces.
Royal lifts.
Topgallant lifts.
Topsail lifts.
Fore lifts.
Main lifts.
Crossjack lifts.
Royal sheets.
Topgallant sheets.
Topsail sheets.
Fore sheets.
Main sheets.
Jibstay reeving-line.
Jib lacing.

Hanks
Royal clewline.
Topgallant clewline.
Topsail clewline.
Clewgarnets.
Fore tack.
Main tack.
Royal yard rope.
Royal halliards.
Topgallant yard rope.
Topgallant halliards.
Topgallant buntlines.
Top bowlines.
Fore bowlines.
Main bowlines.
Topsail buntlines.
Fore buntlines.
Main buntlines.
Leechlines.
Slablines.
Topsail reeftackles.
Reef burtons.

Peak halliards.
Throat halliards.
Spanker brails.
Spanker outhaul.
Boom topping lift.
Boom sheets.
Tack tackle.
Tack tricing line.
Flying jib halliards.
Jib halliards.
Fore topmast staysail halliards.
Flying jib downhaul.
Jib downhaul.
Fore topmast staysail downhaul.
Flying jib sheets.
Jib sheets.
Fore topmast staysail sheets.

TO REEVE ROYAL-BRACES.

To Reeve a Fore Royal-Brace.

Place the eye, when marled, to the lift over the yard-arm, and reeve the other end through a block seized on the fore part of the main topgallant funnel, from forward aft, and pay the end down between the crosstrees, through lubber's hole on deck, and reeve it through a sheave in the fife-rail.

To Reeve a Main Royal-Brace.

Place the eye, when marled, to the lift over the yard-arm, and reeve the other end through a block seized on the fore part of the mizen topgallant-stay. pay the end down between the crosstrees, through lubber's hole on deck, and reeve it through a sheave in the mizen fife-rail.

To Reeve a Mizen Royal-Brace.

Place the end, when marled, to the lift over the yard-arm,
and reeve the other end through a sheave hole in the after-
part of the main topmast-crosstrees, through lubber's hole
on deck, through a sheave in the fife-rail.

To Reeve a Fore Topgallant-Brace.

Reeve the end up through the sheave in the main fife-rail
and lubber's hole, and the block under the main topmast
cross trees, through a leading-block fast to the collar of the
main topmast-stay; if a single brace, splice an eye in the
end, and marl it to the fore-topgallant lift, ready to go over
the yard-arm ; if a double brace, reeve it through the fore
topgallant brace-block, from out in, and make the end
fast close to the block on the collar of the main topmast-
stay.

All line of battle ships, and frigates above the sixth class,
have double topgallant-braces ; the block on the yard-arm,
however, is found inconvenient; a good single brace,
fitted with a whip under the lead, is found to give sufficient
purchase.

To Reeve a Main Topgallant-Brace.

If a single brace, take the end up through lubber's hole,
through a block seized to the foremost shroud of the mizen
topmast rigging, high enough to work over the mizen topsail yard when hoisted. Splice an eye in the end, and place
it over the topgallant yard-arm. If a double brace, instead
of making an eye-splice in the end, it is rove through the
brace-block on the topgallant yard-arm, brought back, and
secured to the foremost shroud of the mizen topmast, close
to the block ; the hauling part is rove through one of the
sheaves of the fife rail abreast the mizen mast.

To Reeve a Mizen Topgallant-Brace.

If single, take the end up through lubber's hole, through
a block either seized to a bolt on the after-part of the main
lower cap, or to the after main-topmast shroud, just below
the crosstrees, from forward aft, form an eye-splice, and
put it over the yard-arm. If double, the end is rove through
the brace-block on the yard-arm, and brought back and
secured alongside the block on the after main-topmast
shroud ; if the block is secured to an eye-bolt in the main

lower cap, the standing part of the brace is secured round
the ass of the block. The hauling part is rove through a
sheave in the fife-rail abreast the main-mast.

NOTE.—For the convenience of working ship, the fore topgallant and
royal-braces often lead forward.

FORE TOPSAIL-BRACE.

To Reeve a Fore Topsail-Brace.

Reeve the end through the sheave in the main bitts, from
aft forward, through a block under the main trestletrees,
through another block fast to the fork of the mainstay, then
through the brace-block on the yard-arm from out in, and
secure the end round the main topmast-head with a half-
hitch, and seize the end back, or take a round turn round the
topmast-head and splice the two ends of the braces together.

The leading-block on the fork of the mainstay leads the
brace clear of the foot of the main-topsail; sometimes the
standing part is made fast to the mainmast-head with a
seizing to the fork of the mainstay, to keep it clear of the
main-topsail, and the hauling part is rove through a leading-
block at the main topmast-head, under the eyes of the topmast-rigging; it it generally considered the fore topsail-yard
is more easily braced up.

MAIN TOPSAIL-BRACE.

To Reeve a Main Topsail-Brace.

Reeve the end through the sheave in the mizen bitts, from
aft forward, up through the leading-block, half way up the
mizenmast, through the brace-block on the yard-arm, from
down up, up to the mizen topmast-head, where it is secured;
but in most cases, in order to relieve the mizen topmast, it is
led through a clump-block at the mizen topmast-head, fast
under the eyes of the rigging, down to the after-part of the
mizen chains; a thimble is spliced in the end, and it is set
up with a lanyard.

MIZEN TOPSAIL-BRACE.

To Reeve a Mizen Topsail-Brace.

Reeve the end through a sheave in the main fife-rail
up through lubber's hole, through a leading block at the
mainmast-head, close up under the cap, stropped to an

eye-bolt, from forward aft, through the brace-block on the mizen topsail yard-arm, from out in, and splice the end to the eye-bolt at the mainmast-head, where the leading block is secured.

To Reeve a Fore-Brace.

Reeve the end through the sheave in the main bitts, from aft forward, up through the block at the cheek of the mainmast from aft forward, take the end forward outside all the rigging, through the brace block on the fore-yard, from out in, and secure the end with an eye-splice round the same eye-bolt, as the block is stropped on at the cheeks of the mainmast head.

The starboard-brace is fitted with a tricing line, in large ships, from the mainstay, so as to be able to frap the brace in out of the way, in shifting main topsail-yards.

To Reeve a Preventer, or Fore Main-Brace.

Reeve the end through the sheave-hole at the fore bitts from aft forward, up through the outer sheave of the double block at the cheek of the foremost head, through the preventer brace-block on the main-yard from out in, and down through the inner sheave of the double blocks at the cheeks of the foremost head; both ends are led through pipes or fairleaders, down through the sheaves on to the main deck, where they are always worked in large ships.

These braces are frequently led across for the convenience of working ship.

To Reeve a Main After-Brace.

Reeve the end through the main brace block on the quarter from in out, through the brace-block on the yard, from out in, turn a double block in the end, reeve a purchase to a single block, which is hooked to an eye-bolt close to the main brace-block on the quarter; this purchase is for hauling the brace taut, after the slack has been gathered in on the long end.

To Reeve a Cross Jack Brace.

Reeve the end through the sheave in the fife-rail of main rigging, through the outer sheave of the double block fast to the necklace at the mainmast-head, through the brace-block on the yard-arm, from out in, and splice the end in one of the links of the main-necklace, close to the double block; these braces are frequently led across for the convenience of working ship.

To Reeve a Royal Lift.

Splice an eye in one end to go over the yard-arm, and marl it to the outside part of the eye of the brace, reeve the other end through a thimble seized to the royal backstay—in large ships, between the royal shrouds, from out in, down into the top; splice a thimble in the end, and set it up with a lanyard.

NOTE.—For the convenience of squaring yards, the ends of the top-gallant and royal lifts are rove through thimbles secured to the eyes of the lower rigging, and belayed to cleats at the lower masthead.

To Reeve a Topgallant Lift.

An eye is spliced in one end, served and marled to the eye of the brace ready to go over the yard-arm; in large ships, where double-braces are used, it is marled to the eye of the brace-block; the other end is rove through a roller or thimble, from out in, and (in large ships through a sister-block seized in the topgallant-shrouds), down inside the topmast-rigging into the top; a thimble is spliced in the end, and they are set up with a lanyard, *i.e.*, the starboard lift of the fore and mizen, and the port of the main, they are called the short lifts. The other lifts, that is, the port lifts of the fore and mizen, and the starboard lift of the main, are rove through thimbles secured by a strop to the eyes of the lower rigging, belayed to a cleat at the lower masthead, and are called the long lifts, so as to admit of the topgallant-yards canting; and is easily let go.

FORE AND MAIN TOPSAIL-LIFTS.

To Reeve a Double Topsail-Lift.

Take the end from the chains up in a line with the third shroud, through lubber's hole, inside the topmast rigging, through the lower sheave of the sister-block, from in out, down to the yard-arm, through the topsail lift-block, from in out, send the end aloft, and secure it round the topmast-head with a half-hitch, and the end seized back.

The lower end is rove through a clump-block in the chains, and in some cases led through a pipe in the ship's side inboard.

MIZEN TOPSAIL-LIFT.

A Mizen Topsail-Lift is Single.

To reeve it. Take the end out of the top, up inside the topmast rigging, through the lower sheave in the sister-block, from in out, splice an eye in the end, worm and serve it, and place it over the yard-arm.

A thimble is spliced in the other end, and it is set up in the top with a lanyard.

A single fore or main topsail-lift is rove in a similar way, only the end is set up in the chains.

To Reeve a Fore and Main Lift.

Take the end up through the lubber's hole, reeve it through the after-sheave in the block at the lower cap, from in out, down before the rigging, through the lift-block at the lower yard-arm, from out in, up through the foremost sheave of the block at the cap, from in out, splice a running-eye in the end of it, worm and serve it, and place it over the yard-arm. In some cases it is clenched, and about two fathoms end left to act as a stopper for the topsail-sheets.

To Reeve Cross Jack Lifts.

Cross-jack lifts are single, being either rove through blocks hooked to the lower cap, or passed over a saddle which is scored out on top of the lower cap, they go over the yard-arm with an eye-splice—a thimble or block is spliced in the other end by which they are set up.

To Reeve a Royal Sheet.

To reeve a royal sheet, take the end up through lubber's hole if led on deck ; if not, out of the top, up between the crosstrees, through the after-sheave in the quarter-block on the topgallant-yard, from in out, up through the cheek or sheave-hole at the yard-arm, up before the lift, and bend it to the clew of the royal with a sennit-eye over a spring toggle.

To Reeve a Topgallant Sheet.

To reeve a topgallant sheet, take the end up through lubber's hole, through the after-sheave of the quarter-block on the topsail yard, from in out, up through the cheek at the yard-arm, before the lift and reef-tackle, up through the clew of the topgallant-sail, and place the sennit-eye over the spring-toggle, which is seized in the clew of the sail.

To Reeve a Rope Topsail Sheet.

Reeve the end through the quarter-block on the quarter of the lower yards, from in out, up through the cheek at the lower yard-arm, through the block in the clew of the sail, from in out, and secure the end round the lower yard-arm with an outside clinch.

To Reeve a Chain Topsail Sheet.

To reeve a chain topsail-sheet, bend a hauling-line to the inner end of the chain, reeve it down through the cheek at the lower yard-arm, in through the rollers underneath the lower yard, through the gin in the slings of the yard, and secure it to the lugs of the whip-block by a bolt; the standing part of the whip is made fast to an eyebolt in the deck, and the hauling part is rove through a sheave-hole in the bitts, or a leading block; the other end of the sheet is secured to the clew of the topsail with clasp hooks or shackled. The cheek at the lower yard-arm is of iron when it is intended to reeve chain sheets.

To Reeve a Fore or Main Sheet.

Splice a hook in the end of the standing part, and hook it to an eye-bolt abaft the channels; reeve the other end through the sheet-blocks in the clew of the sail, from out in, and through the sheave near the standing part inboard.

To Reeve a Jib Stay Reeving Line.

It is taken out inside the jib guy and rove from down up through the sheave hole in the jib-boom end, and bent to the becket in the jib stay.

To Reeve Jib Lacing.

The lacing is spliced in the upper eyelet hole of the jib and rove, over the stay through the eyelet holes, against the lay of the stay.

Hanks.

Wood and iron hoops used for bending staysails and jibs to the stays.

To Reeve a Royal Clewline.

Take the end up through lubber's hole, if led on deck, or out of the top between the crosstrees, reeve it through the quarter-block on the royal yard, from in out, and bend it to the clew of the royal with a sheet bend. In large ships, royal sheets and clewlines are generally worked from the tops, and not led on deck.

To Reeve a Topgallant Clewline.

Take the end up through lubber's hole, through the fore-most sheave of the quarter block, on the topgallant-yard from in out, and bend it to the clew of the topgallant-sail with a sheet bend.

To Reeve a Topsail Clewline.

Take the end up through lubber's hole, reeve it through the foremost sheave of the quarter-block, on the topsail-yard, from in out, through the block which is lashed on the after part of the clew of the sail, from in out, and secure it round the quarter of the topsail-yard outside the quarter-block, with a timber-hitch.

To Reeve a Fore or Main Clew Garnet.

Take the end up through the clew garnet-block on the lower yard, reeve it from in out, down through the clew garnet block, which is lashed or shackled to the clew of the sail from in out, take the end up, and secure it round the lower yard, outside the quarter-block, with a timber hitch.

To Reeve a Fore Tack.

Splice a running-eye in the end of the standing part, and put it over the bumpkin; reeve the other end through the tack-block in the clew of the sail, from forward aft, through the block on the bumpkin, from out in, through the sheave hole in the bulwark inboard. If fitted with slips, fit the standing part of tack with a thimble.

To Reeve a Main Tack.

Splice a hook in the standing part, and hook it to an eye-bolt in the deck, placed for that purpose, near the main tack block; reeve the other end through the block on the clew of the sail, from forward aft, and through the main tack block on the deck from forward aft.

The standing part is sometimes fitted with a slip.

To Reeve Royal Halyards or Yard-Rope.

Reeve the end through the sheave in the bitts, up through lubber's hole, through the sheave-hole in the royal masthead, from aft forward, pay the end down before all, through the grommet and lizard, and bend it to the slings of the yard with a studdingsail halyard-bend.

Two single blocks are kept rove on the yard-rope, and stopped in the top to form a purchase when the sail is set ; one, a hook-block, which is the upper block on the yard-rope, but becomes the lower block of the purchase when rove, is hooked to the lower trestletrees, the other block is fitted with a long strop and eye, the purchase is formed by taking it well up the yard-rope, forming a hitch over the long-eye with a bight of the yard-rope and placing a bight of the yard-rope through the eye in which a toggle is placed, so as to keep it in place, thus forming three parts.

Topgallant purchases, in small vessels, are the same, the toggle is iron, and well served.

To Reeve Topgallant Halyards or Yard-Rope.

Reeve the end through the sheaves in the bitts, from aft forward, up through lubber's hole through the sheave-hole in the topgallantmast-head, from aft forward, pay the end down before all, through the grommet and lizard, and bend it with a studdingsail halyard-bend to the slings of the yard. At sea, a topgallant purchase is used on the yard-rope or halyard.

In large ships it is a purchase rove through two double blocks, the upper block is fitted with two tails, for dogging round the yard rope, the lower block is a hook-block, iron-bound, hooked on deck. When in harbour, the upper block is made fast to the after-shroud, above the futtock-rigging. The main is worked the starboard side, and the fore and mizen the port side of the deck.

To Reeve a Topgallant Buntline.

A topgallant buntline is a single buntline, fitted with two legs, each leg has a running eye spliced in the end of it, which goes over the toggle in the foot of the topgallant-sail, the other end is rove through the thimble of the lizard of the yard-rope, which acts as a buntline-span, then through a block from forward aft, which block is seized to the eye of the topgallant-stay, down into the top, or through lubber's hole on deck.

To Reeve a Foretop Bowline.

Take the end out through the sheave-hole in the head-rail, through the sheave-hole in the bees of the bowsprit, or through a block at the bowsprit end ; splice a running eye in the end, and place it over the toggle in the lower bowline bridle in the leech of the sail.

To Reeve a Maintop Bowline.

Take the end up through lubber's hole through a block
lashed to the eyes of the fore rigging, and bend it with a
running-eye over the toggle of the middle bowline bridle in
the leech of the main topsail.

To Reeve a Mizentop Bowline.

Take the end up through the inner sheave of the double
block the crossjack brace is rove through, splice a running
eye, and put it over the toggle on the lower bowline bridle,
in the leech of the mizen topsail, in a similar manner to the
main and fore.

To Reeve a Fore Bowline.

. Reeve it through the block on the bowsprit, from down
up; splice a running eye in the end, and bend it over a
toggle in the bowline-bridle, in the leech of the foresail.
The fore bowline blocks on the bowsprit are span-blocks,
fitted round and under the bowsprit, outside the inner forestay collar.

To Reeve a Main Bowline.

The main bowline is fitted with a light runner and tackle ;
the runner is rove through a thimble, which is attached to
the lower bowline-bridle, on the leech of the mainsail, by a
slip toggle ; the runner and tackle are hooked forward by
the foremast, and is always shifted from side to side in
working ship, by the first part of quarter-deck men.

To Reeve a Fore Topgallant Bowline.

Take the end out, and reeve it from down up, through a
span block, which is fitted round the jib-boom funnel or
seized to the jib guys, and bend it to leech of the topgallant-sail, with a running eye over the toggle. A main
topgallant bowline is rove up through a sheave-hole, in the
after part of the fore topmast crosstrees ; a mizen topgallant
bowline is rove through a block seized to the main topmast
shrouds.

To Reeve a Topsail Buntline.

Take the end up through lubber's hole through the cheek
of the tressletrees at the topmast-head, from aft forward,
down through the thimble of the buntline-span ; splice a
running eye in the end, and place it over the buntline-
toggle, in the foot of the sail. In reeving a buntline that

has been in use, or with a running eye already spliced in it, reeve it the reverse way, that is, place the eye over the toggle in the foot of the topsail, reeve the other end up through the thimble of the buntline-span, through the cheek of the topmast tressle trees, from forward aft, and pay the end down through lubber's hole on deck, and reeve it through its proper sheave in the bitts.

Q. What are buntline spans, and their use?

A. Buntline spans are simply two pieces of rope, about 2 ins. or $2\frac{1}{2}$ ins. in size, according to the size of the topsail, and about one fathom and a half in length, with a thimble spliced in one end, through which the buntlines are rove, the other ends are knotted abaft the tye (in harbour) with a reef knot, and round the neck of the tye block at sea; the reason the buntline span is secured round the neck of the tye block at sea, is to prevent the foot of the sail rising above the yard, also to spill the sail in taking the third or fourth reef in.

To Reeve Fore and Main Bowline.

Reeve the buntlines, through the upper sheave of the buntline-block, then reeve both ends through the double-block, which is hooked to the foremost eyebolt of the lower cap on either side, from aft forward, down through the sheave holes in the fore part of the top; round the buntline-block, close up to the double block, then bend the ends of the buntlines to the foot of the course, either by toggling or clenching them. The buntline-whip is rove through the lower sheave of the buntline-block, and both ends led down through lubber's hole on deck, and are rove through blocks or sheave holes. Two single blocks, in one strop, on end, are sometimes used instead of fiddle-blocks as buntline blocks; they are called shoe-blocks. When there is sufficient drift, buntlines are sometimes rove with single legs, and double whips. The ends of the legs are rove through thimbles, spliced into the inner holes at the foot of the courses, and made fast to the outer holes.

To Reeve Leech Lines, Fore or Main.

They are rove through a double-block under the top from in out, down through the leech-line blocks that are seized on the jackstay of the lower yards before the sail, and are clenched or toggled to the leech of the sail; there are two on each side in large ships, but only one in small vessels.

To Reeve Fore or Main Slab-Lines.

They are rove through a double-block, on the quarter of the yard, from in out, through the slab-line blocks seized on the jackstay of the lower yard, between the yard and the sail, down abaft the course, and are clenched or toggled to the leech of the sail, in a similar way to a leech-line; when there are two leech-lines of a side, there are also two slab-lines; in taking a course in they act the same as a brail would to a fore and aft sail.

To Reeve a Bunt Slab-Line.

It is a single rope rove through a tail block, fast to the slings of the lower yards, it leads down abaft the sail, and is clenched to the foot.

To Reeve a Topsail Reef-tackle.

Take the end up through lubber's hole, inside the topmast rigging, through the upper sheave of the sister block, from in out, down through the sheave at the yard-arm; through the reef-tackle block, from in out, and secure the end round the goose-neck with an inside clinch.

To Reef the Second Reef-tackle.

To reeve the second reef-tackle, take it up through lubber's hole through a tail-block at the topmast-head, from in out, down through the block on the yard-arm, and bend it to the second reef-tackle cringle in the sail with a half-hitch, and the end seized back, or with clip-hooks if a single reef-tackle.

The second reef tackle cringle is placed between the second and third reef-cringles.

If a double reef-tackle, it is rove through a block toggled or hooked to the cringle in the leech of the sail, and secured with an inside clinch round the goose-neck of the topsail-yard.

To Reeve a Reef Burton.

Reeve the end of the fall through a leading block at the lower cap, from in out, through a cheek in the lower yard-arm from in out, then through a block which is secured to the reef-cringle in the leech of the sail by clip hooks, from in out, and make the end fast to the boom-iron with an inside clinch, the other end of the fall is led on deck, with sufficient length to admit of lowering the sail on deck; thus, in shifting or bending courses, there is no necessity for using a Burton.

To Reeve the Peak Halyards.

Take the end up the port side, through lubber's hole, and reeve it through the port sheave of the double-block, which is iron-stropped and hooked to the after part of the mizen lower cap; then down abaft the top, through the outer block on the gaff, from forward aft, up through the starboard-sheave of the double-block at the cap, from up down; down abaft the top again, and through the inner block on the gaff, from aft forward, send the end aloft, and secure it round the neck of the double-block with a running eye.*

The standing part of the peak-halyards is frequently made fast with a running eye round the mizen topmast head, in which case they are rove through the inner block on the gaff, first, from aft forwarded, and through the outer block last, from forward aft, but in the same way as before, through the double-block on the after part of the lower cap.

* N.B.—This applies to the boom-mainsail of a brig.

To Reeve the Throat-Halyards of a Spanker.

Take the end up the starboard side, abaft the mast, reeve it through the foremost sheave in the chock, abaft the try-sailmast, from starboard to port; down through the throat halyard-block on the jaws of the gaff, from port to starboard up through the after-sheave in the chock, from starboard to port; then send the end down, and secure it with a running-eye over the neck or lower part of the block on the gaff. If the gaff is fitted with a double-block, or a span with two single blocks round the jaws, the standing part is made fast round the neck of the upper block, or through a hole in the chock, with a stopper-knot.

Peak-Brails.

Span-blocks are fitted on the gaff or the inner and outer peak-brails. The outer blocks are single, and seized round the gaff two-thirds out; the inner blocks are double, and seized on, one-third out on the gaff. Both the inner and outer peak-brails are rove through them.

The throat-brails are rove through a block seized to the jaws of the gaff.

Throat-Brails.

The middle brails are rove through single blocks fitted with a span round the trysail mast, half way down, or seized to the luff of the sail.

R 3498.

L

Small vessels are only fitted with one peak-brail.

A treble block is now seized to the jaws of the gaff, which takes the peak and the throat-brails, therefore a fiddle-block is now used on the gaff for the inner peak-brails.

To Reeve Brails.

They are each in one piece of rope, and when the sail is bent and hoisted, the position for the brails is determined on ; they are middled, and the bight of each brail seized to the after-leech of the sails, as marked, and rove through their respective blocks, from aft forward down on deck.

To Reeve a Spanker-Head Outhaul.

When a spanker is fitted at the head with an outhaul and inhaul, the head of the sail is attached to small iron hoops which travel on an iron rod underneath the gaff.

The outhaul is fitted with a pendant and whip. The pendant is rove through a clump-block, which is lashed to the gaff end ; one end of the pendant has a thimble and hook spliced in it, for hooking to the head-earring thimble in the sail, the other end has a thimble, or one of the blocks of the whip spliced in it ; the other block of the whip is fitted with a hook, which is hooked to a strop at the jaws of the gaff. It is frequently made of chain, in which case a treble iron-bound block is hooked to the lower cap instead of a double-block for the peak-halyards, the third sheave is used to reeve the chain outhaul through.

To Reeve the Outhaul.

Reeve the end up through the starboard outer sheave of the treble-block, from forward aft, down through the sheave in the end of the gaff, and shackle it to the head-earring thimble of the spanker ; an iron-bound single block is shackled to the other end, through which a whip is rove to another iron-bound block, hooked to the deck by the mizen-mast.

To Reeve a Spanker-Foot Outhaul.

Reeve the end up through the sheave in the boom-end through a clump-block, fitted either with a lashing-eye or a clip-hook, to the clew of the sail, from forward aft, and secure it over the boom-end by an eye splice ; sometimes it is fitted with a pendant and whip, in which case a block is spliced in the end of the pendant, and the other block of the whip is hooked to an eyebolt, under the jaws of the boom.

To Reeve the Topping-Lifts.

The standing part is spliced round a thimble to an eye-bolt attached to an iron band round the boom, about 12 ft. from the outer end, and is rove through a clump-block, iron-bound—in a brig, bolted to the main tressletrees, and in a ship, bolted to the mizen tressletrees, from aft forward, down, through the snatch on the boom. A thimble is spliced in the end for hooking the tackle to.

The tackle is rove through a single and a fiddle-block, the standing part of the fall being spliced in the ass of the single-block; the fiddle-block is hooked to the weather-topping lift, and the single-block to an eye-bolt under the jaws of the boom. A stopper is fitted round the boom, inside the snatch, for stopping the topping-lift in tacking, so as to shift the tackle.

When the topping-lift is fitted single, after the end is rove through the clump-block at the tressletrees, a double block is spliced in the end and a fall is rove to a single block, hooked either in the chains or by the mast.

BOOM-SHEETS.

Spanker-Boom Sheets.

In large screw or sailing ships there are two double blocks on the boom, and three single blocks each side of the ship aft, one acting as a leading block; the standing part of the sheet is spliced in the eye-bolt at the boom-end.

For small screws and paddle-wheel steam-vessels there are two double and two single blocks, the single block being on the boom, the standing part is made fast to an eye-bolt in the boom-end; where there is a stern gun, the blocks in the quarter should be fitted with a shackle.

In brigs, boom-sheets are rove through two double blocks on the boom, and two double blocks and a leading block inboard on the quarter. Reeve the end through the leading block, from forward aft, through the lower sheave of the block on the boom from aft forward, through the lower sheave of the double block inboard from forward aft, so on until the fall is rove in full, making the end fast round the boom, end with an eye-splice, or splicing it into an eye-bolt.

To Reeve Tack Tackle.

It is rove through two blocks for bousing down the tack of any fore and aft sail.

The Tack-Tricing Line.

The tack-tricing line is a double whip, the upper block secured to the jaws of the gaff, and the lower block is fitted with a tail, which is bent to a thimble in the lower part of the luff of the sail.

To Reeve the Flying-Jib Halyards.

Take the end up the port side, abaft all, reeve it from aft forward through the flying-jib halyard-block, and pay it down on deck the port side of all the stays, splice a clasp-hook on a swivel in the end, and hook it to the head of the flying jib.

To Reeve the Jib-Halyards.

Take the end up the starboard side abaft all, reeve it from aft forward, through the jib halyard-block, then make a bowline with the end round the jibstay, pay it down, splice a thimble, with a clasp-hook on a swivel in the end, and hook it to the head of the jib.

To Reeve Fore Topmast Staysail-Halyards.

To reeve the fore topmast staysail halyards, take the end up the port side, through the fore topmast staysail halyard-blocks (which is shackled the port side of the topmast-necklace) from aft forward, down before all, through the block which is hooked to the head of the sail, send the end aloft, and secure it to a link in the topmast necklace close to the halyard-block. These halyards are of great use in shifting the fore topsail or jib-boom.

To Reeve a Flying-Jib Downhaul.

Reeve it through the sheave hole in the head-rail on the port side, take it out underneath the man-ropes, and over the jib-guys, through the flying-jib downhaul block, at the flying jib-boom end, from down up, through the three upper hanks, and bend it to the head of the sail, or over the thimble in the halyards, with a sheet bend. The flying-jib is attached to the flying-jibstay by a lacing ; the tack is secured in like manner to the jib by a tack lashing round the flying-boom end.

To Reeve a Jib Downhaul.

Take the end out on the starboard side through the sheave-hole in the head-rail, through the jib downhaul-block at the jib-boom end, up through the upper hank or grommet,* and bend it to the head of the jib or over the thimble in the jib-halyards, with a sheet-bend.   The luff of a jib is attached to the jibstay by hanks and lacing, and the tack is secured to the jib-boom end with a tack lashing, which is spliced in the tack thimble, two or three turns being passed round the jib-boom, and through the thimble in the tack of the jib, and the end hitched round its own part; sometimes it is fitted with a strop and toggle instead of a tack-lashing.

To Reeve a Fore Topmast Staysail Downhaul.

Reeve the end out on the port side, through the head-rail, through the downhaul-block on the bowsprit end, from down up, up through the three upper hanks, and make it fast with a sheet-bend to the head of the sail.   Tack lashing is spliced in the thimble in the tack of the sail, and passed two or three times round the bowsprit, each turn being passed through the thimble in the tack of the sail; the end is hitched round all parts of the lashing.   Fore topmast staysails are seized to hanks round the port fore topmast stay.   If a lacing is used instead of hanks it is only rove through every other eyelet-hole in the luff of the sail, and round the stay; being seized to the eyelet-holes, it is not rove through.   The sheets are fitted with whips and a pendant.

To Reeve Flying Jib Sheets.

The sheets are fitted exactly in a similar way to the jib-sheets, and connected in like manner to the clew of the sail. In small vessels they are single, similar to the jib-sheets, and attached to the sail in the same manner.

To Reeve Jib Sheets.

Jib-sheets, in large ships, are fitted with double whips and pendants, an eye being formed in the bight of the pendant, and attached to the clew of the jib by a strop and toggle; in some cases they are lashed or fitted with a shackle and screw pin.   In small vessels the jib-sheets are single.

---

* In addition to the lacing of a jib, there are always two or three hanks or a grommet, at the head of the luff.

To Reeve Fore Topmast Staysail Sheets.

Pendants and whips are used, the bight of the pendant is made fast to the clews with strops and toggles, and the whips rove through the blocks in the ends of the pendants.

The standing part is made fast to a bolt just before the cathead, and the hauling part is rove through a sheave hole in the bows.

To Reeve a Fore Bunt-Whip.

It is a single rope, with a clasp-hook in one end, to hook to the bunt becket, and rove through a single block, lashed to one of the upper links of the lower slings ; the hauling part being led on deck.

To Reeve a Topsail Bunt-Whip.

A bunt-whip consists of three single blocks, forming a runner and tackle. The runner-block is fitted with a long tail, which is secured round the topmast-head, or a thimble in the strop, and lashed under the crosstrees, or to the neck-lace ; one end of it has a hook spliced in it for hooking to the bunt-becket—the other end, the upper block of the tackle, is turned in it. The lower block of the tackle is fitted with a tail, or a thimble, in the strop of a block, and is secured to the eyes of the lower rigging ; when not in use it is hooked to a strop, to the eyes of the lower rigging, and kept up and down the mast; the hauling part is worked from the top.

The Long Bunt-Whip.

This is simply a single rope, rove through a block, under the topmost crosstrees with a hook spliced in one end for hooking it to the bunt-becket; the hauling part is on deck. It is used when hauling out to, or furling from a bowline.

BRAILS.

Peak-Brails.

Span-blocks are fitted on the gaff for the inner and outer peak-brails. The outer blocks are single, and seized round the gaff two-thirds out ; the inner blocks are double, and seized on, one-third out on the gaff. Both the inner and outer peak-brails are rove through them.

The throat-brails are rove through a block seized to the jaws of the gaff.

Throat Brails.

The middle brails are rove through single [blocks fitted with a span round the trysail-mast, half-way down, or seized to the luff of the sail.

Small vessels are only fitted with one peak-brail.

A treble block is now seized to the jaws of the gaff, which takes the peak and throat-brails, therefore a fiddle-block is now used on the gaff for the inner peak-brails.

To Reeve Brails.

They are each in one piece of rope, and when the sail is bent and hoisted, the position for the brails is determined on, they are middled, and the bight of each brail seized to the after-leech of the sail, as marked, and rove through their respective blocks, from aft forward down on deck.

Lazy Guy.

Is a pendant with a hook placed in one end and a single block in the other; the fall is rove through another single block with a hook, the standing part is spliced in the ass of the block, in the pendant.

When in use, the pendant goes round the boom, and hooks to its own part between the topping-lifts and sheets, the block of the fall is hooked in the main chain for a brig, and the mizen for a ship; it is used when running free, to steady the boom.

Jaw Ropes.

A jaw rope is a piece of rope rove through a hole in the jaws of the boom or gaff, from out in. A stopper-knot is worked in the end to keep it from coming through; it is passed round before the mast through a number of round pieces of wood, called trucks, through another hole in the jaws of the boom or gaff on the opposite side, from in out, and a figure-of-eight knot is made in the end, to keep it from slipping through; it is to a boom or gaff what a parrel is to a yard.

Vangs, or Peak-Downhauls.

Vangs in large ships are double, and in small vessels single. There is an iron band round the gaff a short space, or about one-seventh in from the gaff end, with an eye-bolt on either side of it; to these eyebolts, the vang-blocks, which are single iron-bound blocks, are hooked with clasp-hooks.

The vangs are rove through the blocks, the standing part is spliced, if double, round a thimble in an eye-bolt in the ship's side, close to the fife-rail, or eye-splice put over the under part of a belaying pin, the hauling part rove through a sheave close to it.

In large ships they are fitted with a pendant and whip; the standing part of the pendant is spliced round a thimble in the eye-bolt in the gaff, and a single block is spliced in the other end, through which the whip is rove, the hauling part being rove through a sheave in the fife-rail, and the standing part secured, as described for a vang.

A Single Vang.

The end is merely spliced round the thimble in the eye-bolt on the gaff, and the other end rove through a sheave in the fife-rail.

To Reeve Lower Studdingsail Outer Halyards.

Take the end up before the top, through the span-block at the foretop masthead, from in out, down before the boom through the block at the topmast studdingsail boom-end, down on the forecastle, and bend it to the middle of the yard, to which the outer half of the sail is laced, with a studding-sail halyard-bend.

The halyards are sometimes bent only one-third out, according to the size of the sail.

The inner halyards are simple double whips; the upper block being fitted with a tail, which is hitched to the collar or the forestay; the lower block is either fitted with a hook or tail, and made fast to the inner corner of the head of the lower studdingsail.

To Reeve Lower Studdingsail-Tack.

Reeve the end out through the sheave-hole in the gangway, through the tack-block at the swinging boom-end, and bend it to the clew of the sail with a sheet bend, or a running-eye and cross toggle, the long and short sheets are formed out of one piece of rope. The sheets are rove through the thimble in the inner clew, according to the length required, crossed and seized, the long sheet is rove through a tail-block, fast to the foremast dead-eye, through one of the ports inboard, the short sheet is merely passed over the netting inboard, and is only used for taking the sail in.

To Reeve a Tripping-Line.

Take the end up abaft the foreyard, and reeve it through a block under the top, or secured to the foremast-shroud of fore-rigging, through a block on the inner yard-arm of the lower studdingsail-yard, through a thimble in the after-part of the sail, and bend it to the tack with a sheet-bend.

TOPMAST STUDDINGSAIL.

To Reeve the Topmast Studdingsail-Halyards.

Take the end up through lubber's hole, through the span-block at the topmast-cap from in out, down through the jewel-block on the goose-neck of the topsail yard-arm, between the yard and the boom, down abaft the lower yard inside the brace, and bend it to the yard to which the head of the sail is laced with a studdingsail halyard-bend one-third out.

To Reeve the Tack.

Take the tack up outside of the backstays and lower rigging, out to the lower yard-arm under the brace, reeve it from aft forward, through the tack-block at the topmast studdingsail boom-end, then in over the fore-brace, down on deck, and bend it with a sheet-bend to the clew of the sail.

The hauling part is rove through the inner sheave of a double block, secured by a tail to the foremost shroud of the main rigging, the boom-brace being rove through the outer sheave of the same block, or through two sheaves in the ship's side, just before the gangway.

To Reeve a Topmast Studdingsail-Downhaul.

Reeve the end up through the downhaul-blocks, which is seized to the outer clew of the sail, up abaft the sail, through a thimble on the outer leech; splice a running-eye in the end, and place it over the outer yard-arm inside the earring.

Topmast Studdingsails

Are fitted with two sheets, a long and a short one; the long one is worked from the deck, and the short one from the top, passing under the heel of the boom.

To Reeve Topgallant Studdingsail-Halyards.

Take the end up through lubber's hole, through the span-block at the topgallantmast head, from in out, down through a block at the topgallant yard-arm, before the yard, into the top, and bend it to the yard to which the sail is laced with a studdingsail halyard-bend one-third out.

To Reeve a Topgallant Studdingsail-Tack.

Reeve the end out through a block seized below the after dead-eye in the top, up, under, and outside the topsail-brace, through the tack-block at the topgallant studdingsail boom-end, in over the brace, and bend it with a sheet-bend to the outer clew of the sail.

The downhaul is bent to the inner yard-arm and led into the top.

The sheets are led over the topsail-yard into the top. Topgallant studdingsails have only one sheet. They are set and taken in from the top.

When blowing fresh, and a topmast studdingsail is set, the lower studdingsail-halyards are often converted into a martingale for the topmost studdingsail-boom; by taking an over-hand-knot in them above the boom, placing a toggle to prevent the knot from jambing, and hauling down on the under-neath part, which is either rove through an eye-bolt in the forecastle or secured to a cleat.

LOWER YARDS—JEER FALLS.

To Reeve the Long Main Jeers.

Both ends of the fall are fitted with beckets for bending a reeving line to. Reeve the end through the sheave-hole of the main-bitts, the starboard side of the main deck, from aft forward, up through the fair leader in the upper deck aloft and through the starboard sheave of the upper jeer-block, under the main top, from aft forward, down through the starboard jeer-block on the yard from forward aft, up through the port sheave of the upper block, from aft forward, down through the port jeer-block on the yard, from forward aft, and secure the end either round the strop of the other block, to the tressletrees, or round the lower masthead; the fall thus rove forms five parts. When used, the hauling part is brought to the after capstan, on the main deck, in all large ships. In small vessels it is worked on the upper deck.

The fore-jeers are rove in a similar way, commencing on the port-side first, and are worked in all large ships by the foremast capstan on the main deck.

When the main and fore-yards are up, and hung by the slings, the long jeers are unrove, and the sea jeers rove exactly in the same way with respect to the lead through the jeer-blocks, only the end of the falls do not come on deck, they are expended round all parts of the fall and hitched ; in the event of the chain-slings carrying away, the short jeers take the weight of the yards, and prevents them from being sprung, which sometimes occurs.

The cross-jackyard is sent up and down by the mizen burton, which is two double blocks.

To Reeve Truss Pendants and Falls supposing them to be of Chain.

Reeve them through the clump-blocks which are iron-bound and shackled to a bolt in the after part of the trestle-trees, from aft forward, through the thimble of the truss-strop on the yard, from up down, through an iron clamp abaft the mast, which has a division in it, one for the upper, the other for the lower pendant, so as to keep them from riding, and also to keep them up in place, and shackle them to the truss-strop on the opposite side of the yard.

The ends of the pendants hang about two-thirds of the way down to the deck, and have a double iron-bound block shackled to each, through which the falls are rove.

In reeving the pendant the standing part will be inside the hauling part of the one rove first, and outside the hauling part of the one rove last.

To Reeve the Truss-Fall.

A single iron-bound block is hooked to the deck, abaft the mast with a ring in the ass of it for the standing part of the fall to be spliced, the end of the fall is rove up through the double block from forward aft, down through the single block from aft forward, up through the double block from forward aft, and then through a sheave in the fife-rail.

A tricing line is fitted to the truss pendants, it is spliced in a thimble fast to the same shackle as the double or upper block of the fall, or about half-way down, and rove through a single block seized to the after-shroud above the futtock-rigging, so as to light them up in working ship. Small ships have only a single iron bound block in the pendant for the falls.

When a fore or main-yard is fitted with rope pendants, the standing part is secured round the yard with a running-eye, and the fall is rove through the sheave holes in the after-part of the trestletrees in the following way : the standing part of the fall is rove with a running-eye round the truss-pendants, rove through the inner sheave on the trestletrees, from forward aft, through the block in the truss-pendant, from aft forward, through the outer sheave in the trestletrees, from forward aft, and then through a sheave in the fife-rail on deck.

The cross-jack trusses are always fitted in this way. The single block in the end of the pendant is seized in what is termed a soft-eye, which is to admit of the block being turned out easily in sending the yard down.

To Reeve a Yard-Tackle Whip.

Take the end up through the upper sheave of the fiddle-block in the yard-tackle pendant, from in out, through the lower block, from out in, up through the lower sheave in the fiddle-block, from in out, and splice the end in the ass of the lower block. The hauling part is rove through a leading-block, placed as convenient.

A yard-tackle pendant and whip is fitted with two tricing-lines, viz. : a quarter and bill tricing-line.

To Reeve the Quarter Tricing-Line.

The end is rove through a leading-block fitted with a tail, or seized to the after-part of the lower yard on the quarter, out through a block seized to the jackstay, which hangs down abaft the yard, and sufficiently far in to bring the pendant, when triced up taut, along the yard ; the end is secured with a running-eye between the two sheaves of the fiddle-block, the hauling part is rove through a sheave in the fife-rail on deck.

To Reeve a Bill Tricing-Line.

The end is rove through a block seized close up to the seizing of the eyes of the lower rigging, the third shroud from forward, an eye is spliced in the end, it is then rove through the thimble in the lower block of the whip, and placed over the bill of the hook.

The hauling part is rove through a sheave next to the quarter tricing-line in the fife-rail on deck.

When the yard tackle and whip are triced up, the lower block of the whip is hooked to a strop round the same shroud, and close to the bill-tricing line-block.

Rolling Tackle.

A luff-tackle is used for this purpose, the single block being hooked to the strop on the yard, the double block to a strop round the lower masthead above the necklace; the end of the fall is rove through a leading block or spare sheave in the bitts.

Frequently the yard tackle pendant and whip is used instead of a rolling-tackle, by letting go the quarter and bill tricing-lines, bringing it along the yard, and hooking the single block of the yard-whip to a strop round the lower masthead, above the necklace, and hooking a snatch block to the same strop for the hauling part of the fall, so as to give it a fair lead on deck, where it is rove through a leading block or spare sheave in the bitts.

To Reeve Fore or Main Topsail-Tyes.

Fore and main topsail-yards, in large ships, are fitted with two tyes, one on either side, a long and a short tye; the long tye is used for shifting topsail-yards. In the lower end of the tye is spliced a long-eye in which the fly-block is seized; the other end is rove (if the starboard-tye) through the starboard hanging block at the topmast-head, shackled to the topmast necklace from aft forward, down through the starboard tye-block, which is a swivel-block, bolted to the iron band round the topsail-yard, from aft forward; the end is then sent aloft, hauled taut round the topmast-head, hitched to its own part, and the spare end stopped down to the foremost shroud, leaving sufficient drift for the fly-block to hang in a line with the lower cap; hook the lower halyard-block to the after part of the chains, and reeve the halyards.

The standing part of the halyards is spliced in the ass of the upper fly-block and rove through the lower block, for the fore, from aft forward, through the upper block, from forward aft, and then through the sheave in the topsail-halyard bitts, or through a leading block hooked to an iron spur in the ship's side, from forward aft.

A main is rove in a similar way, only the hauling part is led forward; and in large ships it is led through a pipe on to the main deck, through a leading-block, and there secured to a Samson-post.

A mizen topsail-yard, in small vessels, has only a single tye, which is rove through the sheave in the topmast-head, and shackled to the yard.

The halyards are rove on the port side exactly, and in the same way as the fore, and in line of battle ships worked on the poop.

In large ships the tye is generally rove on the bight in the following way : there is only one tye-block on a mizen topsail-yard, the tye is rove through either the starboard or port hanging-block at the topmast-head, from aft forward, down through the tye block on the yard, if rove through the starboard masthead-block first, then reeve from starboard to port through the tye-block on the yard, up through the port hanging-block, from forward aft, splice a long-eye in each end of the tye, and seize the fly-blocks in. The halyards are rove in a similar way to the fore.

Preventer Braces.

For lower yards, the yard-tackle pendant and whip is used, the bill and quarter tricing-lines are let go, the single or lower block of the whip is hooked, if the fore, in the main chains, and if the main, in the mizen chains, the hauling part is rove through a sheave in the ship's side, or leading-block inboard.

For Topsail-Yards.

The sail-tackles are used for preventer-braces, or in some ships, tackles, fitted like sail-tackles, are kept in the tops ready to be used as preventer-braces, so as to have the sail tackles always available for shifting topsails.

The pendant of the tackle goes round the yard inside the brace-block, and is hooked to its own part ; the lower block is hooked, if a fore topsail-yard, in the main chains, and the hauling part is rove through a tail block secured to the foremost shroud of the main rigging, about the same height up as the double block for the topmast studsail-tack and boom-brace. If for a main topsail-yard it is secured in a similar way, the lower block being hooked in the mizen chains, and the hauling part is rove through the sheave where the main topmast studdingsail tack was formerly rove when it was used in the Navy.

Rolling Tackle for a Topsail-Yard.

A top-burton, or jigger, is used for this purpose ; the single block is hooked to the quarter strop, and the double block to a strop round the topmast, above the parrell ; if a jigger is used, the hauling part is in the top, but if a burton, the hauling part is sent down through lubber's hole on deck.

LOWER OR SWINGING BOOM.

To Reeve the Topping Lifts.

They are taken up on either side, inside the fore-rigging, rove through a clump block, from in out, seized between the second and third shrouds of the fore-rigging, through another clump-block, fitted with a tail for a lizard, which is made fast outside the lift round the yard-arm when getting the boom out; when the boom is square, or fore and aft, the tail-block is rounded close up to the block, seized between the second and third shroud of the fore-rigging, and the tail is coiled snugly down inside the futtock-rigging.

To Reeve a Fore-Guy.

Reeve the end out through a fair lead in the forecastle-bulwark, through a sheave on the bees of the bowsprit, from in out, through a clump-block on the spritsail-gaff, seized between the jumper and jib-guys, from in out, under the jib-guys, and splice the end round a thimble, through an eye-bolt about one-fourth in from the end of the boom.

To Reeve an After-Guy.

Reeve the end out through the lower sheave in the after-part of the waist nettings, and splice the end round a thimble through an eye-bolt secured to the same band as the eye-bolt and thimble for the fore-guy.

TOPMAST STUDDINGSAIL-BOOMS.

To Reeve a Topping Lift.

Take the end up out of the top, inside the topmast rigging, through the upper sheave of the fiddle-block at the topmast-head, from in out; splice an eye in the end, and place it over the boom end; when in use the other end is set up by a jigger in the top.

OF MASTS.

Lower Masts.

Q. How is a fore or main runner and tackle fitted, and the fall rove?

A. Twice the length of the mast from the deck to the upper part of the trestletrees is the length of the runner, a long-eye is spliced in one end to seize the double block of the fall in, similar to the topsail halyard-block in the topsail-tye.

The length of the fall is four and a half times the length of the mast from the lower cap to the deck.

The standing part is spliced in the ass of the single block, the hauling part is rove through one of the sheaves of the double block in the end of the runner, then through the single, and through the double block again; when in use the end is rove through a single leading-block, which is hooked to a strop or eye-bolt, as convenient.

Topmast.

A top-tackle-pendant has a thimble spliced in one end to hook the upper block of the top-tackle-fall to.

If a main, it is rove up through lubber's hole, through the top block, hooked to the after eye-bolt, the starboard side of the lower cap, from aft forward, through the sheave in the heel of the topmast, from starboard to port. Make the end fast to the foremast eye-bolt on the port side of the lower cap with a half-hitch, and seize the end back, taking care to well parcel the pendant first in the wake of the eye-bolt. The fore or mizen is rove through the sheave in the heel of mast from port to starboard.

The pendant is fitted sufficiently long to house the mast, and allow the upper block of the tackle to be below the futtock-rigging.

To Reeve the Fall.

The upper block is a treble or double iron-bound swivel-block, according to the size of the ship, hooked to the thimble in the end of the pendant; the lower block is a similar block, they are not always both swivel-blocks, in some cases the lower block is a swivel, and the upper a standing block, and *vice versâ*; it is more convenient to have them both swivel-blocks, so as to move readily; take the turns out of the fall in swaying the topmast. The lower block is hooked to an eye-bolt, placed for that purpose on the deck the fall is to be worked; in line of battle ships it is either worked on the main or lower deck, a trap-hatch, about three planks in width, being cut in the upper deck to pass all parts of the fall through. The fall is always rove on the standing part, being the shortest part of the fall ; it is rove so as to have the hauling part of the main forward, and of the fore aft.

To Reeve a Fore or Mizen Top-Tackle Pendant-Fall.

Reeve the end through the leading-block which is secured, round the hook of the lower block with a long-eye, from aft forward, up through the trap-hatch, through the upper block from forward aft, so on until the fall is rove in full; the standing part is secured by being hitched round the neck of the upper block, or round the pendant above the thimble; it will greatly depend on the lead you wish, whether it is rove through the inner or outer sheave of the fall blocks first; thus rove, it forms five parts; the main is generally worked the starboard, and the fore and mizen the port side of the deck, depending how the sheave-hole in the mast is cut.

To Reeve a Topgallant Mast-Rope.

Reeve the end through the sheave in the bitts from aft forward, up through lubber's hole, through a sheave in the topmast-cap, or a block hooked to an eye-bolt in the after-part of the topmast-cap, through the lizard, then through the sheave in the heel of the mast, from starboard to port if a main, and port to starboard for a fore and mizen, and make the end fast to the foremost bolt in the topmast-cap, with a half-hitch, and seize the end back.

If the top-gallant-masts are on deck, lay them abreast their respective parts of the ship to which they belong, heels aft, and lightning conductors upwards. The halyards are rove through the sheave in the bitts, the starboard or port side, according as the sheave in the heel of the mast is cut. The main is generally cut from starboard to port, and the fore and mizen from port to starboard, up through lubber's hole, through the sheave in the after-part of the top-mast cap, or a block hooked to an eye-bolt in the after-part of the top-mast-cap, down through the tressletrees, through the fork of the topmast-stays, before all, on deck, the side of the lower stay the mast is, through the lizard, through the sheave in the heel of the mast; send the end aloft, and hitch it to the foremost eye-bolt in the topmast-cap, and seize the end back. Secure the lizard with two good half-hitches through the royal sheave-hole, or a hole made for that purpose, about 18 ins. below it, askant through the mast; great care should be observed in securing the lizard well to prevent accidents.

To Reeve a Boom-Brace.

Reeve the end through the outer sheave of the double block secured by a tail to the foremost shroud of the main rigging, about 10 ft. or 15 ft. above the netting, from aft forward, or through one of the sheaves in the ship's side before the gangway; splice an eye in the end, and place it over the boom-end, inside the topping lift.

A Boom-Jigger

Is fitted with two single blocks; it is used for rigging the boom in or out, or tricing it up ; when used in rigging the boom in or out, the hauling part of the fall is rove through a leading block fast to the bunt of the yard on the after side.

To rig the boom out, the upper block is hooked to a strop round the standing part of the lower lift.

To rig the boom in, the upper block is hooked to a strop to the slings of the yard.

To trice the boom up, the upper block is hooked to a strop under the top, and secured by a toggle above.

Heel-Lashings.

The short one is spliced into the eye-bolt in the inner end of the boom, and secured round the jackstay, so as to prevent the boom moving.

The long heel-lashing is rove through a hole about 1 ft. or 18 ins. from the heel of the boom, an eye is spliced in the outer end, and finished off by forming a wall or stopper-knot, so as to prevent the eye from being drawn through the hole in the boom. This lashing is used to secure the heel of the boom, when it is in use for setting lower or topmast-studding-sails; it is passed round the quarter-iron through the eye spliced in the other end of it, two or three times, to keep the boom from running in, then two or three frapping turns round the heel of the boom and jackstay, so as to keep it from rising.

To Reeve a Boom-Back.

A boom-back is simply a short tricing-line, it is rove through a thimble seized to the foremost shroud of the topmast rigging, high enough to trice the boom up when reefing, furling, or shifting topsails ; the end is then spliced in the same eye-bolt as the tricing-line ; it is of great use in steadying the boom for the yard-arm men laying in or out.

Heel-Lashing.

The standing part is spliced in the same eye-bolt as the tricing-line in the heel of the boom; when the boom is rigged out for setting studdingsails, it is rove through the quarter-strop, and through the strop on the heel of the boom, two or three times, to keep the boom from running in, with two or three frapping turns round the jackstay and boom, to keep the heel down. When the boom is rigged in, it hangs down before the topsail, when the sails are furled it is passed round the topsail and the heel of the boom, to keep the boom snugly down in place. There is a strop and toggle fitted to the eye-bolt in the heel of the boom, and another strop fitted to the jackstay, which goes over the toggle to keep the heel of the boom in place when the sails are set.

SPRITSAIL-GAFF.

To Reeve a Spritsail-Gaff Brace.

Splice one eye in one end, serve it and place it over the gaff-end, reeve the other end through a block, at the eyes of the fore-rigging, from forward aft, and set the end up in the fore chains.

NOTE.—Its use is now abolished in the service.

To Reeve a Spritsail-Gaff Lift.

Splice an eye in one end, serve it and place it over the gaff end, reeve the other end through a clump-block stropped to the upper eye-bolt in the bowsprit cap, from out in, splice a thimble in the end, and set it up to an eye-bolt at the knight-heads.

Jaw-Ropes

Are rove through holes in the jaws of the gaff, and secured round the bowsprit, in a similar way to the jaw-ropes of a boom or gaff round the mast.

A Martingale Jaw-Rope

Is rove through holes in the bees of the bowsprit, and knotted on top; an iron martingale or dolphin-striker has no jaws, it is shackled under the bowsprit.

M 2

To Reeve a Jib-Boom Heel Rope.

To reeve the heel-rope. Reeve the end out through the block hooked to the bowsprit-cap, from out in, in through the sheave in the jib-boom end, take the end out and make it fast to the eye-bolt in the after-part of the bowsprit-cap with a half-hitch, and seize the end back on the opposite side to the block.

Q. How do you reeve a flying jib-boom heel-rope?

A. To reeve a heel-rope. Reeve the end out through a tail-block secured to the jib-boom iron, on the starboard-side, from out in, in through the sheave in the flying jib-boom end, from starboard to port, take the end out, and make it fast round the jib-boom iron, on the port side, with a half-hitch, and seize the end back.

In small vessels the flying jib-boom heel-rope is single, the end being secured at the end of the boom, by being rove through a hole made for this purpose, and knotted.

FOURTH INSTRUCTION.

SECTION I.

(1.) *Mat and Sennett.*

To be instructed in making the following :—

Paunch mat.	Common sennett.	Boats' fenders.
Sword mat.	French sennett.	Put a mat over lanyards of lower rigging.
Eye of a harbour gasket.	Square sennett.	
	Cross point.	
Thrum mat.	Hammock clews.	

Q. How do you make a paunch mat ?

A. Stretch a piece of rope, according to the size of the mat required, in any convenient place, in a horizontal position, and the foxes which are used for making the mat are middled and hung over it, close together, from end to end, or as far as the width required for the mat. Then take the fox nearest the left hand and twist a turn in the two parts ; one part give to the man opposite. The next fox has a turn twisted in its two parts, and one part given back to your partner ; the remainder is twisted round the first, which is given back, and then again round its own part ; and so on with the remainder of the foxes until you get it the breadth required. The bottom of the mat is selvaged by taking a piece of rope the same size as used for the top. The two parts of the foxes which are twisted together at the bottom are divided, and the piece of rope put between them ; the foxes are hitched round it, and the ends put through its own lay with a marline-spike.

This mat is used to take the chafe of the lower yards off the lower rigging in bracing up, and is seized to the lower rigging in the wake of the yards.

Q. How do you weave a sword mat ?

A. According to the length of mat required, two capstan bars or iron bars are slung in a horizontal position at the required distance apart for working the mat off ; hitch one end of the warp (which is composed either of small rope, sennit, or spun yarn, according to what use the mat is required) to the bar at the end on which you intend to finish the mat. The other end is then rove through the first hole in the loom over and under the other bar, from which end you will commence, back through the first slit, over and under the other bar, and continue to wind off as many parts as are required for the breadth you have decided on making the mat, the last turn being rove through a slit and secured to the bar at which you finish off; this done, lift the loom up, middle the fittings, and lay it between the upper and lower parts; then lower the loom, and the parts that were the lowest will rise in the slits and become the uppermost, and thus put a cross in the warp.

A piece of wood made in the shape of a knife, called a sword, is then inserted between the alternate parts of the warp, and the crossing is driven close to the head against the bar over which the warp for weaving the mat is passed; then a turn of filling is passed to secure the crossing, reeving the ends through contrary ways; haul it taut, take out the sword, lift the loom up, and continue to pass the filling, half knot it with two turns.

The loom is generally made of a piece of copper sheet with alternate holes and slits in it.

In making a heavy boom mat a fiddle is used instead of a loom; a fiddle is rigged by slinging a handspike athwartships to a beam overhead, pick up every other part of the warp, and with a piece of nettle stuff passed over the handspike with two round turns and rove round the alternate parts of the warp, trim them up.

The upper parts will thus cross the under parts before and abaft the fiddle; you will, therefore, require two swords. Reeve the filling and secure the first crossing already forward by tricing the parts up by the fiddle, hardening it up with the first sword, then put the second sword in between the crossing and the bar abaft the fiddle, disengage the parts by giving the mat a shake, and with the sword lift the upper ones up; the crossing will then be extended before the fiddle; withdraw the first sword, put it in abaft the crossing, drive it up and secure it with a turn of filling; again lift up the fiddle, keeping the second sword fast (which is never removed); a crossing is again formed at each end; you continue to repeat the operation until the mat is finished.

In weaving a heavy boom mat above five feet wide, a second fiddle is necessary underneath in order to rouse the parts through, rigged with a handspike similar to the upper one.

When the fiddles are in use the upper one is worked by a couple of jiggers, and the lower one by a couple of hands jumping down on it, the upper one being lowered at the same time.

To Finish Off or Selvage the Mat.

When the last turn of filling is past and secured with two turns and a half hitch, lay the lanyard across on the top of the filling, and reeve it back through the vacant hole left by the nettle hauled out, thus go right across, and haul the bights taut down to the lanyard. On slewing the mat round you will find that this will leave the second row of filling bare ; so go on withdrawing the same ends again along the second row, and pointing the same reeving ends as at first through the holes the others came out of, covering the filling, and complete four or five rows of this in the same manner. Then, to cover the last row of filling, and to secure the ends of the nettles, you lay them up and down alternately ; the long ends that you have withdrawn going up, and the short ones that you have been reeving lying down ; haul them taut, beat them in, and then tuck them under the bights of the next lay, the lower ones left handed through the bights on to the right, and the upper left handed to the left.

To finish off the upper part of a lower rigging mat by shouldering or reducing the mat to fit close round the shroud above the dead eye, leave as many nettles out at each edge of the mat as will reduce it sufficiently, then lay the lanyard (to secure the mat above the dead-eye) along the top of the last turn of filling, and go on working on the centre nettles that you have retained, as far up as you intend to go. Knot the filling, tease the ends of the nettles out a bit, place them round the shroud and serve them over. Finish the ends off left out by selvaging.

To Splice a Sword Mat.

Unlay six or eight inches of mat, open the ends out, marry them together, laying one up and one down flat along the mat, withdraw the nettles on one side of one mat and point the nettles of the other mat through the holes they came out of ; all ends will then disappear from that side, and there will be four rows of ends on the other. Turn the mats over, pick out the proper nettles of the side which have been married together, withdraw the ends belonging to one mat, and introduce the corresponding ends of the other mat through the holes, thus repeating the same operation on each mat, and on each side there are now two rows of ends ; marry those together on each side, laying one up and one down, and go on splicing by withdrawing and reeving for two or three rows more in each mat. Leave off with the ends all out on the same side, and finish off as with selvaging.

A cobbler's stitch is used for joining the sides of sword mats together.

Take a filling of roping twine, middle it, and reeve each end through two bights in each mat (if a heavy mat, through three bights at each edge), then reeve the lowermost end back through the same bights as the upper end, which will bring the ends out at opposite sides, draw the mats together, and reeve both ends through two turns in each mat again, passing each other through the same hole opposite ways ; and so work on, like stitching the sole of a boot on; hence the reason for calling it a cobbler's stitch.

Finish off each end by taking a hitch through a bight in the mat of the next lay above, and cut the ends off.

Q. How do you make a thrum mat ?

A. A thrum mat is made by cutting a certain number of yarns of equal length, and reeving them through holes made in the mat, both ends to come through on one side.

Q. How do you make a sea gasket or common sennit ?

A. Take three or four foxes (if intended for tyers it is made of yarns) according to the size you intend to make the gasket, middle them over a belaying-pin and plait three or four of them together, the length you intend to make the eye, then work both parts together to form an eye, and plait them by bringing the outside foxes on each side alternately over to the middle; the outside one is laid with the right hand, and the remainder held firmly with the left hand; work the whole together, adding a fox when necessary; after the eye is properly formed, and you have worked three or four inches down, drop a fox or yarn, and continue to the end with an odd number. When it is a sufficient length, lessen it by dropping a fox at regular intervals. To finish it, lay one end up, leaving its bight down, plait the others through this bight, until they are all worked through it, then haul on the end, till the bight is taut; to secure all parts, cut the ends off, and whip it.

Q. How do you make a harbour-gasket or French sennit ?

A. With foxes something similar to the common sea-gasket, but instead of taking the outside fox over all the rest and bringing it into the middle, you interweave it between them, by taking the outside fox of both sides, and taking it over one and under the other, working it towards the middle, the same as common sennit.

Harbour-gaskets, for lower and topsail-yards, are made of sword matting, and cut off to the required length, leaving enough end to form a Flemish eye each end of the gaskets. Gaskets made of French sennit are only used for topgallant and royal yards, and are always finished off the same as a sea-gasket, by working the ends with English sennit.

Q. How do you make square sennit ?

A. It is made somewhat in the same manner as round sennit, but without a heart. Nettles are used in the same ratio, increasing by fours, but are worked singly instead of in pairs. Having put a whipping round the (eight) ends, divide the nettles, and lay half on each side, bring the uppermost left-hand nettle round underneath all, and up inside two and over two of the right-handed ones ; crossing over the latter ones to the left and making four on each side again, then take the uppermost of the right-hand nettles, pass it underneath, and under two, and over two of the left-handed ones, still keeping four on a side, because the nettle taken up always comes round to its own side again. To proceed, take the upper nettle on each side alternately, and finish off as you finish round sennit.

Cross-Pointing.

Q. How do you cross-point a rope ?

A. Man-ropes are sometimes made of cross-pointing.

To make them.

Take a piece of 2¼ in., or any other size rope, and cut it to the required length, then get it on a stretch ; take sufficient parts of white line to cover the rope, taking care you have an even number, then put a good whipping round all parts where you intend the upper part of your man-rope to be, leaving outside the whipping sufficient length of all parts of the white line to form a man-rope knot when they are worked up into strands.

To Cross-Point the Rope.

Divide the parts, taking every alternate part up, and working round and round continually, taking each part under and over, forming a cross each time. So continue to the end ; it is finished off by unlaying the white line, twisting it into nettles, and pointing it.

Q. How do you make hammock clews ?

A. By taking twelve lengths of three-yarn nettle stuff about 6 feet long, then centre them so as to form an eye of the bight, the eye is served over with a yarn and a throat seizing put on, the ends of the nettles are whipped, this makes one clew of 24 nettles.

A PUDDING FENDER.

Q. How do you make boats' fenders ?

Pudding Fenders are used in the Navy for large boats— such as cutters, pinnaces, &c., &c.—and sometimes on lower yards, to take the chafe on the inside part of the quarter yard.

When fitted as Fenders for Boats.

A piece of rope the required length is cut, and an eye spliced in each end, by which it is set up to small-eye-bolts on the stern ; the rope is then marked where the puddings or fenders are to be worked, one to fit the stem, and two others to fit, one on each quarter, so as to save the sharp edge of the quarters and the stem when lying alongside a ship or boats, or a landing-place ; a number at proper intervals are also worked along each side of the boat, projecting far enough to save her sides also from chafing.

To make a Pudding Fender.

Get your rope, already marked on a stretch, and worm it ; the marks where the puddings are to be formed are filled up with any old stuff, such as old strands, spunyarn, &c. ; in forming it take care the sides intended to be next the boat are flat, and the outer sides a half-round, the largest part is in the middle, tapering gradually off at both ends. When it is formed to the required shape, parcel it with strips of canvas and mark it down, beginning in the middle and marling both ways to the ends. It is then either grafted over or covered with leather ; the latter is the neatest. When fitted as a single fender, for a yard or any other purpose, an eye is worked in each end.

Q. How do you put a mat over lanyards of lower rigging ?

A. The mat is placed on the lanyards of lower rigging outside, the upper end being tapered off and served over, the lower end is secured to the lower part of the dead-eye by a lanyard, the sides of the mat being laced on the inner side.

EXTRA SUBJECTS.
Four-Square Plait.

A four-square plait is made of white line; sixteen parts are generally used, or any other number that will form a square according to the size required; never less than twelve parts ought to be used to form the square properly; it is used for making man-ropes.

To make it.

Put a good whipping on, and secure the ends to any convenient place, and commence by keeping four parts in the middle to form a centre. When made of sixteen parts, keep four parts for the centre working, the remaining parts from left to right, and right to left, passing each part under four and over four, thus in turn each centre part becomes an outside part, and forms a complete square. When it is worked to its required length, the ends are worked into nettles, and it is finished off by pointing it; before commencing it, it must be decided whether you intend working a Flemish eye in the upper end or a man-rope knot, so as to know what length of ends to leave; if a knot is to be worked, the parts are laid up together to form the required number of strands. It is sometimes finished off at the upper end by driving two copper nails through the whipping, so as to form a cross; cut the nails off to the length required, then wold the parts of the nails round with yarns, until the points are covered, then work a Turk's head over it.

A Coach-Whipping Plait

Is used for tails of jiggers or stoppers for fore or main-tacks or sheets, &c., &c.

To make it.

Put a whipping on a piece of rope, leaving the required length for the stopper-knot, unlay each strand, if a three-stranded rope, then divide the three into four parts, work these parts into four foxes, then take the two centre foxes in your left hand, and work the two outside foxes from left to right, and right to left, under one and over one, each fox in turn becoming an outside fox. It is finished off by either whipping the end or working the foxes into nettles and pointing it.

Section II.

Anchor Model.

To be able to point out, to name, and know the use of the following :—

Ring.
Stock.
Crown.
Shank.
Arms.
Flukes.
Bill.
Forelock.
Shackle.
Swivel.
Link.
Stud.
Slip stopper.
Deck stopper.
Compressor.
Controller.
To bend a buoy rope.
Length of a chain cable.
Cable's length.
No. of shackles in a cable.
Length of a shackle.
Where swivels are placed.
Use of swivels.
Connecting piece.
How cables are marked at each shackle.

Which end of a shackle is inboard.
Difference between a cable and an anchor shackle.
How the bolt, pin, and pellet are kept in their places.
Messenger.
Messenger shackles.
Bitting and securing cables.
Bringing to cables.
Heaving in cables.
Securing inner end of bower or sheet cable.
Stream anchor.
Kedge anchor.
Sheet hawse hole.
Bower hawse hole.
Stream cable.
Bringing to a hawser.
Bending a buoy rope.
Bullrope.
Stowing an anchor.
Cat stopper.
Shank painter.

Second catting an anchor.
Parts of a capstan.
Whelps.
Pauls.
To pass the swifter.
Passing nippers.
Racking turns.
Cat back.
Cat.
Fish.
Ground chain.
Cat chain.
Fish pendant.
Single anchor.
Moored.
Mooring swivel.
Moorings.
Short stay.
Up and down.
Heaving away.
Heaving in sight.
Clear hawse.
Foul hawse.
Clear hawse shackle.
Veer cable.
Surging.
Warping.
Kedging.

Q. Name the parts of an anchor ?

A. Ring, stock, crown, shank, arms, flukes, and bill.

Q. What is the ring ?

A. The ring is attached to the upper part of the shank, to which the cable is attached.

Q. What is the stock ?

A. The stock is make of wood or iron ; if iron, it reeves through the lower hole in the upper end of the shank ; if wood, it is built round the shank, at the same place, and hooped and bolted together ; it stands at right angles to the arms, and being much longer, cants the anchor with one fluke down, which causes it to hook to the ground.

Q. What is the crown ?

A. The crown is the lower end of the shank, where the arms or flukes are joined.

Q. What is the shank?

A. The perpendicular or middle piece of an anchor.

Q. What are the arms?

A. The arms are the two triangular pieces at the lower end of the shank, forming hooks, one of which is always hooked or buried in the ground.

Q. What are the flukes?

A. The flukes are the broad triangular pieces within the extreme end or bill of the arms. They are so constructed as to have a greater hold of the ground.

Q. What is the bill?

A. The bill is the extreme point of the arms and flukes.

Q. What is a forelock?

A. A flat pointed wedge of iron, used to drive through the hole in the stock of the anchor, to fix it.

Q. What is a shackle?

A. A span with two eyes and a bolt, attached to the links in a chain cable, at every $12\frac{1}{2}$ fathoms, the bolt is movable, so that the chain can be separated, or coupled as required.

Q. What is a swivel?

A. A strong link of iron used in mooring chains, which permits the bridles to turn repeatedly round, also a swivel link in chain cables, made so as to turn upon an axis, and keep the turns out of the chain.

Q. What is a link?

A. A chain cable is composed of links.

Q. What is a stud?

A. The piece of iron across the middle of each link of chain cables, it acts as a strengthener and prevents the links from collapsing, it also keeps the links endways to each other.

Q. What is a slip or Blake's stopper?

A. A short chain the same size as the cable, with a shackle at one end and a slip at the other, it is shackled to a deck bolt before the bitts, and is used for stoppering the cable to bitt or unbitt it, or when unshackling, to put on the mooring swivel, or to clear hawse, or when the anchor is high enough when weighing, &c.

Q. What is a deck stopper?

A. A short thick piece of rope having a knot at one end, and hooked or lashed to a ring bolt in the deck by the other; it is attached to the cable by the lanyard, which is passed round both, by which means the cable is prevented from running out of the ship when she rides at anchor.

Q. What is a compressor?

A. A contrivance for holding the chain cable by compression.

Q. What is a controller?

A. A contrivance to control the cable and prevent its running out too fast.

Q. How is a buoy-rope bent to a nun buoy?

A. There are two or three ways of bending it.

First, pass the buoy-rope through both upper and lower rings of the buoy, half-hitch and seize the end back, or else secure it with an inside clinch.

Another way of securing it is to pass it through the underneath ring, swab-hitch it over the ring and seize the end back.

Q. What is the length of a chain cable?

A. One hundred fathoms. Two bower and two sheet chain cables are supplied, one of the sheet cables is divided between the two bower cables, thus giving 12 shackles to the bower and 8 shackles to the sheet. The hemp sheet or steel wire hawser supplied in lieu thereof would be used should a fourth anchor be required.

Q. What is a cable's length?

A. Eight lengths or 100 fathoms.

Q. How many shackles are there in a cable?

A. Eight, or one to every length.

Q. What is the length of a shackle?

A. Twelve-and-a-half fathoms.

Q. Where are the swivels placed?

A. One on the first and one on the last length or shackle of cable.

Q. What are the use of swivels?

A. To keep a cable clear of turns when lying at single anchor. If there were no swivels, as a ship swung constantly round to the tide, she would twist her cable full of turns, and bring an unfair strain on some of the links.

Q. What is a connecting piece?

A. A short piece of chain with a swivel placed on first and last length of cable, to keep turns out.

Q. How are cables marked at each shackle?

A. The first length or shackle has a piece of wire round the stud or stay pin of the first link abaft the shackle; the second round the second link, and so on, generally up to 10, when you commence at the first link again.

Q. Which end of a shackle is inboard?

A. The pins or lugs, because if they were forward, instead of aft, they would be liable to catch against the bitts, hawse pipes, or elsewhere, and check or stop the cable running out.

Q. What is the difference between a cable and an anchor shackle?

A. An anchor shackle is much larger than a cable shackle.

In a joining shackle the bolt or pin of the shackle does not project beyond the lugs of the shackle, and is secured in place by a pin passing through a hole in the shackle and bolt. This pin is made to sink into the shackle, and is secured in place by a leaden pellet well beaten down over it.

In an anchor shackle the bolt projects beyond the lugs of the shackle, and is secured by a fore lock.

Q. How is the bolt pin and pellet kept in their places?

A. The bolt is secured by a pin passing through a hole in the shackle and bolt, the pin is fitted into this hole, and the pellet, which is of lead, is placed on the head of the pin and driven in, it expands the upper or larger hole in the shackle being dove-tailed, thus keeping the pin in its place. When necessary to replace the pellets, all lead remaining on the groove should be scraped off, which is termed reaming; should this be neglected, the new pellet will not hold, and the pin will in time work out, also the bolt of the shackle.

Q. What is the messenger?

A. An iron chain having a double and single link alternately, it is used to unmoor or heave up the anchor, it works in iron spurs fastened above the lower rim of the capstan.

Q. What is a messenger shackle?

A. A long shackle connecting the messenger, being of the same size as the messenger to fit the capstan.

Q. How are the cables bitted and secured?

A. Sufficient slack cable is hauled up to form a bight abaft the bitts, which is whipped up by a tackle and thrown over the head of the bitts from amidships towards the ship's side. To weather bitt a cable is to take another turn round the bitt end.

Q. How do you bring to cables?

A. The slack cable is hauled out of the chain locker unbitted and brought to the capstan.

Q. How do you heave in cables?

A. By heaving round the capstan, the slack being payed down the chain pipes into the chain locker.

Q. How do you secure the inner end of bower or sheet cable?

A. In a sailing ship, to slips secured round the main mast, and in steamers to ring bolts in the sleepers on either side. The slips are shackled to necklaces round the main mast, and long enough to reach the top of the chain locker, so a cable can easily be slipped.

Q. What is a stream anchor?

A. An anchor weighing about two thirds of the bower. It is used for warping on, in a tideway or calm.

Q. What is a kedge anchor?

A. An anchor used for light work warping a ship from one part of the harbour to another, or keeping her clear of her anchor in a tideway.

Q. Which is the sheet hawse hole?

A. The outer hawse holes on each side of the bow.

Q. Which is the bower hawse hole?

A. The inner hawse holes on each side of the bow.

Q. What is a stream cable?

A. A small cable for laying out the stream anchor in the event of the ship being on shore, to assist in heaving her off.

Q. How do you bring to an hawser?

A. By taking three round turns round the capstan, the inner part being held to prevent it slipping.

Q. How do you bend a buoy rope, and to what part of the anchor?

A. To the arms or flukes, by half-hitching it round the inner fluke, forming a clove-hitch on the crown, and securing the end by a running-eye, or clinching it over the outer fluke.

A piece of chain, three or four fathoms long, is frequently attached to the end of the buoy-rope, for bending it to the anchor, as it saves the buoy-rope from being chafed on the ground.

Q. Who streams the buoy?

A. The quarter-deck men, and next number from the after part of the fore chains, having previously seen the buoy-rope properly bent, and coiled down in the fore chains, clear for running.

Q. Is there any particular name given to the buoy that is bent to the anchor?

A. Yes, the nun or can buoy; those used in the Navy are made of iron.

Q. What is a bull rope?

A. A hawser rove through a block at the end of the bowsprit, when a ship is moored to a buoy, to keep it clear of the stem.

Q. How is an anchor stowed?

A. By means of cathead stopper and shank painter. If for sea one fluke is brought inboard and secured there by means of lashings.

Q. What is a cat stopper?

A. A piece of rope or chain rove through the ring of the anchor to secure it for sea, at one end a bent link to go over the pin of a tumbler for letting go.

Q. What is a shank painter?

A. The stopper which confines the shank of the anchor to the ship's side, and prevents the flukes from flying off the bill board. Where the bill board is not used it bears the weight of the fluke end of the anchor, at one end is a bent link to go over the pin of a tumbler for letting go.

Q. How do you second cat an anchor?

A. It is done by hooking the cat block to a strop passed round the upper part of the stock down round the shank which brings the ring of the anchor close up to the cathead, and by bousing on the stock tackle brings the stock of the anchor close into the ship's side; by hooking a luff to a strop round the inner fluke the shank is brought close to the bollard heads, when the anchor is well lashed in place. A lashing being passed round the shank and inner fluke to the bollard heads and two eyebolts, placed, one before and the other abaft the fluke for this purpose.

Harfield's Patent Capstan.

(See opposite.)

Directions for Use.

I. *Before letting go.*—Bitt the cable, raise the lever of the bow stopper, and put in the fid (A) under the block.

" Set up " the brake wheel of the cable holder compressor with the lever in the direction of the arrow, *i.e.*, from aft to forward hand taut, then set it back a quarter turn, which will just ease the brake and will leave the lever in position to check and stop the cable without having to shift it into another hole.

II. *To bring up.*—On no account is the bow stopper to be used, but the cable is to be checked by first *gradually* setting up the brake wheel of the cable holder compressor; then *smartly* setting it to " hard up."

III. *To purchase Anchor.*—Remove the fid and drop the lever of the bow stopper ; slack back the brake of the cable holder compressor ; unbitt the cable and take it to the capstan around the guide rollers (B C). See that *all* the pauls are down and pointed the right way.

If the cable as it is hove in will not take itself off the deck it is to be hauled away by hook ropes, and a steady strain maintained so as to avoid a collection between the capstan and the foremost roller (B).

IV. *Upper Deck Paul.*—On no account is the upper deck paul (D) to be used when purchasing anchor. When steam is applied, and the pauls are not " down," they should be pointed the reverse way to the motion, so that should a paul get unpinned and drop, it will not bring up the capstan.

V. *Lubrication.*—Oil may be used for lubricating the capstan bearings, &c.

It is desirable that no grease should get to the friction plates of the cable holder compressor, and therefore a mixture of black lead and tallow is to be used for lubricating their spindle bearings, pressure nuts, and collars.

Q. How do you pass a swifter ?

A. The cut splice in the centre of the swifter is placed over the notch in the end of one of the capstan bars, it is then back-hitched over each bar working both ways from the centre ; when all the bars are hitched the end is rove through a thimble at one end, boused taut and secured.

Q. How do you pass nippers ?

A. The inner end is taken round the messenger, keeping the end between the messenger and cable, the nipper is then expended in round turns round the messenger and cable, the last turn being passed round the cable only.

Q. How do you pass racking turns ?

A. Over and under between the two parts and ends secured with a reef knot.

Q. What is a cat back ?

A. A line for hauling the cat hook about, and which hauls the block to the ring of the anchor for hooking on.

Q. What is a cat ?

A. A purchase by which the anchor is brought to the cathead.

Q. What is a fish ?

A. A purchase by which the crown of the anchor is brought up square for securing.

Q. What is ground chain ?

A. A piece of small chain·shackled to the anchor shackle, and stopped along the cable, of sufficient length to come through the hawse pipe when the anchor is high enough for catting.· The cat chain is then shackled to it.

Q. What is a. cat chain ?

A. A chain which is rove through the cat block, and shackled on to the upper end of ground chain to bring the anchor to cat head.

Q. What is a fish pendant ?

A. The pendant or chain used to hook and draw up the flukes of an anchor towards the top of the bow, after catting, in order to stow -it, it is led through a block at davit head and brought to a purchase.

Q. What is meant by a ship being at single anchor ?

A. A ship riding with one anchor down is said to be at single anchor.

Q. When is a ship moored ?

A. When a ship has two anchors down or secured alongside a jetty or hulk by means of chains or ropes.

Q. What is a mooring swivel ?

A. A revolving iron link used in mooring ship, to prevent the vessel, when swinging, twisting her cable full of turns.

Q. What are moorings ?

A. Two or more anchors laid down with large chains, for a ship to secure to.

Q. What is meant by a short stay ?

A. The cable is said to be a short stay when it grows in a line with the fore topmast stay. Long stay when it is in a line with fore stay. *See* p. 196 (cable a long stay).

Q. What is meant by up and down ?

A. An anchor is said to be up and down when the ship is directly over it.

Q. What is meant by heaving away ?

A. The anchor is said to be away directly it is broken out of the ground.

Q. What is meant by heaving in sight ?

A. An anchor is said to be heaving in sight directly any one can see it from the bows, it is reported foul or clear, as the case may be ; it is " clear anchor " when it hangs fairly by the ring from the end of the cable ; and " foul anchor " if the cable has a turn over one of the arms of the stock or fluke.

Q. What is meant by a clear hawse?

A. A ship is said to have a clear hawse when riding with two anchors down, the cables draw clear of each other ; also when there is no obstruction in her way, such as another ship being anchored too close, preventing her swinging clear of her anchors.

Q. What is meant by a foul hawse ?

A. A ship is said to have a foul hawse when riding with two anchors down, she, by swinging the wrong way, causes her cables to cross each other. If she continues to swing the wrong way until she describes three-quarters or a complete circle, she takes an elbow in her cables. A circle and a quarter form a round turn. A ship anchoring so as to prevent another ship swinging clear of her is said to foul her hawse.

Q. What is a clear hawse shackle ?

A. A long shackle to take the link of the cable with a roller in it. Through that an hawser might be rove to secure the cable while taking turns out.

Q. How do you veer cable ?

A. Veering cable is to light it along the deck and pay it out of the hawse holes.

Q. What is surging?

A. Veering cable suddenly ; or a hawser slipping up the barrel of a capstan is said to surge.

Q. What is warping ?

A. Transporting a ship from one part of a harbour to another by means of hawsers.

Q. What is kedging ?

A. Hauling a ship about a harbour or anchorage by means of small anchors and hawsers.

EXTRA QUESTIONS.

Q. What is meant by shortening in cable ?

A. To heave a certain portion of it in.

Q. What is meant by " cable a long stay " ?

A. An expression used in shortening in cable when the anchor is a short distance ahead, and the cable only forming a small angle with the anchor, or in line with fore stay. *See* p. 195 (cable a short stay).

Q. What is meant by " cable grows " ?

A. A cable is said to grow when it leads in any particular direction. As the cable grows on the port. or starboard bow right ahead, astern, under her bottom, &c.

Q. What is meant by " cable short a peak " ?

A. A cable is called short a peak when it it nearly up and down.

Q. What is meant by " cable under foot " ?

A. The cable is said to be under foot when it is veered quickly before the ship has had time to drop astern clear of her anchor.

Q. What is meant by " anchor coming home " ?

A. An anchor is said to be coming home, or dragging, when it will not hold. It is said to bite well when the lower fluke has a good hold on the ground.

Q. What is meant by " dropping an anchor under foot " ?

A. To drop an anchor under foot is to let go a second anchor without veering cable on it.

Q. What is meant by " backing the anchor " ?

A. To back the anchor is to lash another anchor or pigs of ballast to it.

Q. What is meant by " nun buoy watches well " ?

A. A nun buoy is said to watch well when it floats lightly over the anchor.

Q. What it meant by " bleeding a buoy " ?

A. When a buoy leaks, and you are obliged to make a hole to let the water out, it is called bleeding a buoy.

Q. What is meant by " the buoy watches " ?

A. A buoy watches when it is not carried under the surface by the strength of the tide or other causes.

Q. What is meant by " a spring " ?

A. Leading a hawser from aft, and making it fast to the cable the ship is riding by so as to bring her broadside in any required position by heaving on the hawser.

Q. What is meant by " adrift " ?

A. Slipping or breaking away from moorings.

Q. If sent in charge of a lighter to the dockyard, to bring the chain cables off, how would you stow them in the lighter ?

A. I would stow the anchor end in the lighter first, because it would be the last to go out when alongside the ship.

Q. How would you know the anchor end?

A. By the swivels. The cup of the swivel is always aft, to prevent it catching anywhere as the cable runs out.

Q. How are the swivels kept in a state of preservation?

A. By pouring a mixture of white lead and tallow into the cup.

Q. Where are the chain cables stowed?

A. In the chain lockers.

Q. How many chain lockers are there?

A. Four; two each side of the main mast, two for the bower cables, the third for the chain sheet, and the fourth for the stream, chain, and messenger.

Q. How are the cables got inboard out of the lighter?

A. By double whips, led along the deck outside the bitts.

Q. How do you bend a cable to an anchor?

A. By a ring rope and the fore bowline.

The ring rope is rove through the ring of the anchor, from aft forward, outside, and under all the head gear, in through the hawse-hole, and bent to the fifth or sixth link of the cable and stopped to the first link; the fore bowline is bent inside, to assist in lighting the cable out; also to take the weight off the ring rope. When sufficient slack is outside the hawse-hole, clap on the ring rope, and rouse the cable up to the ring of the anchor, cut the stop on the first link, and shackle it.

Bower Anchors.

The best and small bower; the starboard anchor being termed the best bower, and the port anchor the small bower.

Sheet Anchors.

They are called waist anchors, from being stowed in the waist abaft the fore rigging. One of these anchors is always got ready when lying at anchor in a gale, in the event of the bower anchors not holding or parting.

The bower and sheet anchors are about the same weight.

An iron stock is about one-fifth the weight of the anchor. It is curved at one end, the other is straight, to reeve through the lower hole in the upper part of the shank. A shoulder is fitted in the centre to act as a stop against the side of the shank; it is secured in place by a forelock through the end on the opposite side of the shank, to the shoulder. It is easily disengaged, and laid up and down the shank, for convenience of stowage inboard.

Q. What anchors are supplied to a ship of war ?

A. Two bowers, viz.—best and small bower; two sheet or waist anchors, one stream, one kedge.

Q. Where are the hemp cables stowed ?

A. In the tiers, coiled down right handed.

Q. How is the inboard end of hemp sheet cable secured ?

A. Shackled to a chain stropped round a beam in the heart of the tiers, and lashed down also to one of the adjoining beams.

Q. What side is the sheet cable coiled ?

A. On the same side as the chain sheet is stowed.

Q. Why should both chain and hemp-sheet cables be stowed the same side ?

A. There being a difficulty in bending a rope so large as the sheet cable, it therefore has to be led across the opposite side of the ship when required for use.

Q. Which tier is the stream hemp cable coiled in ?

A. The opposite tier to which the sheet cable is stowed.

Q. How is a hemp sheet cable bent to the sheet anchor ?

A. Shackled to the ganger.

Q. What is a ganger ?

A. Three lengths of chain cable, the same size chain as the bower cable, shackled to the sheet anchor; it keeps the hemp cable from being chafed against the ground.

Q. How is the hemp sheet cable fitted ?

A. By an Elliott's eye in the outer or outboard end, and a ropemaker's eye in the inboard end.

Q. What precaution is taken to preserve the eye in the hemp cable?

A. It is keckled over, which is merely serving over the eye with rope to prevent the cable being chafed on the ground. It is also keckled in the weight of the hawse-hole and cutwater.

Q. What are hemp, sheet, and stream cables principally supplied for?

A. For laying out the sheet and stream anchors in the event of the ship being on shore, to assist in heaving her off.

Q. How many messengers are there supplied to a ship of war ?

A. Only one; a chain one.

Working the Capstan.

Q. Who rigs the capstan ?

A. The carpenter and his crew.

Q. What do you mean by rigging the capstan?

A. The bars being shipped, pinned, and swifted in place.

Q. How are they secured in place?

A. By passing pins up through holes in the drum-head, and corresponding holes in the heel of the bars, the pins are kept in place by a catch, which they fit into, by giving them a half turn.

Q. What do you mean by swifting them to?

A. In each end of the bars there is a notch; a piece of rope called the swifter is passed round in each notch, and swab-hitched to the end of each bar, each turn being hauled well taut, and the ends of the finish well set up together; for this purpose a thimble is spliced in one end of the swifter for the other end to reeve through. While rigging the capstan, the pauls are kept down to steady it.

Q. Who reeves the messenger?

A. The main and fore-top men of the watch below; gunner's mate sees it clear of turns, passed round the capstan, and placed with the long links on the teeth of the sprocket wheel; the armourer shackles it.

Q. How is a messenger rove?

A. A hook rope is passed down the chain locker, bent to the end of the messenger, and run up on the deck the cables are worked on—viz., on the lower deck of a line-of-battle ship, main deck of a frigate, and upper deck of a corvette or smaller vessel, forward round the rollers; the ends are adjusted as to length, hove taut, and joined together by a long or short shackle, as required, in order that it might fit the sprocket wheel of the capstan, thus forming an endless chain, passing round and round the capstan and the roller forward, the teeth of the sprocket wheel taking the long links of the messenger at each turn.

Q. How is it hove taut for shackling?

A. One end is secured by a strand or rope's-end being rove through the third or fourth links from the end, to a ring-bolt in the deck, the capstan is hove round to tauten the messenger sufficiently to bring the end links together for shackling.

Q. How is a hemp messenger fitted?

A. A long lashing eye is spliced in each end, which is grafted over, the messenger is passed round the rollers in a similar way to a chain messenger, and four turns round the barrel of the capstan; in lashing the eyes together, a drift of from four to five feet is allowed between the eyes, so as they will lay fair on the capstan, the heaving-in part being the lowermost. The quarter-deck men are stationed by the capstan with commanders to give the messenger a tap up if it should work too low down on the barrel of the capstan.

Q. What is done in the event of the messenger carrying away?

A. Bouse to the compressor, and stopper the cable at once. Join the messenger together again with a long or short span shackle, according whether it be a long or short link that is carried away.

Q. If it is necessary to bring the opposite cable to, what is done?

A. The ends must be unlashed and passed the contrary way; this is readily done by heaving round until the eyes are close to the capstan; then cast off the lashing, slacken the turns, pass the end of the short leg of the messenger inside between them and the barrel of the capstan, render all parts until the lower turn is brought on the opposite side, re-lash the eyes, and it is ready for heaving in the other cable.

N.B.—Hemp messengers are not now supplied to ships of war.

Preparing to Anchor.

Q. Who clears the anchors away ready for letting go?
A. The forecastle men.

Q. What precautions are taken when a ship is going to anchor?

A. The carpenters remove the bucklers and take the hawse-plugs out. Fore and main-top men range the cables; according to the depth of water the ship is likely to anchor in, sufficient cable is ranged on the deck abaft the bitts, to allow the anchor to reach the bottom without a check, the running part outside. A bar of iron, called the bitt-pin, is shipped in the outer part of the cross piece, to prevent the chain coming off as it runs round the bitts.

Q. How is an anchor hung from the bows ready for letting go?

A. The inner fluke is eased off the bill-board clear, the ring is hung by the cat-head stopper, and the shank by the shank-painter; the inboard end of both being secured to bollard heads or large-size cavil's in the ship's side.

Q. How is an anchor let go?

A. The cathead-stopper and shank-painter, being fitted to go over tumblers, at a given signal are slipped together, and the anchor falls clear of the ship's side into the water.

Q. Who gives the signal?

A. The boatswain, who stands on the knight-heads when the order is given by the Commanding Officer, " stream the buoy," " stand clear of the cable," " let go the best or small bower anchor," whichever it might be. The boatswain gives the order—" one, two, three; let go," when the forecastle men pull together on the jigger (if so fitted), which releases the cathead-stopper and shank-painter together.

First part of forecastle men attend the cathead-stopper, and the second part the shank-painter, which are hauled inboard directly the anchor is gone.

Q. What precaution is taken at the order—" stream the buoy, stand clear of the cable"?

A. The compressor having been thrown back clear of the cable, the chock of the tumbler is taken out, but the pins are kept in place till the order is given—" let go the anchor," when they are taken out, the lever being kept back by hand till the boatswain gives the word—" one, two, three; let go." At the word " let go," the anchor is freed by a smart pull on the monkey tails, which are lanyards, attached to the end of the lever; the man attending the cathead-stopper taking care he does not let go before the man attending the shank-painter does, so as to insure the anchor falling flukes down.

Another Plan of letting go the Anchor.

A span is fitted with one end secured to the lever of the cathead-stopper, and the other to the lever of the shank-painter; a small jigger is hooked to the span, and at the word " let go," the hands attending it give a smart pull, having received the signal that the pins are out, both levers flying back, disengage the cathead-stopper and shank-painter together.

Bending a Cable.

Bower Anchor ready for letting go.   Anchor a Cockbill.

Chain carried away, weighing Kedge
Anchor with Buoy Rope.   Foul Anchor.

Q. What do you mean by an anchor being a cockbill?

A. The shank-painter being eased down and the anchor allowed to hang from the cathead secured by the cathead-stopper only. Merchant ships generally cockbill their anchor when about to come to.

Q. What precaution is taken before slipping a cable?

A. A buoy-rope is passed in through the hawse-hole, and as soon as the armourer has unshackled the cable, the buoy-rope is bent to the end of it and paid out through the hawse-hole again; the buoy is then streamed, the cable paid out through the hawse-hole as far as the slip-stopper; when all is clear and the ship's head has taken the right way, the slip is knocked off.

The buoy marking the end of the cable should have a distinguishing mark from the one marking the anchor.

Q. What is the use of a buoy to an anchor?

A. It marks the position of the anchor, and prevents other ships fouling it; it is also very useful in case of a ship being obliged to slip her cable; it enables her to pick her

BARQUE.

anchor up again ; or in the event of one of the flukes hooking a mooring chain, or in any way becoming entangled with the bottom, by hauling on the buoy-rope, it will capsize the anchor and in all probability clear it.

Q. How is the cable checked when running out?

A. By the compressor being boused to, which binds it against the chain pipes.

Q. Who attends the compressor tackle?

A. The idlers on the lower deck.

Q. When there is sufficient cable out, how is it secured?

A. By being bitted, and by means of deck stoppers.

Weighing Anchor.

Q. What preparations are made for weighing anchor?

A. The slip-stopper is put on before all, and the cable is unbitted ready for bringing-to; the forecastle men reeve and overhaul the cat-fall down; when sufficient is overhauled to allow the cat-block to reach the hawse-holes, it is hauled forward by the cat-back, ready for hooking; they also see the martingale of the fish-davit hooked in place.

Foretopmen trice up the up and down tackle by the inner lower studdingsail halyards, and lash it to the short leg of the lower pendant, and hook the single block to the head of the fish-davit, to act as a topping-lift.

The gunners rig the fish-davit, and reeve the fish-fall when it is hauled forward in place by the fish-back, ready for hooking.

Q. Where is the fish-davit shipped, and how is it secured in place?

A. It is shipped in a shoe, in the fore part of the fore chains, and kept in place by fore and after guys, topping-lifts, and a martingale. The after guy is the largest guy, as it has to bear a very great strain in fishing the anchor.

Q. What is the use of a martingale to a fish-davit?

A. It keeps the head of the fish-davit down in place, when a strain is brought on, when hauling taut the fish-fall.

Q. What would be the consequence if the martingale was not taut before hauling on the fish-fall?

A. The head of the fish-davit would rise, and in all probability the heel slip out of the shoe, and the davit capsize altogether.

Q. What is the use of the topping-lift to the fish-davit ?

A. After the fish-fall has brought the fluke level with
he bill-board, pull up on the topping-lift, at the same time
easing away the martingale ; when in position, lower the
fish-fall, and place the bill of the anchor on the bill-board,
where it is secured by the shank-painter.

Q. How is the cable secured to the messenger for heaving
in ?

A. By rope or iron nippers.

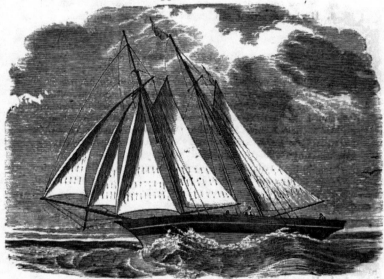

A FORE AND AFT SCHOONER ON A WIND.

Q. How is a rope nipper passed ?

A. The messenger is brought to a cable, as a cable cannot
be brought to a messenger. This is done by taking two round
turns with the after or inboard end of a nipper round the
messenger by one of the inside hands ; the coil or remaining
part of the nipper is then passed over the cable to one of the
outside hands, who, facing aft, passes it round the messenger
and cable, with the sun on the port side, and against the
sun on the starboard side, rousing each turn taut, keeping the
messenger on top of the cable, dogging the end round the
cable and round the end of the next nipper, to prevent it from

slipping; it is held by one of the topmen, who walks aft with it. When far enough aft, and the cable is secured by other nippers following in a similar way, he starts the nipper he is holding and passes it forward again; the nippers are constantly being passed in this way as the cable comes in at the hawse-holes. When there is much sea on, or a great strain, racking turns are passed.

Q. Who passes the nippers?

A. Main and foretop men; foretop men working before, and maintop men abaft the bitts.

Q. What is meant by heaving through all?

A. When the cable is covered with mud it slips through the nippers; to prevent this, buckets of sand are kept close at hand, and the hands passing the nippers keep on throwing sand over the cable as it comes in, and the turns of the nippers are passed thicker; if this is not sufficient, a round turn is taken round the messenger, then another round turn round the cable, with racking turns between.

Q. How is an iron nipper secured to the cable?

A. A shackle, fitted with a hinge at one end, and a slip at the other, holds the messenger and cable together; one of these is only used at a time, the second one being put on as the first gets well aft.

Q. When the anchor is hove up to the bows, what is done?

A. Pipe (avast heaving) when the slip-stopper is put on before all, walk back the capstan until the slip has the weight of the anchor; then off nippers and bitt the cable.

Q. Why is the cable bitted?

A. To prevent the cable running out too freely when the slip is taken off for catting the anchor.

Q. When is the slip knocked off?

A. When the cat is hooked, and all parts of the cat-fall are taut, the boatswain pipes veer, or surge the cable; when sufficient is out to allow the anchor to reach the cathead, the slip is again put on to prevent the cable from running out.

Q. Who hooks the cat-block, and how is it hooked?

A. The forecastle men. It is hooked with the bill of the hook in or towards the ship's side. When all is ready, walk away with the cat.

Q. Where do the men stand to hook the cat.

A. They are slung in bowline knots, and stand on the stock of the anchor; the block having been roused forward by the first cat-back, the second cat-back is rove through

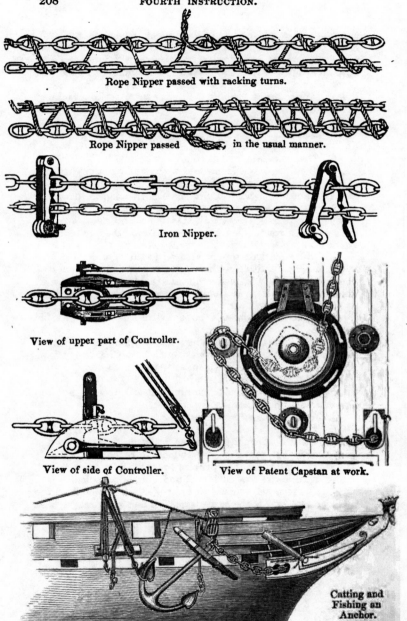

Rope Nipper passed with racking turns.

Rope Nipper passed in the usual manner.

Iron Nipper.

View of upper part of Controller.

View of side of Controller.

View of Patent Capstan at work.

Catting and Fishing an Anchor.

the thimble in the bridle of the cat-block, and led up through the head gratings on to the forecastle, where the standing part is made fast; it takes the weight of the block while the men on the stock guide the hook in the ring of the anchor; the bridle is a piece of rope spliced into two small eyebolts on the fore part of the shell of the block, with a thimble seized in it for reeving the cat-back through; when the cat is hooked, and the cable surged, the small cat-back is unrove. The large one is always kept in place for tricing the block up to the cathead after the cathead-stopper is passed.

Q. Who hooks the fish?

A. The captain of the forecastle; the fish-hook is hauled forward by the fishback, and when in a fair way of catching the inner fluke it is eased up; when hooked, the fish-fall is steadied taut.

Q. What prevents the fish from unhooking?

A. The shoulder of the fluke.

Q. What is a fish-back?

A. A rope bent to the fish-hook to rouse it forward in place for dropping it over the fluke of the anchor; it is half-hitched round the hook, just below the eye, and seized down on the back part of the shoulder of the hook.

Q. How do you reeve a fish-fall?

A. Through the single block in the fish-davit head down through the foremost sheave of the lower fish-block, up through the foremost sheave in the double block, over the davit heads, and so on to the finish; the standing part is secured round the neck of the lower block; the hauling part is rove through a single block lashed to the long leg of the lower pendant.

Q. Why are the cat and the fish-falls rove through the foremost sheaves?

A. Because they are the first to tauten, therefore will not jamb the after parts.

Q. How do you reeve a cat-fall?

A. Reeve it through the foremost sheave in the cat-head, through the foremost sheave in the cat-block, and so on until it is rove in full; the standing part is clinched to the eyebolt under the cathead, or secured with a round turn round the cathead and timber-hitched.

R 3498.   o

Q. Where are the hauling parts of the cat and fish-falls led ?

A. Through leading-blocks hooked to the eyebolts on the opposite side of the deck.

Q. What is done when the anchor is up to the cathead ?

A. The cathead stopper is passed and secured. The stock pendant is put over the outer part of the stock, the stock tackle hooked and steadied taut; the fish is hooked to the inner fluke of the anchor.

Q. What precaution do you take before walking away with the fish-fall ?

A. Unhook the cat-block, and attend the stock-tackle; when all is ready walk away with the fish-tackle, attending the martingale and topping-lift; when the inner fluke is landed on the bill-board, pass the shank painter.

Q. Why is the cat-block unhooked before walking up the fish ?

A. To prevent it being split between the cathead and anchor as the fish brings the anchor up.

Q. How is a stock pendant and tackle fitted, and what is its use ?

A. The pendant is fitted with a running eye in one end to go over the anchor stock, and a thimble in the other for the tackle to hook to; a luff is generally used for the tackle; when in place, and steadied taut, it prevents the inner or lower arm of the stock from scraping the ship's side in fishing the anchor; it is also used when stowing the anchor for sea after the second catting, to bring the stock close into the bill-board.

Q. How is an anchor cleared when hove up to the bows foul ?

A. We will suppose, for example, the anchor comes up flukes uppermost.

Clap the foul-anchor strop on the fluke most convenient, or the crown, hook the cat, and walk the anchor up to the cathead, then hang the anchor by passing an hawser equal to the weight over the thumb-cleat round the fluke, and hitching it to the cathead.

Haul taut the hawser and belay it, ease up and unhook the cat or strop. Overhaul the cat, and hook it to the ring of the anchor.

Ease away the hawser, and walk up the cat at the same time. Clear the cable with ring ropes.

Slue ropes on the stock will be found a great assistance.

Should the anchor come up with the cable round the stock, and the ring turned down so that it is impossible to hook the cat to it, put a strop round the stock in such a way as to insure its not slipping.

Hook the cat to the strop, and walk the anchor up to the cathead, when the cable can be readily cleared, either by ring ropes, or hanging the cable, unshackling it, dipping it round the stock till clear, and shackling it on again.

Hang the anchor, unhook the cat, off strop, and hook the cat to the ring, and cat the anchor.

SECTION III.

(1.) *Model Room.*

To know the names, and describe the uses of, the following Purchases and Tackles.

Single whip.	Gun tackle purchase.	Royal halliard pur-
Double whip.	Quarter tackle.	chase.
Runner and tackle.	Sail tackle.	Purchases on a fore
Runner (for topmast	Top burton.	or main lift.
rigging).	Yard tackle.	Stay tackle.
Spanish burton.	Mizen burton.	Top tackle pendant.
Luff.	Topgallant halliard	Top tackle falls.
Tail jigger.	purchase.	Use of a lift jigger.

PURCHASES.

THEIR NAMES—HOW FITTED—STRENGTH—THEIR USE.

Name of Purchase.	Power gained.	How fitted.	Remarks. General Use.
Single whip.	None.	A rope rove through a single tail block, fixed in any position.	Is a purchase of least power in use; it is used for all light work, discharging luggage from a boat, &c.
Double whip.	Twice.	A rope rove through two single blocks; the upper block is a tail block, the lower one is a moveable hook block; the standing part of fall is secured with a round turn and two half hitches round the yard close to the tail block.	Is used for all common purposes, for clearing boats of things, &c. too heavy for a single whip.
Runner.	Adds an additional power to the purchase it is used with.	Is a rope rove through any moveable blocks.	Is always used in connexion with another purchase, such as the runners, and tackle in staying lower mast, top-Burton and runners, &c., or setting up topmast rigging.
Spanish Burton.	Three times.	Composed of two single blocks, one stationary, secured by a tail, the other is a moveable block.	Used for coaling ship.
Luff tackle.	Three times; four times if used in connexion with a leading block.	Two hook blocks, one double and one single. The standing part of the fall of this tackle is rove through a becket in the ass of the single block, and secured by being spliced round the strop at the neck of it.	Is used for all common purposes where a heavy pull is required, setting up rigging, &c.
Tail jigger.	Three times.	Composed of a double block, fitted with two tails or one, and a single hook block. Standing part of fall is secured in the strop of single block.	Used for setting up topgallant backstays, &c.

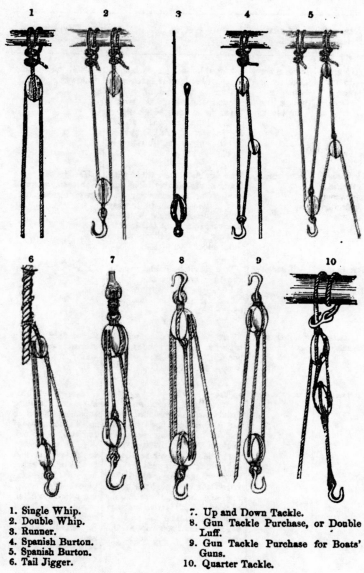

1. Single Whip.
2. Double Whip.
3. Runner.
4. Spanish Burton.
5. Spanish Burton.
6. Tail Jigger.

7. Up and Down Tackle.
8. Gun Tackle Purchase, or Double Luff.
9. Gun Tackle Purchase for Boats' Guns.
10. Quarter Tackle.

Name of Purchase.	Power gained.	How fitted.	Remarks. General Use.
Up and down tackle.	Three times; four times when used with a leading block.	A double and single block; the double block is fitted with a thimble for lashing to the lower pendants; the single block is a hook block, fitted with a long strop, the standing part of the fall is spliced in the strop of the single block.	Used for setting up lower rigging.
Gun tackle purchase, or double luff.	Four times.	Two double blocks, fitted with hooks; the double block intended for the standing part of fall has a score in the ass of the block under one of the sheaves, to form a fair lead in reeving the fall through the other block.	Used as side tackles of guns, and preventer tackles.
Gun tackle purchase for boats guns.	Twice.	Two single hook blocks; the standing part of the fall is spliced in the strop of the block, forming the final lead of the fall.	Used for boats' guns.
Quarter tackle.	Twice.	Two single blocks, each fitted with a long pendant and hook, the lower one with a tongue for stay to hook to.	Hoisting in stores, provisions, water, &c.
Sail tackle.	Three times.	Three single blocks; the strop of the upper block is fitted with a long and short leg, a thimble being spliced in the end of the long leg, and a hook in the end of the short leg; the third block is a leading block, stropped to the strop of the lower block, between the crown of the block and the hook; the standing part of the fall is rove through a becket in the ass and secured round the strop at the crown of the upper block.	Is used for shifting or bending topsails; when in use the long leg of the upper block goes round the topmast-head, and hooks to the short leg of the same block. For staying topmast; often used as a preventer lower brace in small ships, and sending topsail yards up and down.

Name of Purchase.	Power gained.	How fitted.	Remarks. General Use.
Top Burton.	Three times.	Is composed of a double hook block, sometimes fitted with a long strop, and a single hook block fitted with a long strop, and with a long loose strop or tongue.	Used as preventer lifts on topsail yards, setting up topmast rigging, and for other purposes too heavy for whips.
Mizen Burton.	Three times.	A double and single hook block; the standing part of the fall is spliced in the strop of the single block.	Used for sending the cross jack yard up and down, staying mizenmasts, &c.
Runner and tackle.	Eight times.	Consists of three blocks, one double and two single; one of the single blocks is a clump fitted with a thimble as a lashing block, through which the runner is rove. The tackle is rove through the two other blocks. The double block of the tackle is turned in one end of the runner, and a hook and thimble in the other end of runner; the standing part of the tackle is spliced in the ass of the single block, which is fitted with a long strop and a hook.	Used for staying lower masts, and weighing anchor when the capstan is disabled.
Yard tackle.	Three times.	Two blocks; upper block is a fiddle block, turned in the end of the yard-tackle pendant, fitted with a long strop; the lower is a single hook block, fitted with a long strop, in the ass of which the standing part of the fall is spliced.	Used for hoisting heavy weights in or out, such as boats, &c.
Topgallant purchase.	Twice or thrice.	Two single blocks; the topgallant shrouds are fitted with a long and short leg, a sennit eye in each leg; the long leg is rove through a thimble in the crown of the upper block, and toggled to the short leg. The standing part of the fall is spliced in the ass of the upper block; the lower block is a hook block.	This purchase is fitted for the purpose of setting topgallant rigging up smartly; the upper block in large ships is a double block.

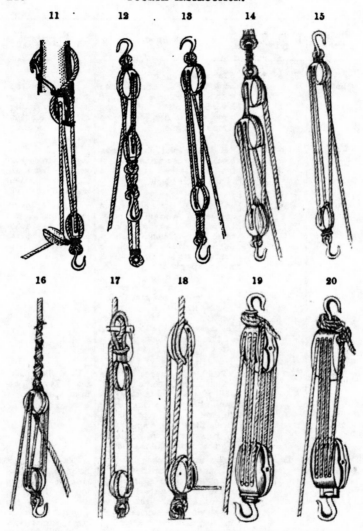

11. Sail Tackle.
12. Top Burton.
13. Mizen Burton.
14. Runner and Tackle.
15. Luff Tackle.

16. Top Gallant Purchase.
17. Top Gallant Halyard Purchase.
18. Lower Lift Purchase.
19. Threefold Purchase.
20. Fourfold Purchase.

Name of Purchase.	Power gained.	How fitted.	Remarks. General Use.
Topgallant halyard purchase.	Three times.	Two single blocks ; the lower block is a hook block ; the upper block is fitted with a long strop, and when in use is toggled to a bight of the topgallant halyards or yard rope, a half hitch is formed with the yard rope round the strop, and the bight put through the upper part of the long strop and toggled ; sometimes a double and single block is used, the double block fitted with two tails ; another plan is a runner and two single blocks.	Is used when the topgallant sails are set for mast-heading the sails.
Lower lift purchase.	Three times.	Two blocks—a double and single block ; the double is the lower block, and stropped to an eye-bolt in the deck close to the mast ; the single block is turned in a half strop in the lift.	Used for squaring or topping lower yards.
Three-fold purchase.	Six times ; seven times when used with a leading block.	Generally fitted with two three-fold metal blocks.	Used for raising the screw in screw ships.
Four-fold purchase.	Eight or nine times.	Generally rove through two four-fold metal blocks.	Used where any heavy purchase is required.
Launches purchases.	Eight times.	Consists of a runner and tackle.	Used for hoisting the launch in or out. When the launches purchase is in use, the pendant or runner is rove through a block at the yard-arm, led over the lower cap, and hooked to the opposite quarter of the yard. This purchase is seldom or never used.

Name of Purchase.	Power gained.	How fitted.	Remarks. General Use.
Forestay tackle.	Three times.	Consists of a double and single block; the double block is the upper block, fitted with a span with a hook in each end. The lower or single block is a hook block; standing part of fall is spliced in the strop of lower block.	Used for hoisting boats or any heavy weights in or out.
Mainstay tackle.	Three times.	Consists of two blocks; the double or upper block is fitted with a long pendant and hook; the single or lower block is a hook block, with standing part of fall spliced in strop.	Used for hoisting boats or heavy weights in or out.
Royal halyard purchase.	Double power.	Two single blocks, the upper one with a long eye and toggle, the lower with hooks and thimble.	For sea service, working with the watch.
Top tackle pendant.	Double power.	A piece of hawser-laid rope fitted with a thimble in lower end, the reeving end pointed, with a beeket in it.	For striking topmasts.
Top tackle falls.	Eight times.	Fitted with two iron-bound double blocks, the upper being a standing block, the lower a swivel.	For striking topmasts.
Lift jigger.	Three times.	A double and single block, the double block fitted with a tail for hitching round the lift, and the lower block fitted with hook and thimble.	Setting up weather topsail lift.

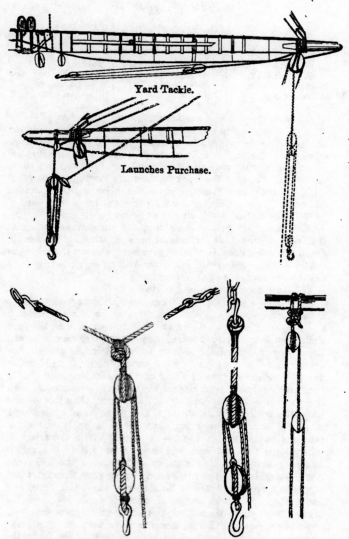

Yard Tackle.

Launches Purchase.

Fore Stay Tackle.   Main Stay Tackle.   Whip upon Whip.

EXTRA SUBJECTS.

I. SAIL MAKING.

To be instructed in the following :—

Sew a seam (flat, round, middle).	Make a sailmaker's splice.	Tabling.
Work an eyelet-hole.	Put a bottom in a bag.	Marl the footrope to a topsail and course.
Work a cringle.		

Q. How do you sew a seam flat round and middle ?

A. To sew a round seam you rub down one selvage according to the width of the seam required, place the other selvage to the bight and sew towards the hook, having the selvage towards you, putting about 112 stitches to the yard, rubbing down from the hook against the sewing. To sew a middle seam you commence from the hook with the canvas flat on the knees, putting from 70 to 80 stitches in a yard.

Q. How do you work an eyelet hole ?

A. Place your grommet on top, and commence sewing at that part of the hole farthest from you, sticking the needle down through outside of the grommet and up through the centre of the hole working from left to right, taking care that the grommet is well covered.

Q. How do you work a cringle ?

A. Unlay a single strand from the size rope your cringle is required to be, whip both ends, reeve the strand through the left-hand eyelet-hole in the sail, having one end longer than the other nearly a third, keeping the roping of the sail towards you. If a thimble is to be put in the cringle, lay up the two parts of the strand together, counting three or five lays, according to the size of the thimble, taking care you always have an odd number of lays; commence with the short end of the strands towards you, then reeve the long strand from you, through the right-hand eyelet-hole, taking it through the cringle, and it will be in the right position to lay up in the vacant space left in the cringle; when done, the one end will hang down inside the right-hand eyelet-hole, and the other end outside the left-hand one; the ends are then hitched by being rove through their respective eyelet-holes, and passed over the leech rope, and under their own part, one hitch being towards you, and the other from you; then tuck the ends under the first two strands nearest the hitch, heaving them well in place; the cringle is then fidded out, and the thimble is put in on the fore part of the sail. The ends of the strands are then tucked back, left-handed, under one strand, and again under two, right-handed, as in the first place, heaving them taut in place at each tuck, the ends are then whipped with two of their own yarns, and cut off.

To Finish a Cringle off on the Crown.

Commence as before, but after laying up the strand together, instead of forming a hitch with each end, the ends are rove through their respective eyclet-holes, and tucked back under two strands of the cringles, and again laid up as far as the crown, forming a four-stranded cringle, and is finished off by tucking the ends under two strands, and crossing them under the crown of the cringle, and cut close off. Cringles in the clews of boom-mainsails, or spankers, also the reef-cringles of fore and aft sails, are made this way, as they are considered much stronger than cringles made on the other method, and do not weaken the leech rope by being tucked under the strands of it. Cringles, when worked in the clew of topsails, arc made in the same way.

Another plan of finishing a cringle on the crown is, instead of laying the strands up to make a four-stranded cringle, it is made like the first, as far as the hitch. After forming the hitch, as in the first plan, instead of tucking the strand under the two nearest strands of the leech rope, it is backed and tucked left-handed under the nearest strand to it in the cringle, then right-handed under the strands towards the crown, both ends being served the same way, the cringle is fidded out, the thimble put in place, the ends whipped and cut off.

N.B.—Thimbles are always entered in the cringles on the canvas side of the leech rope; if entered on the rope side they are liable to take the edge of the canvas, when being forced in place, and carry the stitches away.

In working a cringle in a piece of rope, such as the roping of an awning, the only difference is, there are no eyelet-holes, therefore the strand is tucked under two strands of the rope it is to be worked in; instead of being rove through an eyelet-hole.

Q. How do you make a sailmaker's splice?

A. It is used for splicing the roping of sails together, or a larger to a smaller rope, such as a foot rope of a topsail to the leech rope, clew ropes of jib to the leech and foot ropes ; the leech rope of a boom mainsail, spanker or trysail, to the head or foot-ropes, &c.

Put a whipping on the leech rope, leaving end enough to tuck the strands twice ; then put another whipping on the foot rope to a certain distance, according to the number of times you intend to tuck the strands, which must greatly depend on the relative disproportion of the ropes, and the degree of tapering you intend to give them ; unlay the strands of both ropes to their respective whippings, then heave the turns out of the small rope, on the other side of the whipping to the distance you intend tucking the strands of the large rope ; then heave two or three turns out of the large rope on the other side of the whipping, crutch the two ropes together, and put a stop at the crutch to keep them in place ; tuck the first strand of the foot rope through the corresponding strand of the leech rope left-handed ; reduce it by cutting off a few yarns, and pass it again back-handed round the same strand of the leech rope, and so proceed, working with the same strand of the foot rope round and round the same strand of the leech rope, reducing the strand gradually at each tuck until it is tapered down to nothing ; take care in tapering the strand always to cut the inside yarns ; follow the same process with the other two strands of the foot rope, then tuck the strands of the leech rope into the corresponding strands of the foot rope, twice left-handed ; cut the whippings off, taper the ends down, worm, parcel, and serve them over.

If it is not to be served over, the ends are whipped together with two yarns out of one of the strands.

Q. How do you put a bottom in a bag ?

A. Rub down about 1 inch on the bag and the raw edge of the bottom, and sew towards the hook with the bottom towards you, then turn the bag and table down on the inside.

Q. What is meant by tabling ?

A. Tabling is sewing from the hook with the canvas flat on your knees, putting 70 to 80 stitches in a yard.

Q. How do you marl a foot rope to a topsail or course ?

A. Set the foot rope up taut, allowing sufficient slack of canvas to stretch of rope. You then commence to marl from the leech clew upwards, with white line or small rope, the hitches being made on the fore side of the sail, and a double hitch on every cloth.

To Lengthen a Rope of a Sail with Single Strand.

It is sometimes necessary to enlarge a sail with one or more cloths; to do this, the roping must be lengthened the best way of doing which is by introducing an additional strand, instead of putting in a piece of rope, which could only be done with two long splices, and thereby causing a much larger portion of the sail to be ripped than in the present instance.

There are several methods given of performing this operation, but as they come to the same thing in the end, there is very little difference in them, only in the mere wording. Some recommend the rope to be cut in the centre first, where you propose introducing the additional strand, while others prefer cutting the strands at the extremities first: however, it is a mere matter of taste which you do.

For example, it is required to give a sail one cloth more spread, it will therefore be necessary to lengthen the head and foot rope.

To do this, rip the rope off four cloths; that is, two cloths each side of the place you intend to lengthen the rope. The width of a cloth is 24 ins., which will allow a drift of 8 ft. for inserting the new strand.

If a 3-in. rope, it will take 2 ft. for splicing, allowing 6 ins. to each strand; cut the strands at the distance of 2 ft. 6 ins. from each other, as in Plate 1.

Cut one of the strands at A, and unlay it to C; then cut one of the strands remaining at C, and unlay it to B, laying the strand A up again as far as B; then cut the only remaining strand at B, which will be the centre, when your rope will be in two parts; by following this plan, the wrong strand cannot possibly be cut; the rope will appear as represented in Plate 2.

Marry the long end A to the end B, then lay up the long strand C in the lays of the strand A, and marry it to the other strand B, which represents Plate 3.

Take a strand about 9 ft. or 10 ft. in length, of the same size rope, and marry one end to the short strand A, as shown in Plate 3; then fill up the space left from A to C, by laying in the new strand, and marry the other end to the short strand C; you will then have four splices or knots, and it will appear as in Plate 4.

Then finish off, if a foot rope, as with an ordinary long splice, from which it will only differ in appearance by

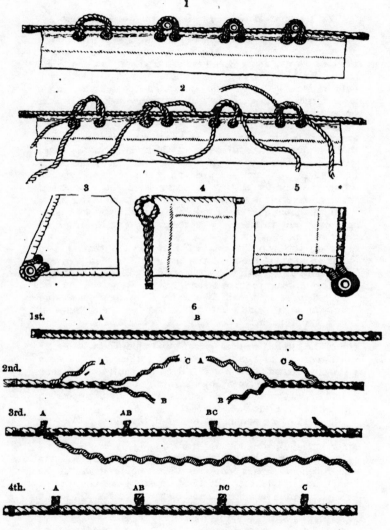

1. Cringles Finished.
2. Making Cringles.
3. Cringle in Clew.
4. Head Earring Cringle.
5. Clew of Sail.
6. To Lengthen a Rope with a Single Strand.

having to knot and tuck eight ends instead of six. Stretch
the splice, put a west country whipping on the ends, and
cut them off within 1 in. of the rope.

In laying the new strand in, care must be taken to exactly
follow the lay correctly, or it will not come in the right
position to knot the ends A and C.

The strands of a head rope are merely crossed, and both
strands whipped together underneath by a couple of yarns
out of one of the strands, not knotted and tucked, as in a
long splice; in sewing the sail to the head rope, the rope is
cross-stitched over the ends where tucked.

This is one of the neatest operations that can be performed by a sailmaker; but if not laid up right the first
time, it becomes very troublesome, and generally ends in a
failure.

A rope of a fore and aft sail can be shortened on the
same plan, as low as 6 ins., where too much slack rope has
been put on, and there is not enough rope to make a long
splice.

Sail Exercise.

Now that it has become a general practice throughout the
service to stow courses and topsails away in the sail-room,
furled, ready for bending, the gaskets are sewed in the head-
rope of the sail for this purpose, and the bending strop is
seized in place, ready for hooking the sail tackle to.

A Bending Strop

Is simply a pair of bail slings, only unlike slings, one bight
is not rove through the other, but merely seized together
with spunyarn when in use. The strop or slings are passed
round the bunt of the sail after it is made up for bending,
one bight is passed down abaft the sail, up before all, and
seized to both parts of the other bights, sufficient length
being left on the upper bight for hooking the sail tackle to.
This plan of fitting a bending strop is not, however, very
safe, as everything depends on the seizing.

The bending strop is sometimes seized to the head-rope of
the sail, as well as to act as a preventer in the event of the
other seizing slipping or carrying away; but the best and
securest plan of fitting it, is to have two eyelet-holes worked
in the head of the sail, just below the head-rope, the sail

R 3498.

P

being strengthened in the wake of the eyelet-hole by a patch of canvas. Cut the bending strop to length, reeve it from aft forward, through one hole, then from forward aft, through the other hole, splice both ends together, thus the splice will be on the after part of the sail; when covered with canvas a strop fitted this way can scarcely be seen, and is always in place; it is generally drawn through the eyelet-holes when the sail is set close to the foremost bight, and hangs down abaft all; in furling, it is tucked in the sail out of sight.

When used for bending, it is rendered through the eyelet-holes, the bight on the after part of the sail being passed round the bunt of the sail, up before all, and seized to both parts of the bight on the foremost part of the sail; for this purpose the strops or slings are marked and seized each side of the eyelet-hole, to prevent it slipping, leaving sufficient length on the bight on the fore part of the sail for hooking the sail tackle to. A strop fitted this way, for all the seizing might slip or carry away, would never allow the sail to fall on deck.

To Furl a Course on Deck for Bending or Shifting.

Stretch the sail taut along the roping next the deck, hitch the earring to any convenient place, to keep the head taut. Gather all the slack sail over towards the foot, then lay the second reef-band on the head, haul the second reef-earring taut out. Bring the leech taut in as far as the inner leech-line cringles, leaving the toggles out over the head ready for bending the leech-line, and if a fore course, leave the bowline cringle out to bend the bowline.

Bring the clews in over the head of the sail, about 4 ft. from the midship roband on either side, then lay the bunt-line toggles about a foot over the head, between the clews, ready for bending the buntlines to.

Extend the hands along the head of the sail, as if they were on the yard, and gather up, as in furling, until they come to the skin, then all step across the sail again, kneel down, and roll it taut up, making a snug furl, pass the gaskets, footing them well taut, pass the bending strop, and seize it in place ready for hooking the stay-tackle to. Stretch the head-earring along the head-rope, as near the bunt as possible, and stop them, ready to be got hold of as soon as the sail is above the fore or main yard.

The sail is now ready for bending or stowing away.

Q. How are topgallantsails and royals made up for stowing away?

A. Stretch the head of the sail taut along the roping or after part next the deck. Gather all the slack sail over towards the foot, then carry the sail towards the head in a similar way to a topsail or course, making three folds of it. Bring the clews towards the bunt till the leech rope of each fold lays inside the leech rope of the other; then take the clews out over the leech rope again, roll the sail taut up, leaving the robands out, and the bight of the head-earring hitched round the sail. Secure the sail with ropeyarn stops. It is then ready for stowing away.

Q. How do you make gaff-topsails up for stowing away?

A. A gaff-topsail is made up on the head, the tack is brought in towards the head, so as to square the foot. The foot is then laid along the head rope, and the sail rolled taut up and stopped with spunyarn stops, ready for stowing away.

Q. How do you make a jib or staysail up for stowing away in the sail bins?

A. Stretch the after-leech along the roping or port side next the deck. Bring the head and tack towards the sheet, until it nearly forms a square, then roll up taut on the after-leech, and secure it with ropeyarn stops; the sail is then ready to stow away.

Q. How do you make a boom-mainsail, spanker, or trysail up, for stowing in the sail-room?

A. On the after-leech; double the head and foot in towards the middle of the sail, roll it up snugly, and secure it with ropeyarn stops, it is then ready for stowing away.

Q. How are studdingsails made up?

A. Rolled taut up on the outer leech, secured with ropeyarn stops, and the tally is left out.

Q. How are boat's sails made up?

A. Rolled taut up on the after-leech, secured with spunyarn stops, and the tallies left out. Avoid making boat sails up on the head, as it stretches the sail in the heads, and spoils its set.

Q. How are awnings made up?

A. Stretched taut along the deck, both parts brought together, and rolled taut up on the ridge rope, which is fitted with stops, for securing it.

Bending and Shifting Sails.

Q. How do you bend a course?

A. Supposing the course to have been stowed away, furled ready for bending, with the bending strop seized in place.

The sail is brought on deck and laid athwartships under its respective yard, roping of the head next the deck.

The stay-tackle is then hooked to the bending strop, and having ascertained the sail is clear of turns (if necessary it should be swayed up and down for this purpose, and lowered again), bend the gear, hook the reef-burton blocks, either to the first or second reef-cringle, as directed, taking care it is over the tacks and sheets, bend the leechlines and buntlines; the head rope of the course is marked in the wake of the leechline blocks, to these marks the leechlines are stopped either with a roband or a yarn, care being taken that the leechlines are clear of each other, the inner one being stopped inside the outer one. The tack and sheet-tackle is now fitted with a ring on the shoulder, to which the clew-garnets are shackled, instead of being lashed to the clew, so in shifting courses, one shackle answers the purpose of all three.

Shackle the tackle and sheets, and lash or shackle the clew-garnets in place.

Hang the clews to the strop of the stay-tackle block.

When all is ready, man all the gear and stay-tackle, overhauling the tacks and sheets well. At the order " sway away," take down the slack of clew-garnets, and walk all the gear up together; see if the leechlines have been stopped with care, so as to come up taut to each leechline block; the head of the sail will haul taut along the yard, and a few hands will be able to bring the sail to the jackstay; when the head-earrings are secured, the robands passed, slablines bent, and the bunt-whip hooked to the bunt becket, and hauled well taut, cut the seizing of the bending strop and leechlines if stopped with yarns. Hook the reef-tackle blocks to the reef tackle cringles, toss the sail well up, and pass the lanyards of the gaskets round the jackstay, round the clew-garnets, taut up to the quarter blocks, and steady taut the tacks and sheets. Pass the clew-hangers.

Q. How do you bend a course made up not furled?

A. The sail is laid athwartships, under the yard to which it belongs, cast adrift on deck, and the gear bent. The leechlines and buntlines are stopped to the head of the sail.

The reef-tackles are hooked to the first reef-cringles. Tacks and sheets are shackled, and the clew-garnets are lashed to the clews; when ready, man the reef-tackles, leechlines, and buntlines, and clew-garnets, and walk all the gear up together.

As soon as the head-earrings are fast and the robands secured, shift the reef-tackles to their own cringles and bend the slablines. The sail is then ready for either setting or furling.

Q. How are the top-gallantsails and royals bent?

A. They are always bent on deck, and brought to the yard with head-earrings, and robands, the same as a topsail.

Q. How do you bend a jib?

A. To bend a jib. Reeve 'the stay through all parts of the lacing, from head to tack, and then bend the reeving-line to the becket of the stay; reeve the downhaul up through the lacing, from tack to head, and bend it with a sheet-bend to the head of the sail; hook the halyards to the head-cringle, pass the bight of them round under the foot, and all parts of the sail, and stop the bight to its own part, bend the clew-rope, pull up on the halyards, when high enough haul out on the reeving-line and downhaul, easing the halyards as required. Pass the tack-lashing, bend the jib-pendants, cast off the clew-rope, put on jib-purchase, and set the stay up; cast off the bight of the halyards from round the jib, and hoist the sail.

Q. How are staysails bent?

A. A fore topmast staysail is passed out on the bowsprit, the holes in the luff of the sail are usually seized to hanks on the port or lower fore topmast stay. The halyards are hooked to the head of the sail, and the downhaul is rove up from tack to head, through the three upper hanks, and bent to the head of the sail, the tack-lashing is secured in place, and the sheets or pendants are toggled to the clew, the sail is then ready for setting or stowing.

When a fore topmast staysail is brought to the stay with a lacing, it is passed through every alternate hole only, in the luff of the sail, and round the stay, the lacing being seized to the holes it does not pass through.

Main topmast and topgallant staysails are generally bent in the foretop, they are brought to their respective stays with lacings. The topgallant staysail stay is generally marked, and the head of the sail is seized to it when the stay and

HEADSAILS.

T Chain Strop.   Jib Sheet.

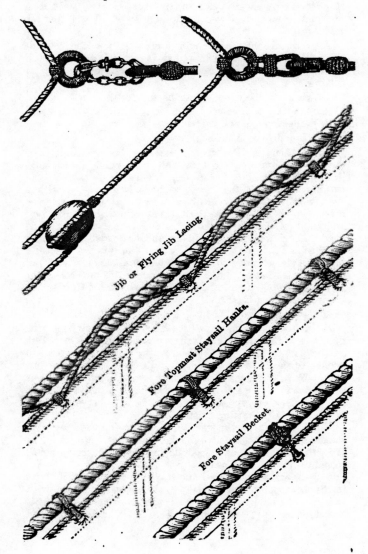

Jib or Flying Jib Lacing.

Fore Topmast Staysail Hanks.

Fore Staysail Becket.

halyards are in one. Halyards, downhaul, and sheets are bent in the usual way.

The storm staysails are laid abreast their respective stays, they are brought to the stays' with beckets. Luff-tackles are used for sheets. Halyards, downhaul, and tack-lashings are bent and secured in the usual way.

Q. How are storm trysails bent?

A. They are brought to smaller gaffs than those used for the regular trysails, beckets being used instead of a lacing; all the other gear is bent in the usual way.

How to bend a Boom-Mainsail, Spanker, or Trysail.

All gaffsails are brought to the gaff in a similar way.

The gaff is lowered down low enough for the hands to work conveniently, and steadied in place by the vangs, over to the side of the deck the sail is lying. A score is made under the gaff abaft the jaws, with an eyebolt on either side of it. The head-earring thimble or hook of the sail is placed between the two eyebolts, and a bolt passed through the three, with a head at one end, and secured with a forelock at the other. It is, however, sometimes shackled. The head of the sail is brought to the starboard side of the gaff or the roping next the gaff, and laced in a similar way to a studdingsail, or in roundabout turns round the gaff, and through two holes in the head of the sail from the throat towards the peak. The peak-earring is secured with two outer turns, two thumb-cleats being nailed to the gaff end to keep them out in place, or a hole for the purpose bored through, and with four up and down or inner turns. If a new sail, the lacing should be passed slack, and the head on no account stretched in hauling the peak-earring out. In bending a spanker or trysail dip the head of the sail through the brails; as soon as the head is secured, sway the gaff up, seizing the hoops on above the reefs as the sail rises, splice the lacing in below the hoops, selecting a soft, greasy piece of rope for this purpose, reeving the end through the cringles before the mast, from side to side, as the sail rises.

If a boom-mainsail or spanker, bend the tack-tricing line, and, if required, hook the tack-tackles. If a trysail, secure the tack-lashing.

The after-clew of a boom-mainsail is secured to the boom-end by an earring, or shackled before the sail is hoisted.

The outhaul-block is hooked to the after-clew of a spanker, and steadied out in place. A piece of rope, called a lazy sheet, is spliced in the clew of a trysail, to secure it until the sheet is hooked.

Q. How do you bend a gaff-topsail?

A. The gaff-topsail is bent to the gaff-topsail yard on deck, in a similar way that a studdingsail is to a studdingsail yard.

Q. How are studdingsails bent?

A. There are holes in the yard-arms for hauling the earring out to; the head of the sail is secured to the yard with hitching turns, sometimes a grommet is fitted in one of the head-earring cringles of the sail, which goes over the yard-arm, two thumb-cleats being nailed on the yard to keep the grommet from slipping in. The other earring is hauled out in the usual way. Tyers are also substituted instead of a lacing.

Q. How are boatsails bent?

A. In a similar way to all fore and aft sails, being roped on the port side; they are brought to on the starboard side of the gaff or yards; never stretch the head of a new boatsail in bending it, as it will ruin its set for ever after.

Shifting Courses Furled.

The men on the lower yards stop the leechlines and buntlines to the head of the sail, unhook the bunt-whip, cast off the clew-hangers, the lanyards of the gaskets from the jackstays, and secure them round the sail, also the lanyards of the bunt-gaskets round the bunt, cast off the robands and inner turns of the head-earrings, keeping fast the outer turns until the order is given to "ease in"; the earrings are then let go, and the sail is lowered by the buntlines and reef-tackles, the gear unbent and bent to the other course, as already explained in bending courses, the stay-tackle is then hooked to the bending strop, when all is again ready for swaying the sail up.

Reefing and Furling Sails.

Q. How do you reef a course?

A. For this purpose the sails are either taken in altogether, or the clew-garnets and buntlines well raised, the reef-tackles hauled close out.

When the sail is properly laid for reefing, the hands go aloft and lay out.

The earring is passed outside the rigging, on the yard-arm, which answers the same purpose as a reef-cleat on a topsail-yard, and through the reef-cringle, from aft forward, taking as many turns as possible, passing it through the reef-cringle each time ; as the whole strain of the tack comes on the reef-earring, sufficient number of turns should be taken to be equal to the same amount of strain as the leech-rope. The second reef is taken in in a similar way.

The second reef is seldom, if ever, taken in in the main-sail.

As soon as the earrings are secured, toggle the reef-beckets, overhaul the reef-tackles, and lay in, when the sail can be again set.

Should the sail be hauled close up, see the leechlines and slablines are overhauled sufficiently to admit of the earring being hauled out.

Q. How are reef-pendants to a boom-mainsail fitted ?

A. They have a stopper-knot fitted at one end, and the other end is pointed with a becket in it.

Q. How is the reef-tackle hooked to it ?

A. A bowline-knot is formed in the end of the pendant to which the reef-tackle is hooked.

Q. How is a reef-pendant rove in the sail ?

A. The pendant is rove through an eyebolt at the boom-end through the thimble of the reef-cringle to which it belongs, down through a cheek fitted with a sheave on the other side of the boom, the end brought in and stopped round the boom ready for use.

The eyebolts and cheeks for the reef-pendants on the boom-end are fitted on alternate sides so that the pendants work clear of each other.

Q. How do you reef a boom-mainsail ?

A. Haul in the sheet, lower the peak and throat halyards to slack the after-leech and luff of the sail sufficiently to haul the reef-pendant down, and to secure the luff of the sail. Hook the reef-tackle, which is always kept hooked under the boom, to a bowline-knot in the end of the first reef-pendant, and bouse it well down, and belay the reef-tackles to a cleat under the boom, secure the thimble in the tack to the thimble in the first reef-cringle, by passing a tyer through each thimble three or four times, tie the reef-points over the foot, shift the tack-tricing line block up to the first reef-cringle, ease the sheet and hoist the sail again.

This also applies to a cutter's mainsail, or a spanker, when the after-clew is shackled to the boom end; when the second reef is to be taken in, the first reef-pendant is stoppered and hitched round the boom, and the reef-tackle unhooked, ready to hook to the second reef-pendant.

The first and second reef-pendants are always kept rove.

Q. How do you reef a spanker or trysail?

A. Brail the sail up, easing away the outhaul for a spanker and the sheet for a trysail, lower the throat and peak halyards to the required distance, so as to insure slack-sail enough to enable you to take the reef in; steady taut the vangs, and if a spanker, the boom-sheets; if the first reef, secure the thimble in the clew, and the tack-thimble to the thimbles in the first reef-cringle in the after-leech and luff of the sail with a tyer; a regular earring is generally fitted to the after-leech, then tie the points over the foot. Shift the outhaul, if a spanker, to the thimble in the first reef-cringle in the after-leech, and the tack tricing-line to the first reef-thimble in the luff.

If a trysail, hook the sheet to the first reef-cringle in the after-leech, hitch the tack-lashing to the first reef-cringle, when complete, ease the vangs, and sway the gaff up in place, ease down the brails, and haul on the outhaul or sheet.

The other reefs are taken in in a similar way.

Q. How do you furl a course?

A. When all the gear is hauled taut up, the sail is laid in the right position for furling, the leechlines bring the leeches taut along the head of the sail, and the clew-garnets carry the clews of the sail up to the bunt of the yard.

At the order "lay out," the outer hands on the yard get hold of the leech as quickly as possible, and pass it in towards the bunt, taking care to form a skin in doing so.

The hands on the quarter and bunt of the yard gather the foot of the sail on top of the yard in the bunt, and then they work all the slack-sail in between the clews and the yard, towards the bunt on both sides, equalizing as much as possible the sail on each quarter of the yard; by doing this the sail will be light at the yard-arms, and a good bunt will be formed; as soon as the bunt-becket can be reached, hook the bunt-whip, and pull up on it, let go the buntlines, and foot the sail well down in the bunt skin.

All hands on the yard look towards the bunt, and give one good skin up together, pass your gaskets and clew-hangers, and lay in, and down from aloft smartly.

Q. How do you furl a topgallantsail or royal ?

A. At the order "lay out," get hold of the leeches and hand them taut in from the yard-arms, gather the foot of the sail on top of the yard, in the bunt, working all the slack sail in between the clews and the yards, shake the sail down into the skin, equalize the bunt, having as much sail on one quarter as on the other, then skin the sail well up, and pass the gaskets.

Q. How is a jib stowed at sea ?

A. The hands on the jib-boom get hold of the foot of the sail and lay it taut along the jib-boom to form a skin, keeping it under their breasts, they then gather up all the slack sail into the skin thus formed, and pass the stops.

A footline should be fitted to all jibs in large ships, to assist the men on the boom to get the foot of the sail taut along, and keep it in place ; it is most useful in bad weather.

Q. How is a jib furled in harbour ?

A. The second or third cloth from the after-leech is taken for a skin, according to the size of the jib, for this purpose ; the seam of the cloth, be it the second or third, whichever is to be your skin, is stopped to the jibstay above the lacing, and brought taut in along the jib-boom ; if it is the third cloth, the first and second will hang down between the furlers and the jib-boom ; all the slack sail is then picked up, and laid under the third cloth, the first or second on one side, and the fourth and fifth on the others, are then tucked under the slack sail, thus the third cloth forms a complete cover for the sail ; the gaskets are then passed.

Q. How do you furl a boom-mainsail ?

A. After the boom is crutched, lower the gaff down, so as when the hands stand on the boom they will be able to reach over the gaff to pick the sail up, the boom acting as a foot-rope.

Steady the gaff taut by the vangs, and a rope's-end round it as well.

Man the Boom.

First the hands will get hold of the slack sail, about 4 ft. from the head, the same side of the gaff as they are standing, and lay it on top of the gaff under their breast, so as to keep it in place for a skin, then pass the after-leech taut in towards the jaws, leaving little or no sail at the peak. Gather up all the slack sail from the foot, then lean well over the gaff and get hold of the slack sail kept for the skin, shake the sail well down in the skin thus formed, toss it well up together so as to have no wrinkles in the skin, and pass the gaskets.

Q. How do you furl a spanker or trysail?

A. Haul the lee-brails close up, or if laying head to wind, haul the starboard or port-brails up as convenient, steady through the slack of the other, form a skin with the after-cloth, gather all the slack sail in, pass the gaskets; when furled this way they are fitted with covers.

Q. How do you furl a trysail with the gaff lowered down?

A. When the gaff is lowered down, steady it well taut with the vangs, and, if necessary, by passing a rope's-end round it. Make a rope fast to the peak and jaws, to act as a foot-rope; where a gaff-topsail is fitted, the gaff-topsail sheet will answer this purpose.

Take the clew up to the jaws, gathering the after-leech along the head of the sail, then gather all the slack sail up from the foot, forming a skin, with the sail near the head, when skinned well up, pass the gaskets, and cover the sail.

When a spanker or trysail is fitted with covers, they are secured by one long gasket being passed with roundabout turns round the sail and gaff.

Q. How do you furl a gaff-topsail?

A. Bring the sheet and tack in square with the head, roll it up taut, so as to form a good skin. It is generally secured with centipede gaskets round the yard; in a cutter it is usually fitted with a cover, and stowed on the main boom.

Q. How do you furl a studdingsail?

A. Studdingsails are furled square on their heads, tack sheet and downhaul cringles being left out, the sail being secured with centipede gaskets.

II. Sailing Launches and Cutters.

To be instructed in the following:—

Heaving the lead and calling the soundings.	Working a dipping lug in a cutter.	Shaking out reefs.
Steering with a wheel.	Getting masts up and down.	Making tow ropes fast.
Working the launches under sail.	Reefing boat's sails.	Laying out hawsers.

Q. How do you heave the lead and call soundings?

A. To take soundings a man stands on the weather gunwale, or on a platform fitted for the purpose, with stanchions and breast rope.

The lead is thrown forward while the vessel has headway, if the depth of water corresponds with the mark on the line, say its blue bunting, the leadsman calls out " by the mark thirteen," if its a deep there is no mark upon the line, such as four, six, eight, or nine fathoms, he calls out " by the deep four, &c."

If he judges the depth to be a quarter or a half more than a particular fathom, as, for instance, six, he calls out, and a quarter six, or and half six, if its six and three quarters, he calls out quarter less seven, and so on.

Q. How do you steer with a wheel?

A. The tiller is brought in connexion with the wheel by means of ropes or chain; the action of the wheel is the same as in all vessels, that is to say, whichever way you wish the boat's head to go, you turn the wheel in the same direction, the rudder acting on the boat, the tiller or yoke being the lever, and the wheel and ropes the purchase by which power is gained.

Working a Launch under Sail.

A CUTTER ON A WIND.

Part III.

Q. If sailing in a stiff breeze, what precaution would you take in placing your crew ?

A. All hands should sit on the bottom boards, as little of them as possible ought to appear above the gunwale ; keep the men out of the bows, and in a heavy sea always endeavour to keep a boat's head on to it.   Never allow the crew to sit to windward, and should they be sitting to windward in a breeze, and you are about to pass a ship, make them resume their proper places on the thwarts before you are under her lee ; there is always an eddy wind under the stern of a ship lying head to wind, and invariably a great indraught of water ; frequently, boats passing close under the stern of large ships are suddenly taken aback, and were the crew in such a case sitting on the weather gunwale, or all hands over the weather side, it might be the means of capsizing the boat, and causing some fatal accident.

Q. If blown off the land in a boat, what would you do to keep her head on to the sea, and prevent her drifting to leeward ?

CUTTER BEFORE THE WIND.

A. Securely lash all her spars, oars, &c. together.   Make a span of any rope you have in the boat equal to the strain that will be brought on it ; to the span, when properly bent to the opposite ends of the largest spar, bend the end of a cable, if you have one in the boat; if not, the end of the painter, or any long piece of rope, before launching the spars overboard; the longer scope you can give, the easier the boat will ride; this has been known to answer well.

Q. If using oars in a light wind, what precaution would you take when the breeze freshens?

A. In using oars under sail, in light winds, always boat them directly the breeze freshens, or at least, the lee oars, to prevent the possibility of catching a crab, that is, the oars becoming entangled in the water, the blades going in the opposite direction to which you wish, the loom flying forward against the hands using the oars, and in five cases out of six capsizing them backwards off the thwarts in the bottom of the boat, causing confusion among the other hands, and is often the means of three or four others on the lee side catching crabs, which ends either in splitting and carrying away the lee gunwale, or in capsizing the boat.

Q. When about to sail, what ought you strictly to observe?

A. Great care should always be taken in seeing a boat's sails well and properly set, so as to render her manageable; also sightly to other ships.

A great deal is done in handling a boat, in having the sails properly trimmed, and the crew or any weight on the boat judiciously placed; all weight, as much as possible, should be kept out of the bows and stern, and placed amidships; you can easily tell by the helm if a boat is in trim or not.

When in trim, she will carry her helm nearly amidships; by being obliged to give much weather or lee helm, the rudder is dragged across her stern, and the boat's way is retarded.

Q. How would you make sail in a boat rigged with gaff sails?

A. Always set the jib or stay-foresail before setting the gaff-foresail, taking care to steady the runners hand taut first. The jib and stay-foresail act as a forestay, and if the gaff-foresail is set before either of the head sails, the foremost head is dragged aft, and causes the after-leech of the gaff-foresail to hang slack; but should circumstances oblige you to set the gaff-foresail first, ease off the gaff-foresail sheet, and slack the runners, so as to allow the mast to go forward in its proper position when you set the head sails.

Q. What precaution would you take in belaying a sheet?

A. A sheet should never be belayed, but always kept in hand; as the safety of the boat's crew might depend upon this, a careful trustworthy hand should always be selected for this duty.

Weather helm is often produced by allowing the bowman to sit right forward, and press the boat by the head, also by carrying a press of sail; attention to the jib or mizen sheets, in a boat where the sails are well set, will invariably relieve the helm.

Q. If working to windward among shipping, or into an harbour, and in doubt as to whether you will weather any particular object, what ought you to do?

A. It is always safer to tack, as invariably there will be some tide running, and if a lee tide, and you shake the boat up, she loses her way, becomes unmanageable, the consequence is, you foul the danger you have tried to avoid, and will cause, in all probability, some damage to your boat; should the masthead foul the bowsprit or spanker-boom of the ship you are trying to weather, she is nearly certain to capsize, and most likely drown some of your crew.

Q. Being unable to fetch a ship, what assistance can she render you?

A. If it is blowing hard, or in a strong tide way, keep as much as possible in her wake, so as to pick up a buoy or small boat when veered astern from the ship for your assistance, a deep-sea lead-line or small hawser is generally used for this purpose; as soon as you have picked it up and secured it to your boat, she is walked up alongside by all hands on board the ship clapping on the line veered astern.

Q. What preparation would you make if in charge of a boat under sail, before going alongside a ship, and what guide have you for properly laying your boat alongside the gangway?

A. Much depends upon the judgment of the coxswain in going alongside a ship; the general rule, however, is to get the main-yard end on, but this must greatly depend upon whether the ship is in a tide way or not, or whether the boat is light or heavily laden. In coming alongside, unship the bowsprit, see the boat has been properly baled out, fenders out, slings, if possible, should be hooked, and everything ready for the boat to be hoisted up if you know she is not to remain down, and always remember that a heavily laden boat carries her way much longer than a light boat.

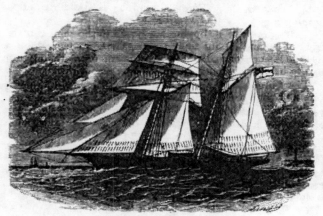

TOPSAIL SCHOONER YACHT.

THINGS TO BE OBSERVED.

Never put the helm down suddenly. When about to tack always ease it down; putting the rudder right across the stern deadens a boat's way; about three-quarters down will be found quite sufficient for any purpose.

It should ever be borne in mind by young and inexperienced seamen, that you cannot carry as much sail on a wind as you can running before it, therefore before rounding to, or hauling on a wind, great caution should be observed, and the sheets and halyards kept well in hand, ready to shorten sail at the shortest notice; the crew for this purpose ought to be properly stationed.

Great care should be observed in running in a fresh breeze dead before the wind; if taken by the lee you are nearly certain to capsize the boat if the sheets and halyards are not well in hand. When unable to lay your course by the wind coming on the sheet quarter, haul up a little, lower your sail and shift over, and resume your course.

Working a Dipping Lug in a Cutter.

Large boats, such as launches, pinnaces, and barges, are generally rigged with gaff-sails, that is, as fore and aft schooners, or with standing lugs.

R 3498.

Q

The smaller boats, such as cutters, gigs, jolly-boats, &c., are rigged with either standing or dipping lugs.

Q. What is the difference between a standing and a dipping lug ?

A. The tack of a dipping lug hooks to the stem, and the tack of a standing lug to the mast, therefore every time a boat tacks or wears, the after yard-arm of a dipping lug has to be dipped round the mast, from aft forward.

There are many opinions as to the best method of dipping a cutter's lug, the simplest and best plan is to dip the fore yard-arm, a small line from the fore yard-arm to the centre of the boat is useful in giving a check to the yard when lowered sufficiently for dipping ; by this method the sheet is kept hooked and the smallest portion of the sail is dipped, instead of ballooning the whole sail round the mast. This plan is adopted in the training service. The halliards are rove the reverse way to the other system of dipping, viz., from the traveller from aft forward.

Q. How low would you lower a lug for dipping ?

A. There ought to be a dipping mark on the halyards, to prevent the necessity of lowering the yard more than is necessary for dipping the after yard-arm round the mast, and also to keep the sail high enough, so as to have sufficient of the sail aback before the mast to carry the boat round and insure as little slack sail as possible on top of the men sitting on the foremost thwarts ; if in a cutter, one of the men stationed on the after-thwart should keep the mizen-sheet in hand, so as to ease off, in case the boat comes-to in re-hoisting the sail.

Q. Where would you belay the halyards of a lug sail ?

A. Always to windward.

Q. How do you dip a lug in wearing ?

A. Just before the wind is right aft lower your sail to the dipping mark, gather it forward, dip the after yard-arm round before the mast. Shift the hauling part of your halyards to windward, and as soon as the wind is on the other quarter re-hoist your sail ; never, if possible, allow a boat to gybe in a fresh breeze, as it will be very difficult to lower the sail down, the halyards will be between the mast and the sail, and the sail will be binding hard against the mast.

Q. How is a downhaul fitted to a lug sail ?

A. The halyards are generally cut sufficiently long to

admit the end of the hauling part to be fitted with an eye, and hooked to the traveller before hoisting the sail.

Q. How do you take a lug sail in?

A. Check the sheet, haul down on the downhaul, and the luff of the sail at the same time, so as to spill the sail; never gather down on the after-leech, as it causes the fore part of the sail to fill, and binds the traveller to the mast, so as to prevent its running down freely.

Q. Where would you bend the halyards of a standing and dipping lug?

A. The proper distance to sling a dipping lug is one third from the foremost yard-arm, and a standing lug one quarter, so as to insure your sail to set well.

Q. What precautions would you take before making sail?

A. Before stepping the mast, see the halyards are rove, and that nothing will be required aloft, and when once the mast is stepped, see the ends of the halyards are within reach, so there will be no necessity for any of the hands to stand on the thwarts; never allow a man to go up the mast, many fatal accidents have occurred in this way; if there is anything wrong at the mast-head, such as the halyards becoming unrove, unstep the mast and rectify it. Ship the rowlock plates, see the halyards hooked clear, also the sheet clear for hooking; never haul the sheet taut aft if on a wind before the halyards are well up.

Q. If on a wind, and the halyards require a pull, what precaution would you take?

A. Always ease the sheet off before getting it.

Q. If sailing on a wind, and caught in a squall with a lug sail, what would you do?

A. Let go the fore sheet at once, and put the helm down; and as the wind often shifts in a squall, it is a safe precaution to lower the foresail down until you see the extent of the squall, and whether the wind is likely to remain steady; if taken aback, the sail would so bind against the mast that there would be great difficulty in getting it down, it would most likely cause the boat to gather stern way, and if blowing fresh, would create such confusion among the crew, which might perhaps induce them to stand up in the boat, and in all probability capsize her. Many accidents have occurred this way, causing the loss of many valuable lives; also through not shortening sail in time. This also applies to a boat schooner-rigged.

Q 2

Q. If sailing with the wind abeam, and caught in a squall, what would you do ?

A. Keep the sheet flowing, and the halyards clear for running.

Q. How do you reef boat's sails ?

A. Lower the throat and peak halyards until you have sufficient slack sail to secure the earring and reef points, easing off the sheet as necessary. When the reef is in and the tack of the sail secured reset the sail.

Q. When ought you to reef in a boat ?

A. Directly she begins to wet, or show any inclination of being crank ; never allow the boat's crew to stand up ; when reefing, the men should be properly stationed before you

Different Rig of Boats.

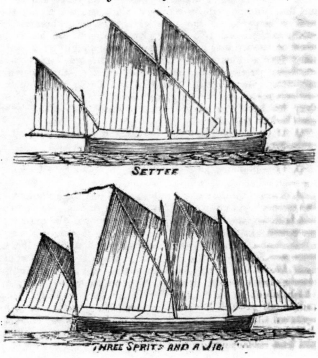

SETTEE

THREE SPRITS AND A JIB.

begin, so each man might know what he has to do without confusion; the hands not engaged in reefing should be made to sit perfectly still; keep the boat under command, but the sails should be lifting, the halyards checked, and the sail lowered sufficiently for the men to handle without rising in the boat.

Q. What is to be observed in taking a reef in a boat-sail.?

A. Never roll the foot of a sail, as it holds more water, and tends to force the boat to leeward.

Q. How do you shake out reefs?

A. The reef is first shaken out, keeping the sail set, then when ready the halyards are lowered, the tack and sheet shifted and the sail set again as soon as possible.

Q. How do you get the masts up and down?

A. In getting a mast up the mast should be launched aft far enough to place the heel in the step, the after hands lifting at the head, the foremost hands hauling on the shrouds which are passed forward at the same time as the mast is raised and clamped. In getting the mast down the shrouds are passed forward, the mast is then unclamped and eased down, the after hands looking out for the head. Care should be taken never to stand up in a boat unless absolutely necessary.

Q. Making tow ropes fast?

A. In towing alongside a ship, get your tow-line from as far forward as possible from the ship you are towing alongside; if towing astern, the shorter your tow-line is the better. Never make a tow-line fast, but toggle it with a stretcher through the aftermost of the foremost sling-bolts, so as to be able to slip it in case of any emergency; use the lazy painter as a frapping to frap it into the stem.

If towing astern of a ship, with many other boats, never allow them to make their painters fast to the stern of your boat, as it will strain her, and perhaps start the stern-post or stem; when about to be cast off, always have your oars in hand ready for use. The largest and heaviest boats should tow nearest the ship.

Q. How would you tow a spar?

A. The smallest end first.

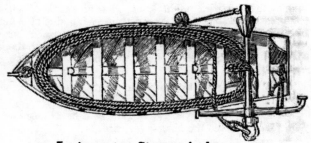

Laying out a Stream Anchor.

Towing.

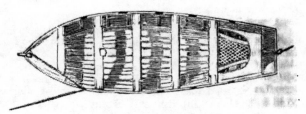

Towing Alongside.

Hauling a Boat up on a Beach.

Laying out Hawsers.

If ordered to lay a warp out, coil enough of it forward in the boat to take two round turns and two half-hitches the instant your boat gets to the buoy or ship you are going to secure to.

If you are going to lay a warp to windward, or against a tide, coil the whole of the warp in the boat, pull to the place you are ordered to, make it fast, and drop down on the ship, paying out as the boat goes; this is called making a guess warp of it, as you have to well judge your distance to your ship, and in many cases, when you have paid the warp out too quickly you are unable to reach the ship, and another boat is obliged to bring a line to your assistance, which denotes a lubberly way of performing the duty intrusted to you.

Hill and Clarke's Boat Lowering Apparatus.

Instructions.
To Disengage.

When the boat is up at the davits ready for lowering, the claw (fig. 28, p. 261) must be pulled back clear of the hook (fig. 29, p. 261).

A man in each end of the boat should take hold of the toggle lines attached to the rings of the falls and pull them clear of the hooks when boat is waterbourne (figs. 22 and 23, p. 259). In rough sea, however, the rings will clear themselves when the boat is lifted by the water sufficiently to slacken both the falls simultaneously (*see* fig., p. 247, *also* fig. 21, p. 258); but one end of the boat will not unhook without the other, *see* fig., p. 249.

The fore and aft safety line may be used by the men to steady themselves upon entering the boat; but must not be unfastened from the falls.

To Hook on.

When the boat comes alongside in ordinary weather the rings must be taken in the hands and hooked on (as in figs. 11 and 14, p. 254), by first passing the upright part of the hook through the ring, then, with the hand, pushing the bottom of the ring up under the curved part of the hook. The claw must then be thrown over to lock them together.

When the sea is rough the ring should be simply hooked in the curved part of the hook, and locked by claw (as in fig. 27, p. 260).

In very bad weather the claws should be secured by passing the small line attached to the claw down through the centre of ring, and fastened the same round the bottom of the hook, or by a piece of rope being jammed through the hook under the ring (*see* figs. 25 and 26, p. 260). Either of these make it impossible for the boat to wash away from the ship in very rough weather.

To attach Fore and Aft Line.

When possible the fore and aft line should be hooked on before the falls are tautened and the boat hoisted up (fig. 18, p. 257). Should the boat be raised without the fore and aft line being attached, then it must be done when the boat is taken in on the chocks, or one end must be temporarily hung by passing the boat's painter over the davits' head, and the fall slackened. Then the lanyard in the centre loosened, and the after ends are hooked on again hauled as taut as possible, and made fast (fig. 30, p. 262).

The loose end of the lanyard should be fastened round one of the thwarts to prevent the line falling overboard when the boat is disengaged (fig. 17, p. 256).

It is not necessary to use the fore and aft line when the ship is at anchor or in harbour, but should be always on at sea to prevent one end of the boat unhooking before the other (*see* p. 258).

INSTRUCTIONS TO SHIPS' CARPENTERS FOR FITTING BOATS.

The hooks must be fixed in the ends of the boat, as shown in either figs. 1, 4, or 6, when possible, keeping the distance between the hooks from 6 to 10 inches greater than the width between the davits. *Great care must be taken to place the back or long part of hook towards the centre of boat as shown in figs.* 1, 4, *and* 6. A piece of small line is spliced into the join pin of the safety lock for pulling the lock clear of the hook (fig. 29).

When fitted with the double shackle, as in figs. 1, 2, and 3, to the ordinary sling pans of the boat, the old ring should be cut out, and the double shackle, fig. 2, must be fastened in the chain, and the length of the sling itself tautened as much as possible ; the steadying lines should, when possible, be made of rope, in order that they may be hauled taut to keep the slings rigid.

When fitted with the keel bolt, as in fig. 4, through the thwarts, the old ring bolt should be taken out and the new bolt, fig. 5, be put through the keel, when possible, a few inches nearer the ends of the boat and clinched, great care being taken that the *lower end* of the *slots* in the top of the bolts be always turned towards the *centre of the boat.* When the turnover keel bolts are used, they must be let into the thwart, as in figs. 8, 9, and 10, and the pin side be turned towards the centre of the boat.

When fitted with the crutch bolt, as in fig. 6, in the ends of the boat, the common ring bolt must be taken out and the new crutch bolt, fig. 7, fixed in the lower bolt of the crutch bolt in the bow end will have an eye for the purpose of attaching the boat rope to.

The links in the rings to be fixed in the lower tackle blocks (*see* fig. 14), and a toggle line, 2 feet long, spliced in the small side eye of the rings (fig. 15).

The fore and aft line should be made of two pieces of wire rope (fig. 16), with a thimble spliced in each end, the two pieces together being about 1 foot 6 inches shorter than the distance from davit to davit, and fastened by a lanyard of manilla or other rope passed through the thimbles five or six times, and left long enough to fasten the end loosly round one of the thwarts of the boat, to keep it from falling overboard.

When the rings are fastened into the hooks, and the locks thrown over to secure the same, the end thimbles of the fore and aft line are hooked into the hook links and the lanyard hauled tight, the boat is then raised and ready for use (figs. 17 and 18).

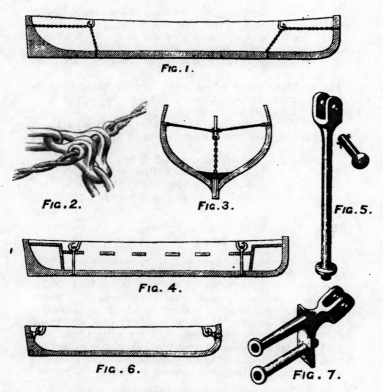

FIG. 1.

FIG. 2.

FIG. 3.

FIG. 5.

FIG. 4.

FIG. 6.

FIG. 7.

SPECIAL FITTINGS FOR YACHTS, BOATS, &c., ENABLING THE HOOKS
TO BE TURNED BENEATH THE SEATS WHEN NOT IN USE.

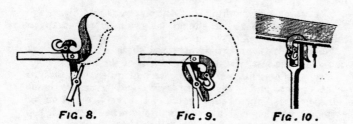

FIG. 8.

FIG. 9.

FIG. 10.

Fig. 1. Long boat or cutter fitted with slings. Hooks attached by means of *double shackles* into slings.

Fig. 2. *Double shackle* and steadying line, used for fixing hooks into slings of long boat or cutters.

Fig. 3. Section showing method of keeping hook and sling in position by steadying lines to side of boat.

Fig. 4. Life boat or whale boat showing hooks fitted in *keel bolts passed through thwarts and fixed in keel.*

Fig. 5. *Keel bolt* used in fig. 21.

Fig. 6. Sketch showing fitment of short jolly boat or dingy ; hooks fixed in stem and stern by means of crutch bolts.

Fig. 7. *Crutch bolts* for dingy used in fig. 21.

Fig. 8. Hook in position, fitted with automatic stop.

Fig. 9. Hook out of use, fitted with automatic stop.

Fig. 10. Hook fitted to *turn over bolt* with *pin stop.*

HILL AND CLARK'S BOAT LOWERING AND SELF-ACTING DETACHING APPARATUS.

The apparatus, in its complete form, places the lowering of a boat with its full crew from ships of any size *entirely under the control of one man.* As soon as the boat reaches the water it ensures a perfectly *automatic and instantaneous* detachment from the ship, without requiring any attention from those in the boat. It can be readily fitted to any vessel having the ordinary appliances, which are all retained.

We may take for granted that the following qualities are necessary in an effective boat apparatus :—

The boat should be lowered square by one man (described on p. 261).

The same apparatus, which is used in lowering and disengaging the boat, must also be used in attaching and hoisting up.

The water, and nothing but the water, should disengage the boat, and no power should be given to any man to release the boat before it has reached the water.

Now, the most important of these three qualities is undoubtedly the last, viz., the detachment of the boat.

Every sailor will know what man's judgment is; and to what extent, under the most trying and critical circumstances, it is to be relied upon. The very adoption of systems which depend upon man's judgment to release the boat tends to increase the risks rather than diminish them ;

for we hear of many instances of men erring in their judgment, when detaching the boat from the ship by means of levers and tripping lines long before the boat has reached the water—in very many cases losing the men and destroying the boat, and this has happened in such calm weather that the common old tackle could have been used with safety. The first and great danger, therefore, to provide against is to remove from everyone the power of disengaging a boat before it has reached the water. After it has reached the water it is necessary to give a more safe and ready means for the disengagement of the boat than the common hook and ring, which so often causes an accident, either through releasing one end of the boat before the other, or doing injury to the men by jamming their fingers and hands in their attempts to overhaul the falls.

To enable the water, and nothing but the water, to disengage the boat from the ship, it was first of all necessary to devise a self-acting or automatic hook, and in inventing this there were four distinct things to keep in mind.

First.—To give an effective detaching hook and ring, combining in their solid construction the simple and well known common hook and ring, but giving in their new form more security and less danger.

Second.—The hook should be easily and readily disengaged without any necessity for the men to overhaul the falls ; at the same time enabling the disengagement to be done without risk of jamming the men's fingers.

Third.—It should be a hook more readily hooked on in a seaway than the common hooks and rings now in use, and more secure when hooked on.

Fourth.—The same hook to combine in itself the principle of a self-acting or automatic action, to be readily applied and used at the wish of the Captain or Commander of the ship.

Principle of the Hook and Ring.

The bare principle of the self-acting detachment of the hooks is shown by the two engravings below.

The hand represents the davit, and the cord represents the fall, to which the ring is fastened. The *hook* is supposed to be attached to the boat. Now so long as a strain is maintained on the cord (as by the weight of the boat) the ring keeps in its place, as shown in fig. 11 ; and the greater the strain the more securely does it do so. But the moment the cord is slackened (as by the boat, and with it the hook,

being lifted by the sea), the ring naturally falls away from
its oblique position, as shown in fig. 12. It is prevented

Fig. 11.
Hook and Ring attached,
cord strained.

Fig. 12.
Hook and Ring detached, cord
having been slackened.

from being again engaged by the back or upright part of
the hook (H, fig. 13), so that when the boat drifts away the
ring slips completely clear.

Fig. 13.

The hook A with the lock
E, thrown back, which
is used for securing the
ring in the hook when
attached; P shows pin
for attaching the un-
locked cord.

Fig. 14.

Hook and Ring at-
tached. F, hook or
ring of lower tackle
block. D, shackle
to which slings of
boat are attached.

Fig. 15.

Ring B, with hook
link C and tog-
gle line.

One hook, fig. 13, is fixed at each end of the boat by the several means described at pages 5 and 6, and has its companion ring, fig. 15, attached to the lower block of each fall, by the intervention of a link C, which has a hook G, forged on its side, the use of which is described hereafter.

If it could be ensured that a boat would always descend evenly and into moderately sized waves, nothing further than that which has already been described would be necessary. But in heavy weather, a sea may strike one end of a boat and lift it; that end would be unhooked, and drop when the wave retired, while the other end would remain hung up out of the water. Again, should one end of the boat be *lowered* into the water before the other, the effect would be similar.

To prevent this, and ensure that *both ends of the boat shall be detached at the same instant* the safety line is employed, fig. 16.

Fig. 16

This is a wire or other rope fitted with thimbles. It runs fore and aft, and is hooked on at each end to the hook link C before referred to (figs. 14 and 15). It is then hauled taut in the middle with a small lanyard, and the effect is to draw the lower table blocks towards each other, and pull the rings and hooks into a slanting position, as in fig. 17. This is done by the boat being temporarily hung at one end by passing the painter or boat rope over the davit head and slackening the fall, then the lanyard hauled as taut as possible and made fast (*see* fig. 30).

The effect of this is, that a portion of the strain borne by one ring is transmitted to the other, so that neither ring is ever sufficiently relieved of strain to become detached until both are relieved together by the boat being properly waterborne.

Then both rings, having no strain, instantly detach themselves, and the boat becomes free, leaving the safety-line in the boat itself (fig. 21).

The loose end of the lanyard should be tied to one of the seats to prevent the fore and aft line falling out of the boat.

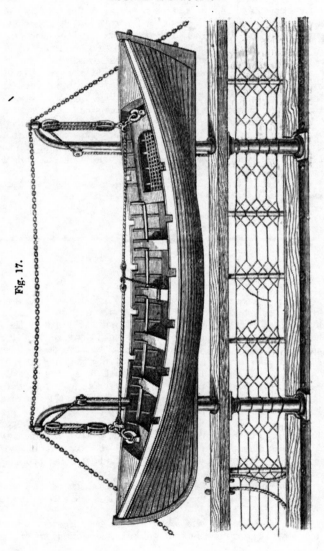

Fig. 17.

Upon reference to figs. 18, 19, 20 it will be seen that as
long as one or both falls are kept taut the connexion will
remain fast; but that immediately on the falls becoming
slack by the boat floating or becoming waterborne the connexion ceases, for the rings, falling down by their own
weight, free themselves (fig. 21). The rings once loosened
from the close grip of the curved body of the hooks can
never again resume their connexion with them, or in other
words "foul," except they are forced to do so by the inten-
tional action of a man's hand. The reason of this is obvious.
When the rings have been attached, by being passed over
the upright head and hooked under the curved body of the
hooks, they do not (owing to the former parts projecting
over the latter) hang freely, but they are in a slightly inclined position. Naturally, therefore, the first impulse of
the rings on being released from the body of the hooks is
to fall into a vertical position, and having once done so,
they can never again become attached, unless intentionally
hooked on.

From the foregoing remarks it will be seen that a slight
lift of the boat is necessary to automatically release it from
the tackles. At sea there is almost at all times sufficient
rise and fall of the water to effect this. If, however, a boat
is lowered in very smooth water, while there is headway on
the ship, or when the ship is at anchor in a tideway, and
consequently a towing strain on the falls the boat is easily
and readily released by a slight jerk on the toggle lines,
which are fixed in a small eye on one side of each of the
rings (figs. 22 and 23).

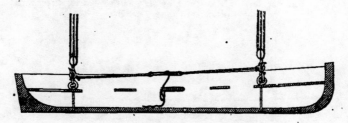

Fig. 18.

Showing boat hanging at davits ready for lowering.

R 3498.   R

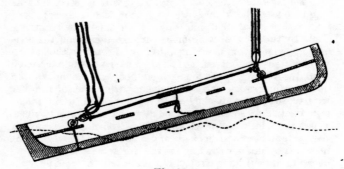

Fig. 19.

Showing boat lowered stern first into water ; *neither end yet disengaged.*   Dotted line shows water line.

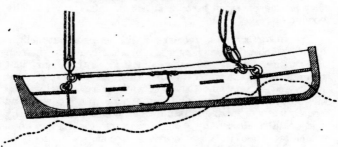

Fig. 20.

Showing bow of boat struck by sea; *neither end yet disengaged.*
Dotted line shows water line.

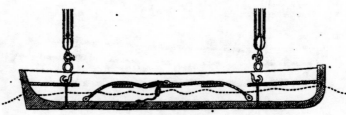

Fig. 21.

Showing boat water-borne, *both falls clear, safety line also disengaged.*

Hooking on.

In ordinary weather the rings should be hooked as in figs. 14 and 24 ; the upright part of the H (fig. 13, p. 8)

Fig. 23.

to be passed through the centre of the ring, and the bottom part of the ring to be pushed by the hand up under the curved part of the hook.

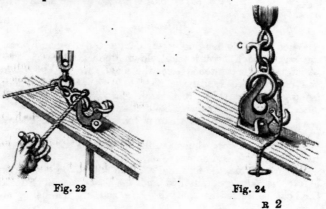

Fig. 22.   Fig. 24.

R 2

The fore and aft hook *e* (fig. 15) to be always turned towards the middle of the boat.

When the sea is rough, the rings should be hooked simply in the curved part of the hook, and locked by claw, as in fig. 27. The boat must then be properly hooked when hoisted, as in fig. 17.

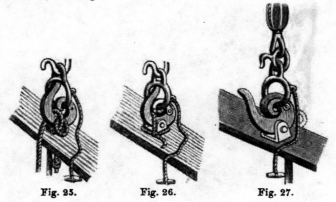

Fig. 25.   Fig. 26.   Fig. 27.

Should the locks become broken or disabled, the rings can be secured in their places by a piece of rope or the end of the fall being passed through, as shown in fig. 25.

In very bad weather the lock may be fastened down by a piece of spun yarn, as an extra precaution to secure the boat.

Unlocking.

When a boat is hanging at the davits ready to be lowered, the lock of each hook is shut down upon a piece of cord, which has a loop hitched over the small pin P; the other end of the cord is fastened to the davit, or upper block, leaving two or three feet slack (fig. 28). As the boat descends the lock is thrown back clear of the hook.

Or the locks can be thrown back by hand, if desired (fig. 29).

The piece of rope shown in fig. 25 can be withdrawn in both ways described above.

When possible, the fore and aft line should be hooked on before the falls are tautened and the boat raised. Should the boat be raised without the fore and aft line being attached, the boat must be temporarily hung one end by means of the man rope or boat rope, and the fall slackened; then the lanyard in the centre loosened, and, after hooking ends on, be hauled taut, and made fast. The loose end of the lanyard should be tied to the seat, to prevent the line falling out of the boat.

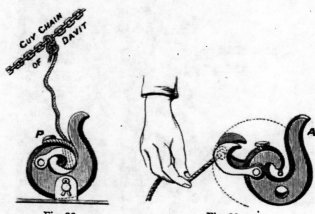

Fig. 28.　　　　Fig. 29.

It is not necessary to use the fore and aft line when the ship is at anchor, but it should be always on at sea, *to prevent one end of the boat unhooking before the other.*

The lowering gear (fig. 31) consists of a simple method of "*marrying*" the falls together, so that one cannot run out without the other, and therefore the boat must descend on an even keel. The two falls are run from the davits over rollers or thumb blocks fixed on the top of the bulwark of a ship in the ordinary way (fig. 31, *cc*), and then passed together, side by side, over and under small revolving rollers fixed on a plate attached to the inside of a ship (fig. 31 *b*). The result of this is that when the boat is being lowered, should a foul take place in either tackle, the other will not unreeve itself or run out, and the boat must remain fast. By this arrangement, the friction, combined with the *adhesion* or *sympathy* between the two ropes, is so complete, that a single man is able to work both falls together, either on board the ship or in the boat itself, and besides that, he may with perfect safety discard one rope or fall altogether,

TO FASTEN THE FORE AND AFT LINE FOR SEA USE.

Fig 30.

THE LOWERING GEAR.

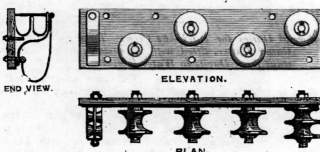

END VIEW.

ELEVATION.

PLAN.

Fig. 31.

and lower the boat with the remaining one alone.   The two
falls, before passing into the *"marrying plate,"* are separated
by a double crutch, as shown.

This lowering gear does not in any way interfere with
the ordinary method of raising the boat from the water, as
the falls are thrown out of the *"marrying plate"* in a
moment.   When the boat is hauled up, the falls are again
passed into the *"marrying plates,"* and the boat is again
ready for lowering.

By this method of lowering boats, it is impossible for a
foul at either of the blocks at the davit heads, a place
almost inaccessible to sailors in a heavy sea, except at great
risk.   The foul will always occur at the *"marrying plate,"*
which anybody on board can readily clear.

Extra Subjects.

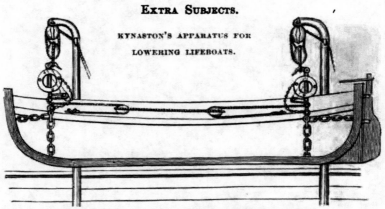

KYNASTON'S APPARATUS FOR
LOWERING LIFEBOATS.

*Special Duties for Lifeboat's Crew.   Twenty-five feet, ten
Oared Cutter, fitted with Kynaston's Hooks.   Jackstays from Davits to Water-line, &c.*

First hands up slip gripes.   Each man on entering the
boat will put his cork jacket on, and take his place on his
respective thwart as quickly as possible.

Stroke-Oarsmen see plug in, safety-pins out of after-
hook, and attend after-lizard.

Bowman.—Out safety-pins of foremost-hook, attend boat-
rope, and see it ready for slipping, boat-hooks ready for
use.

Second thwart attend lizard.

Coxswain.—Have whip clear for slipping, and ship "tiller." The rest of boat's crew sit down and hold on to "life-lines."

At evening quarters pins are taken out, plugs put in, and the boat-ropes seen into the boat, and clear from forward.

Life Belt.

On getting into the boat each man should put his life belt on as quickly as possible, putting his right arm through shoulder-strap No. 1, and his left arm through shoulder-strap No. 2; dipping his head through the cross, No. 3,

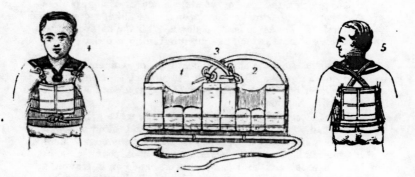

having the corks outside; bringing the strings round and tying them in front, which will cause the belt to close.

Figure 4 shows the belt tied in front.

Figure 5 shows it as it appears behind.

The life belts supplied to Her Majesty's ships weigh five pounds, have a buoyancy of twenty pounds, and are capable of supporting one man.

Extra Questions.

Q. How would you haul a boat up on a beach, or launch one?

A. All boats ought to be fitted with a hole in the fore foot, about 1 in. in diameter, for the purpose of placing an iron bolt or a strop to hook a tackle to, or bend a rope's-end, for the purpose of hauling her up.

Before leaving the ship to haul a boat up on a beach to scrub her bottom, or for any other purpose, see a boat's anchor and a luff-tackle in the boat, place her thwarts or stretchers under her keel, bury her anchor in the beach well up, bend a rope's end to the ring of it, and make a long strop, so as to allow sufficient drift to hook the tackle to a strop round the iron bolt in the hole in the fore foot of the boat, or to a strop rove through it; hook the single block of the luff to the strop secured to the ring of the anchor, and the double block to the strop in the fore foot of the boat, man the tackle, leaving sufficient number of hands each side of the boat to keep her in an upright position, and walk her up (*see plate, page* 246).

To prevent the anchor coming home or rising, place a stretcher or an oar under the upper arm or fluke, and station a couple of hands to keep it down. This also applies to launching a boat which has been left high and dry by the tide.

Never attempt to haul a boat up, or launch one, by clapping a number of hands on her painter, as it only tends to bury her bow in the sand or mud, and you stand a chance of starting her stem.

If not fitted with a hole in the fore foot, make a rope fast round her stern, well down to the keel, and hitch it round the bow, and hang it by a rope's-end over the boat to keep it from falling under the keel, to which hook your tackle, or bend a rope's-end to it, and clap all hands on it, leaving a sufficient number of hands each side of the boat to keep her in an upright position.

Q. When laying on your oars under sail, what precaution would you take?

A. Heave them out of their rowlocks, and let them rest abaft on the gunwale.

Q. What ought the crew to do in the event of a boat being capsized or swamped?

Q. As a rule, everyone should remain by her, as she will assist those that cannot swim to keep afloat, and those that can swim will, with the help of the boat, be able also to render valuable assistance, and insure confidence to the former.

Never go away in a boat without your shoes, as it will give your ship a slovenly name, as also smoking in a boat, lounging on the gunwale, hailing a ship or boat in passing, or the shore. STRICT SILENCE should always be observed, for the credit of the ship you belong to.

Never leave a boat without leave, and never sit on the gunwale.

If a boat has stern way, put the helm the opposite way you wish her head to go, as it has the opposite effect to what it has in head way.

If sent to another ship on duty in charge of the boat, deliver your message, and return to your boat immediately. If required to remain alongside in a tide way, make fast to the swinging boom, unless ordered to lay off on your oars.

Always clearly understand a message you are to convey, also the answer given, before leaving the respective ships.

If under sail, and meeting another boat on opposite tacks, the boat on the port tack gives way to the boat on the starboard tack; that is, she passes to leeward of her; boats going free, or running before the wind, give way to boats on a wind.

If sent to convey stores or luggage keep the weights as much amidships as possible; above all things see the well clear, ready to bale the boat out if required.

Before going alongside of a ship under weigh or hove to, observe if she has head or stern way.

Never overload a boat, more particularly with men or sand; the former may be attended with loss of life, and it should always be remembered that sand is much lighter when dry than when wet.

A boat fast to the swinging boom, or astern, may be kept clear of the ship by making a wash deck bucket fast overboard to her stern.

If going up a river, where a bridge is too low to admit of your passing under, or any weight that cannot be moved, and it only requires a foot or some inches for the gunwale of the boat to clear, take the plug out, and sink her to the required distance.

If in charge of a boat under sail, get your oars out directly the wind falls light; nothing denotes laziness so much as to see a boat drifting about under canvas waiting for a breeze.

Always learn your boat's recall, which in well regulated ships is painted on a board; also the general recall, secured in a safe place in the boat, sometimes on the back-board.

When in charge of a boat watering with casks, or taking

in provisions, always, if possible, stow the midship casks with slings on, ready for hoisting out.

Never take more in a boat than she will carry; great judgment is required, whether in loading a boat with luggage, provisions, or water, not to risk the safety of the boat or crew.

If watering from the beach, keep the end of the suction hose in a tub, or a piece of rag round the brass strainer on the end of the suction hose, as the least thing drawn in, such as small gravel, will choke the valves and stop the work.

If sent to take another boat in tow, pull well ahead clear of her oars without fouling her, and directly you have the end of her painter inboard and secured, give way; when well done it causes no delay; but should you pull alongside of her, or get athwart-hawse, you considerably delay the work, and in many instances lose more ground than you can possibly gain for some time again.

In a cutter, or any large boat, if sent to weigh an anchor or any heavy thing over the stern, place the rope over the roller fitted to the gunwale, and ship the awning stanchion over it, which is fitted with two legs, so as to prevent the possibility of its slipping, flying over the quarters, and capsizing the boat; also take care to keep your crew well forward, to counterbalance the weight brought on the stern.

Paddle-box boats are stowed upon the tops of the paddle-boxes, and are most useful in embarking or disembarking troops, baggage, coaling, or for provisioning and watering ship.

Q. How are boats built ?

A. All cutters, gigs, and small boats are generally clinker, commonly called clinker-built boats.

Launches, pinnaces, barges, and paddle-box boats are either carvel or diagonally-built boats.

Q. What is a clinker, or clinker-built boat?

A. Where the lower end of one plank in the side of a boat overlaps the next plank below it.

Q. What is a carvel-built boat?

A. When the planks lie in a fore and aft direction flush with each other, the edges close together, and caulked to make them water-tight.

Q. What is a diagonally-built boat?

A. A diagonally-built boat resembles a carvel-built boat, only the planks lie obliquely across the boat's timbers, instead of fore and aft.

Q. What wood are boats built of?

A. In the Navy they are built of elm or mahogany; light gigs are built of fir.

Q. Name the purchases used for hoisting boats in and out?

A. For a launch, a regular purchase is fitted, called the launches purchase, consisting of a runner and tackle at the yard-arms.

Stay-tackles, fitted with a span between the fore and main mast, and the fore and main tackle to the lower pendants or preventers.

Q. How do you secure the lower yards for hoisting a launch in or out?

A. The top burtons are hooked to the lower cap and the lower yard-arms, to assist the lifts, taking care to have an equal strain on each; luffs are hooked as rolling tackles to the quarter strops on the lower yards, and to strops round the hounds of the lower masthead, to strengthen the yard in the bunt and assist the trusses.

Q. What precaution would you take before hoisting a launch, or any other heavy boat in?

A. Pass all the movable gear out of her.

Q. What purchase is used for hoisting a pinnace or barge in?

A. Yard and stay-tackles.

Q. In hoisting a boat in, in a sea way, when there is a motion, or a ship is rolling, what precaution ought to be taken?

A. A luff-tackle should be hooked in a fore and aft direction, the fall led in on the forecastle, and steadied well taut, to keep her from surging; a sufficient number of men should be stationed in the boat, to keep her clear of the ship's side and sheet anchor.

Q. Name the principal parts of a boat?

A. Keel, keelson-board, stem, stem-board, sternpost, and sternboard; rudder-irons, knees, timbers, thwarts, stern-sheets, head-sheets, gunwale, thole-pins or rowlock-holes.

III. Fitting Rigging.

With an eye splice.
With a fork and two lashing eyes.
With a throat seizing on a bight.
With a cut splice.
With a horse-shoe splice.
Cutter stay fashion.
With end turned up.

With wooden dead-eyes.
With iron dead-eyes (new pattern).
Topgallant and royal rigging and stays.
Blocks where single strops are used.
Blocks where double strops are used.

Where two single blocks are used.
Clothing a bowsprit.
Fitting bobstays.
Rigging a lower yard.
Rigging a topsail yard.
Rigging an upper yard.

With an Eye Splice.

To splice an eye in standing rigging of hemp or wire rope with three or more strands.

To Splice an Eye in a Three-Stranded right-handed Rope.

A. Bend the end of the rope down, having first opened the strands (as in fig. 1), leaving the middle strand on top of the rope. The middle strand is forced under any convenient strand in the rope (according to the size of the eye required) from right to left (as in fig. 2).

The left-hand strand is then forced from right to left, over one strand and under the next on the left (as in fig. 3).

Now turn the rope round to the left, so as to bring the remaining or right-hand strand on top of all (as in fig. 4).

The right-hand strand is then forced from right to left under the strand of the rope immediately on the right of the one the first or middle strand was placed under (as in fig. 5).

In placing this strand, if a half turn is taken out of it, it will lay closer.

In completing the splice it is immaterial which strand is used first, as each is taken over one strand of the rope, and under the next one.

In large ropes each strand is halved before being spliced in, to form the second layer.

In a left-handed rope the strands are put in from left to right.

To Splice an Eye with more than Three Strands.

The second strand from the left is forced from right to left under any convenient strand (as in figs. 2 and 6).

The left-hand strand is then forced under the same strand and also under the next one on the left, thus laying under two strands, then turn the rope over as in fig. 4, work each of the remaining strands in as the right-hand strand of the three-stranded rope, (fig. 5.) working round towards the right hand, each strand is then halved and the splice finished as before.

With a five-stranded rope, the centre strand of the five is forced under the most convenient strand, then the next strand on the left under one, and the left-hand strand of all under two strands, as in fig. 6, then the two right-hand strands as before.

In splicing wire rope, as soon as one layer is finished, a temporary seizing of spun yarn must be put round everything before dividing the strands, ready for the next layer.

Each strand is put in three times in order to taper the splice down better.

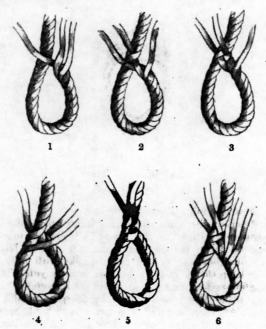

1   2   3

4   5   6

With a Fork and two Lashing Eyes.

Is made like an eye-splice; it is used in fitting lower and topmast.stays. A piece of the rope intended for the stay is cut off according to the length of eye required, allowing sufficient length on both ends, one end to be tucked once and a half in the rope where you intend to form the fork; the strands are scraped and marled down ready for serving over. A Flemish eye is formed in the other end, and a corresponding Flemish eye is also formed in the end of the stay for lashing abaft the mast, as shown in the plate. It is wormed, parcelled, and served over. The shoulders of the Flemish eyes and of the fork are cavilled or shouldered over, which is to pass layers of spunyarn down each side of the crutch of the fork and eyes, to preserve the rope and prevent the wet from entering.

Fork Splice (for Stays).

Q. How do you splice wire rope?
A. Precisely the same as splicing hemp rope, only taking the precaution when the marline-spike is entered under the strands you wish to put your first tuck into to beat the strands on either side of the marline-spike with a hammer, so as to keep them open, or else, as soon as you withdraw the marline-spike, before you could possibly enter the end of your strand, the opening made by the spike would close; when the strand is entered, a hemp strand, kept ready for the purpose, is dogged round it, brought to the windlass bolt,

and set well taut, heaving the strand close in place, taking great care your strand, being hove in, is kept quite straight; once kinked it could never be straightened again. The ends are generally put in once, two-thirds, and one-third, as it cannot be tapered down like hemp. The windlass bolt is a bar of iron, stuck in the stool, used by riggers for splicing. It is worked in a similar way to hemp rigging, and with equal ease. Non-riggers are getting familiar with it.

In splicing an eye with more than three strands, the second left-hand strand is tucked from right to left under the first convenient strand.

With a Throat seizing on the Bight.

A throat seizing on the bight is sometimes used as a temporary seizing. The rope to be used is middled, and the ends passed through the bight, a sufficient number of turns are passed, say 7 or 8, and riding turns are passed back towards the bight, both ends are then expended in cross turns and secured with a reef knot.

With a cut Splice.

Cut Splice, 1st.

Cut Splice, 2nd.

R 3498.

S

A cut splice is sometimes used to form the collar in the bight of a rope to be fitted for pendants, jib guys, breast back stays, odd shrouds, and various other purposes.

To make the Splice.

Middle the rope, cut it in two at the centre of the bight. Mark each piece of rope to the length you intend the eye or collar to be, lay the ends across the opposite standing parts, open the strands to the required length for making the splice, then proceed as if making an eye splice ; the ends are put in once.

With a Horse-Shoe Splice.

It is so named from resembling a horse-shoe in shape, and is used for joining topmast shrouds or backstays when there is an odd one of a side, and it is desired to form an eye on the bight; it is also used sometimes for jib-guys. It is formed by splicing the two ends of a piece of rope into the topmast shroud or backstay, one end on either side of the bight ; where the eye is to be formed, the strands are entered once and a half, marled down, and served over. The length of the piece of rope to be used for this purpose is one-third the length of the eye required, allowing twice the round of the rope on each end in addition for splicing. The ends are tucked under the strands in splicing, exactly the same as when forming an eye-splice.

Horse Shoe Splice.

Cutter Stay Fashion.
COMMON DEAD EYES.

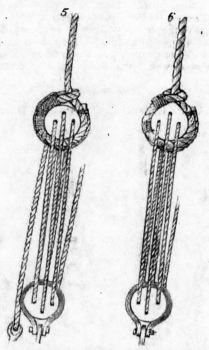

5. Cutter Stay Fashion (Racking Seizing).
6. Cutter Stay Fashion (Throat and Quarter Seizings).

A. After all the shrouds are over the masthead, and steadied taut alike by means of strands round the shrouds, and rove through the lower dead-eyes with as much strain as they will bear, mark the rigging off for turning in as follows:— Put a mark on the foremost and after shroud about 6 ft. from the channels, fasten a line to the mark on the foremost shroud, haul it taut aft, and secure it to the mark on the after shroud, then mark each shroud where the line cuts, which will be for the lower part of the dead-eye, then put another mark below it, at the distance of half the round of the dead-eye, and once the round of the rope, which will be the mark for the nip or crown of the dead-eye ; then bring the end round the standing part of the shroud so as to have the marks in their proper places, the ends of the shrouds in and aft, and heave the two parts together, as close as the standing part of the shroud will allow, by means of a Spanish windlass, put a rope-yarn strop to keep them in place, and then put the seizings on, place the dead-eye, and beat the nip of the shroud well down, this is done by putting a good

With end up.

DEAD EYES.   PATENT DEAD EYES.

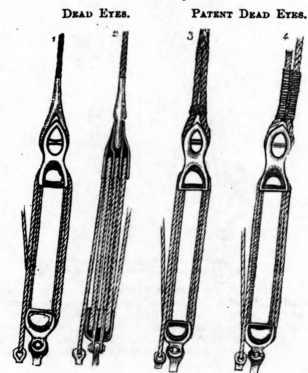

1. Front View. ⎱ Spliced in.
2. Side View. ⎰
    3. Splice and Seizing.
4. End turned up (Racking Seizing).

strand over the nip and beating it down with a commander, until the shroud takes the score of the dead-eye in all parts.

N.B.—In Portsmouth Yard a racking seizing is now used, instead of a throat and quarter-seizing, as formerly.

Topgallant and Royal Rigging and Stays.

Q. How do you rig a topgallant and royal mast ?

A. Topgallant rigging is placed over a funnel, which is made of copper to fit above the hounds of the topgallant-mast; being of a smooth surface, it does not chafe the eyes of the rigging.

HEART.

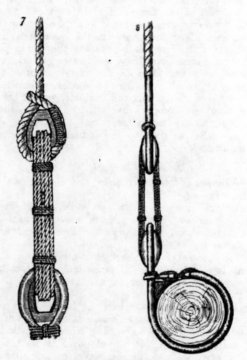

7. For Lower Stays (Side View).
8. Fore Stay Collar Lashed on the Bowsprit (Front View).

To rig a Fore Topgallant Funnel.

Send the gantlines down before all, and make it fast to the stays, about 6 ft. below the funnel, stop it to the funnel; pull up on the gantline, and place the funnel over the hole in the topmast cap, in readiness to receive the topgallant-mast, stop the stays to the cross-trees; send the gantlines down abaft the top for the starboard pair of shrouds, place them over the funnel, then send the port pair of shrouds up and place them; then the starboard pair of backstays, then the port pair of backstays and place them.

The main and mizen topgallant masts are rigged in a similar way, with the omission of a flying jibstay.

Main and mizen royalstays are now rove through sheaves in the after-part of the fore and main topmast crosstrees. Iron jacks, or arms, are also fitted to the lower rim of topgallant funnels. The fore has six, the main five, and the mizen two. On the fore the blocks for the flying-jib halyards, fore top-gallant-buntlines, and the topgallant studding-sail-halyard, are shackled to the four foremost ones, Jacob's ladder being shackled to the two after ones. On the three foremost lugs of the main, the main topgallant buntlines, and topgallant studdingsail halyard-blocks, are shackled, Jacob's ladder to the two after ones. The mizen Jacob's ladder is shackled to the two lugs which are on the after part of the funnel.

Royal Funnels.

A royal funnel is made of copper, and similar in shape to a topgallant funnel.

A false royal masthead is fitted to go far enough down the funnel to be secured by screws; it is in every way the shape of the royal masthead, fitted with the lightning conductor, and a hole for the spindle.

Place the royalstays and backstays on the funnel, reeve the signal halyards and put the truck on. Send it up, and place it over the topgallant funnel, ready to ship on the head of the mast.

Sway on the mast-rope, when the head of the mast is through the topgallant funnel, place the royal funnel and truck, and reeve the royal halyards; when the mast is high enough, settle the topgallant funnel down in its place, and when the sheave is above the cap, reeve the topgallant yard-rope; shackle the span-blocks for topgallant studdingsail halyards and Jacob's ladder, abaft to all the jacks attached to the funnel. The spindle goes with a screw into the false masthead.

N.B.—In most cases the flying-jib halyards block-strop is worked round the chafing grommet when the funnel is not fitted with jacks.

A fore topgallant stay is rove through the dumb-sheave in the jib-boom end, through the dolphin-striker, and set up to one of the knight-heads.

The main and mizen are led through a hole in the lower caps, and set up, the mizen in the main, and the main in the fore-top.

The fore royalstay is rove through the dumb-sheave in the flying jib-boom end, through the lower part of the dolphin-striker, and, like the topgallant stay, is set up to one of the knight-heads.

The main and mizen are rove through a sheave in the after part of the main and fore-topmast crosstrees, and set up to a thimble secured to the eyes of the lower rigging, the mizen in the main, and the main in the foretop.

Blocks where Single Strops are used.

Nearly all blocks are stropped with a single strop, such as blocks of luffs, up and downs, &c.

Blocks where Double Strops are used.

Lower brace blocks, upper jeerblocks, screw purchase blocks, cat blocks, &c.

Blocks where Two Single Strops are used.

Topsail brace blocks, lower jeer blocks, &c.

Q. How do you clothe a bowsprit?

A. On whichever plan a bowsprit is rigged, the rule is, the clothing is commenced at two-thirds the length of the bowsprit from the knight-heads, but owing to the long bows ships now have, this must depend on the length of the cut-water.

There are two plans for clothing a bowsprit—viz., heart plan, or the strop or bale-sling plan.

HEART PLAN.

This plan is generally adopted in Portsmouth Dockyard.

Inner bobstay collar.
Inner bowsprit shroud collar.
Inner forestay collar.
Middle bobstay collar.
Outer bowsprit shroud collar.
Outer forestay collar.
Outer bobstay collar.

N.B.—The bobstay collars are placed the diameter of the bowsprit apart.

Strop or Bale-sling Plan.

Inner forestay collar.	Outer bowsprit shroud
Inner bowsprit shroud collar.	collar.
Inner bobstay collar.	Middle bobstay.
Outer forestay collar.	Outer bobstay collar.

In this way the forestay is placed inside, for convenience in removing the collar if necessary.

An extra bobstay is fitted, reaching from the lower stem-hole to the bowsprit, just inside the cap called the cap-bobstay.

In rigging a bowsprit, the first thing to be done is to rig a stage for the men to work on, as follows:—Take two top-mast studdingsail-booms, or any other spars of that description, rig them out of the head-port over the rail, hook the double block of a luff to the cap of the bowsprit, and the single block to a lashing on the end of the spars; haul them out, and secure their heels on the headrails; lash a third spar across the outer ends, to keep them open, and secure them to the end of the bowsprit by a lashing. Lash two planks athwart them, one near the inner, the other near the outer end of the spar; then lay as many planks as required to form a platform, nailing them for security to the two athwart-ship planks.

The bowsprit is supported at the hole in the bows, which it passes through by wedges, the same as the lower masts are at the partners; it is also secured by chain or rope gammonings, two in number, inner and outer gammonings, which are passed over the gammoning-fish, on the bowsprit, and through holes in the stem.

The gammoning-fish or saddle is well tarred, the ends of the chain are passed over the bowsprit from the starboard side, through the holes in the stem, and over the bowsprit, and shackled to their own parts underneath; the turns are then passed with the other ends, so that the foremost ones on the bowsprit are the after ones in the stem; each turn is hove taut, as it is passed, by reeving the gammoning through snatch-blocks made fast to the bobstay-holes on the cutwater, bringing the bight through the hawse-hole, and toggling on to tackles led from the capstan.

Before coming up the tackles, the chain is secured, by nails driven through it, into the fish or gammoning pieces,

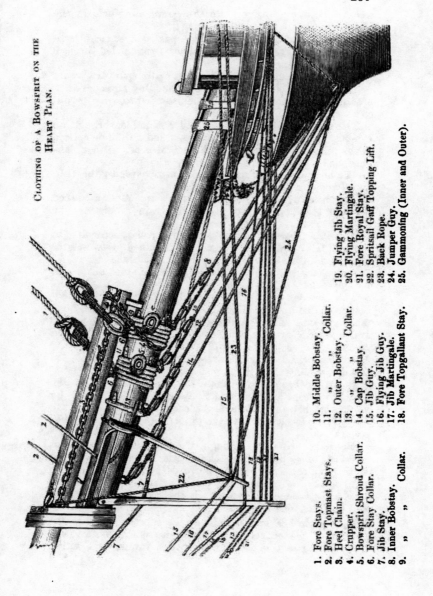

CLOTHING OF A BOWSPRIT ON THE HEART PLAN.

1. Fore Stays.
2. Fore Topmast Stays.
3. Heel Chain.
4. Crupper.
5. Bowsprit Shroud Collar.
6. Fore Stay Collar.
7. Jib Stay.
8. Inner Bobstay. Collar.
9.   „   „   Collar.
10. Middle Bobstay. Collar.
11.   „   Outer Bobstay.   Collar.
12. Outer Bobstay.   Collar.
13.   „   Cap Bobstay.
14. Cap Bobstay.
15. Jib Guy.
16. Flying Jib Guy.
17. Jib Martingale.
18. Fore Topgallant Stay.
19. Flying Jib Stay.
20. Flying Martingale.
21. Fore Royal Stay.
22. Spritsail Gaff Topping Lift.
23. Back Rope.
24. Jumper Guy.
25. Gammoning (Inner and Outer).

also by the wedges driven into the gammoning-hole in the stem.

The last turns are frapping turns, passed over some well-greased hide, and set up by a tackle or a runner led through a block on the bumpkin.

In rope-gammoning, racking turns with spunyarn would be used, instead of nails. Chain-gammoning stretches after much use, and should therefore be attended to, when about to set up rigging.

The man-ropes are spliced round a thimble, through an eye-bolt each side of the bowsprit-cap, and a thimble spliced in the other ends, to set up to the knight-heads with a lan-yard, and attached to the forestay by stirrups.

The bowsprit is secured outside downwards by the bob-stays, and sideways by the shrouds.

The forestays pull upwards, and are always placed between two bobstays, so as not to strain or distress the bowsprit.

The inner bobstay or inner forestay collar, according to the plan the bowsprit is to be rigged, is lashed on two-thirds the length of the bowsprit from the knight-heads.

All collars, before being placed, are well fidded out. The bobstay-collars are lashed on top.

The forestay-collars below, and the bowsprit shroud-collars on the quarter of the bowsprit, the lashings are hove taut by means of a Spanish windlass; when all the collars are in place, cleats are nailed to keep them from shifting in or out.

In some cases they are fitted without being lashed, the thimble reeving through its own part.

Bowsprit-shrouds are usually of chain, secured to the collar by a rope lanyard, and to the eye-bolt in the bow by a slip; all bobstay collars are placed the diameter of the bowsprit apart, which leaves a proper distance for the other collars.

Bobstays are rove through the hole in the cutwater, middled, and spliced, and the hearts seized in, ready for setting up, the drift for the lanyards between the heart in the bobstay, and the heart in the collar is, for the inner bob-stay, the diameter of the bowsprit, the middle one 3 ins. less, and the outer one 6 ins. less.

The lanyard is half the size of the bobstay; if wire, the lanyard of the bobstay is the same size as the bobstay, and the standing part is made fast with a running-eye, either

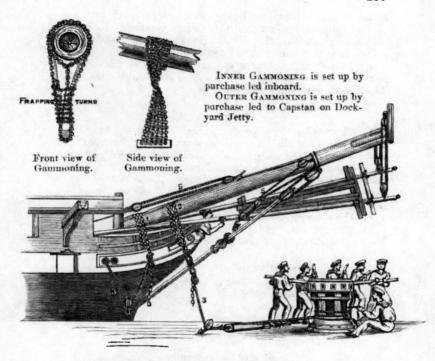

FRAPPING TURNS

Front view of
Gammoning.

Side view of
Gammoning.

INNER GAMMONING is set up by
purchase led inboard.
OUTER GAMMONING is set up by
purchase led to Capstan on Dockyard Jetty.

GAMMONING A BOWSPRIT, AND SETTING UP A BOBSTAY.

round the bowsprit close to the collar, or round the heart in
the collar ; reeve as many turns as you can without riding,
well tar and grease them, hook the double block of a luff, to
a strop round both parts of the bobstay near the cutwater,
and the single block to the lanyard, bring the end of the fall
through a block hooked to a strop round the bowsprit, haul
through the slack, and make a cat's-paw in it, hook the
double block of another luff to it, and single block to the
knight-heads, and haul every turn taut.

The standing parts of the lanyards should be made fast on
opposite sides alternately, so as to endeavour to keep the
blocks of the luff clear of each other in setting up.

After each bobstay has been drawn into place, shorten up for a final pull, and walk all three down together ; rack the turns, and pass the riders, rack these again, and when the last turn is taut, rack the end to the other part.

Sometimes the bobstays are set up on both ends of the lanyards, this is done by reeving one end through a leading block made fast round the bowsprit.

Bumpkins.

The bumpkins are stepped, one each side of the bows, to a beam fitted for the purpose, they are secured downwards and sideways by chain guys, shackled to the bows, and set up to the bumpkin-end, to eye-bolts attached to an iron band that is on the bumpkin-end, and clamped to one of the cross-beams of the head-rail ; it is tapered off at the end, to prevent the foretack blocks from slipping in.

Q. How do you get a bowsprit-cap on ?

A. Bowsprit-caps are put on and taken off with the jib-boom, in a similar way that a lower cap is with a topmast.

How do you Rig a Main Yard?

1st. Next the slings, on either side, jeer-blocks.
2nd. Topsail-sheets blocks.
3rd. Truss-strops.
4th. Clew-garnet blocks.
5th. Rolling tackle-strop.

At the Yard-Arm?

1st. Chafing-grommet.
2nd. Foot-ropes.
3rd. Head-earring strop.
4th. Jackstay.
5th. Yard tackle pendants.
6th. Brace-blocks.
7th. Lift-blocks.

Leech-Line Blocks.

There are two on each side of the yard, and the general rule for placing them is, the outer one is seized on the jack-stay, about 6 ft. inside the quarter iron; the inner one about the same distance outside the clew-garnet block ; but before seizing them on for a full due, their proper position should be determined on when the sail is bent.

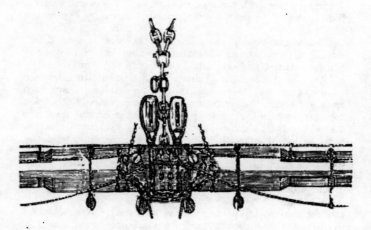

BUNT OF A LOWER YARD.

Slab-Line Blocks.

There are two on each side of the yard, fitted with tails, they are hitched to the jackstay, alongside the leech-line blocks. These blocks hang down before the yard, and abaft the courses.

There are two double blocks fitted also with tails, made fast to the jeer-block strops; they also hang down before the yard, and abaft the courses, to lead the slab-lines on deck.

Bunt Slab-Line Block

Is a single block fitted with a tail, made fast to the slings of the yard, and hangs down before the yard and abaft the course.

The only difference in rigging a main or fore yard is, a main yard has preventer brace-blocks on the fore side by which the yard is worked.

The jeer blocks are single thick, double-stropped, having long and short legs.

The blocks stand fore and aft on top of the yards, the two eyes of the strops are lashed the fore side of the yard, leaving sufficient room between the blocks for the slings, the lashing is passed rose-seizing fashion, and should be

half the size in circumference of the stropping of the block.
There are two such blocks on both the fore and main yards.
The crossjack yard is sent up and down by the mizen
Burtons.

The topsail-sheet, or quarter-blocks, are single thick,
double-stropped, stand athwartships under the yards outside
the jeer-strops, and are lashed on top of the yards.

The size of the lashing should be. half the circumference
of the strop, and is passed rose-seizing fashion ; there is a
span put round the strops, under the yards, above the blocks,
to keep them in their place ; the two eyes of the span are
lashed together. After passing sufficient number of turns,
take a half-hitch with the end of the lashing, round the
middle part of all turns of the lashing, expending the end
by passing frapping turns in a fore and aft direction round
the centre and both parts of the span.

The truss strops are usually of rigging chain ; they are
four in number, two for shackling the standing parts to, and
two for the hauling parts to reeve through ; they are lashed
on the same as rope strops, the starboard truss standing
part up and inside, the port truss standing part down and
outside.

The clew garnet-blocks are single stropped, standing
athwartships, and are lashed at twice the length of the block
outside of the truss-strop, the blocks underneath the yard a
little before the centre, so as to be clear of the topsail-sheets.
The size of the lashing should be one third the circumference
of the strop, and passed rose-seizing fashion.

Rolling-tackle strop is generally a grommet ; an eye is
formed in it and parcelled over on top of the yard, abaft the
jackstay, and then it is driven taut up on the quarter, at
two thirds out from the slings, to the quarter iron.

Lower-yard slings are two pieces of chain, the length of
each piece is about 2 ft. more than once the round of the
yard, more or less, according to the size of the yard; there
is a ring welded in one end of each piece, and a long link at
the other end, to receive the bolt of a shackle that connects
the slip; in reeving them round the centre of the yard the
ends with the rings come up the aft side, and the two ends
with the long links come up the fore side, and reeve through
the ring; the slings are hauled well taut, and seized to the
ring, taking care to keep the ring well forward ; a shackle
with its bolt through the two end links is connected to the
slings, the slip goes through the shackle ; the other end of

the slip is shackled to the two ends of a piece of chain called the masthead slings.

A chafing-grommet is a common grommet put on the yard-arm, and beat well down for the rigging to lay on.

Q. How are foot-ropes fitted ?—if to go over yard-arm with standing eye—if over goose-neck with a welded thimble.

A. Foot-ropes are rove through the stirrups, the eyes are put over the yard-arms, and beat well home, or a thimble over the goose-neck; the eyes of the stirrups are placed over the eye-bolts of the jackstay, which are previously well served or hitched with spunyarn; the thimbles in the other end of the foot-ropes are secured abaft the yard, in the bunt, to the slings. The length of the foot-rope, from the fork of the eye to the thimble, should be one foot less than the yard is from the centre to the shoulder of the yard-arm. It has been found convenient in large ships to put quarter foot-ropes, which, crossing the bunt from each quarter, enables the men to get a footing on that part of the yard.

Head-Earring Strop

Is a strop with a thimble seized in it, placed over the yard-arm, and beat well home to the foot-rope.

Jackstays.

The ends are rove through the eyebolt over the eyes of the stirrups, a thimble is then spliced in each end, the eyes over the yard-arm are beat well home to the head-earring strop, a lanyard half the size of the jackstay is placed in one thimble, and rove through the other, by which it is set taut up in the bunt of the yard; a space of at least 6 ins. is left between the two thimbles for this purpose.

N.B.—All jackstays on lower and topsail yards are now of wire rope, and the thimbles are seized, not spliced in.

Yard-Tackle Pendant.

In large ships they are fitted to remain on the yards, the eye is put over the yard-arm, and beat close home to the jackstay; in small ships they are fitted with a hook and thimble, and put on when required for use.

N.B.—Now the yard-tackle pendant is made of wire rope, it is fitted to a strop that goes over the yard-arm with union thimbles.

Brace Blocks.

Put the strop over the yard-arm, and beat it close home to the yard-tackle pendants, with the head of the pin of the block upwards. The yard-arm strops are single; those on the blocks are double, so that the blocks may lie horizontally. For greater ease in bracing up, the preventer blocks on the main yard are placed on the fore side.

Lift Blocks

Are single, and single-stropped. Put the strop over the yard-arm, and beat it close to the brace block.

Q. How do you rig a main topsail yard?

A. 1st. Tye-blocks are iron-bound, with swivel and lugs, and are connected by a bolt and forelock to an iron band round the yard, the ends of the bolts are covered with leather, and the edges of the iron stopping smoothed down, to prevent them cutting into the masts. Tye-blocks and boom-irons should always be fitted to spare yards.

2nd. Parrel.

3rd. Quarter-blocks. These are double blocks, for the topsail clew-line and topgallant-sheet to lead through, single strop lashed outside parrel, and on top of the yard, lashing half the size of strop.

4th. Rolling tackle strop, is a grommet-strop made round the yard, with a thimble seized in it, and is placed half way out from the centre of the yard to the shoulder or cleat.

A pendant, for sending the topsail-yard up and down, is fitted with a running-eye round the quarter of the topsail-yard, the other end has an eye spliced in it; it is well parcelled for hooking the sail tackle to, and is lashed close outside the quarter-strop, on the opposite side of the yard.

At the Yard-Arms.

1st. Chafing grommet, fitted the same as lower yard.

2nd. Foot-ropes, fitted with an eye to go over the yard-arms, and beat close home to the chafing-grommet; an eye spliced in the other end, and seized to the opposite quarter of the yard; sometimes the outer eye goes over the goose-neck instead of the yard-arm; when fitted this way an additional stirrup is required on the shoulder of the yard-arm.

3rd. Head-earring strop, fitted the same as a lower yard.

4th. Jackstay, fitted the same as lower yard.

5th. Brace-blocks. The strop is put over the yard-arm and beat close home to the jack stay.

6th. Lift-blocks, if double lifts; if single lifts, the standing part of lift; in the case of single lifts, the eye goes over the yard-arm close to the brace-block; in the case of double lifts, the strop of the block goes over the yard-arm, and is beat close home to the strop of the brace-block.

7th. Second reef-tackle block. The blocks on the topsail-yards for the second reef-tackle are attached to the strop with union thimbles, the strop going with lashing eyes round the yard-arm outside all rigging.

8th. Flemish horse. A thimble is spliced in the outer end which goes over the goose-neck, an eye is spliced in the inner end and is seized inside the shoulder, at the distance of once and a half the length of the yard-arm from the shoulder. Not required when foot ropes go to goose-neck.

Topsail-yards (now that reef-beckets have come into general use) are fitted with two jackstays, so that by having two rows of toggles, the reef-beckets may be more clear of each other, when there are two or more reefs in.

The only difference in the rigging of a fore and main topsail yard is, there are no jewel-blocks to a main topsail-yard, now that main-topmast studdingsails are done away with in the Navy.

The difference in rigging a mizen topsail-yard from a main or fore is, the Flemish horse is fitted with clip-hooks to the eyebolt at the yard-arm, and the brace-blocks face forward.

A parrel to a topsail-yard is what a truss is to a lower yard, or a traveller on a boat's mast is to the yard of the sail it is hooked to. In consists of two pieces of rope which are wormed, parcelled, and served, and an eye spliced in each end; one piece is shorter than the other, and is placed, the centre of the short leg on top of the centre of the long leg, seize them together with two short flat seizings, fill up the cutling with strands, and cover the parrel with leather. When in use the parrel is placed abaft the topmast, taking care to have the seam of the leather outside. The long legs are passed underneath the yards, up before all, and lashed to the short legs with a piece of rope called a parrel lashing; in shifting topsail-yards, only one lashing is cast adrift, so the parrel always remains fast to the yard. A small greasy mat is secured to the yard between it and the mast. The length of the long leg, when fitted, will be from eye to eye, twice the round of the yard, and two thirds the round of the topmast; and the length of the short leg, when fitted from eye to eye, will be two thirds the round of the topmast; allowing four times the round of the rope on each leg for splicing the two eyes, will give the proper length to cut the rope for fitting a topsail parrel without waste; the ends are put in once and a half.

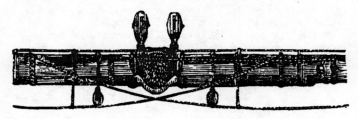

BUNT OF A TOPSAIL YARD.

Q. How do you rig a topgallant yard ?
A. 1st. The slings. Put a strop on the centre of the yard with a thimble seized in it.

2nd. The parrel.

3rd. Quarter blocks, which are double for the royal sheets and topgallant clewlines to reeve through.

4th. A grommet-strop, placed one third out from the centre with a thimble seized in it. Through this the lizard is rove when the yard-rope is stopped out.

At the Yard-Arms.

1st. The foot-ropes.

2nd. Head-earring strop.

3rd. The jackstay.

4th. Braces.

5th. Lifts.

The jackstay is secured to the yard by strips of leather nailed over it.

Royal yards are rigged in a similar way.

Topgallant Parrel.

A topgallant parrel consists of two strops, one long, and one short ; the long strop is spliced round the yard, and has two seizings on it, one close to the yard, the other to seize a thimble in. The short one is spliced round the yard with a thimble seized in it; they are served with spunyarn, and, like a topsail parrel, are covered with leather.

The long strop is put on the port side of the fore and mizen, and on the starboard side of the main topgallant yard. The parrel lashing is spliced in the eye of the long strop. When secured in place, the lashing comes on the quarter of the mast; pass three or four turns with the lashing through the thimbles of the strop, and hitch it round its own part.

To Fit the Parrel.

For the long strop. Take once the round of the yard, once the round of the mast, and once the round of the rope, which would be the length to marry the strop; then allow sufficient to splice it.

The short strop is spliced round the yard with a thimble seized in it.

The Length to fit it.

Take once the round of the yard, once the round of the thimble, and twice the round of the rope. The strands of the splice are put in once and a half, and served all over. The strops are spliced, served, and the seizings put on before placing them on the yard.

N.B.—A royal parrel is fitted in a similar way.

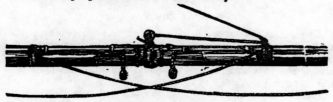

BUNT OF A TOPGALLANT YARD.

SETTING UP RIGGING.

(2.)

To be instructed in the method of setting up Rigging and staying Mast:—

Staying lower mast.	Setting up topmast rigging.	Marking rigging for ratlines.
Setting up lower rigging.	Setting up topgallant rigging and backstays.	Putting on ratlines.
Bringing to a lanyard.		Securing spars for sparring down.
Staying a topmast.	Setting up bobstays.	Commander.

EXTRA SUBJECTS.

SECTION IV.

Standing rigging is composed of pendants, shrouds, stays, and backstays; each mast is supported forward by stays, aft by backstays, and sideways by shrouds; the pendants are for applying extra purchases for additional support, staying the mast, or setting up the shrouds; the foremast is supported forward by the bowsprit, therefore the latter has an additional number of shrouds, bobstays, &c. to meet the strain thus brought on it.

Iron masts are rigged similar to wooden; iron yards occasionally have bands with eyes for lifts, braces, clew-garnets, &c.

Iron bowsprits are seldom or never used in the service, those ships that are supplied with iron masts, such as rams, have wooden bowsprits for running in, which are fitted as follows :—

Bobstay-chain—set up with slip and screw.

Bowsprit }
Shrouds }   do.   do.   do.

Heel-pendants—do.   do.   do.—Blocks iron 2 No.
Do. tackles 2 No.

To Rig a Lower Mast.

The masts are supposed to be placed in their proper positions by means of wedges driven in at the partners. A measuring batten is placed against the mast to indicate the stand, also to guard against bellying the mast in setting up the stays and shrouds.

Gantlines are always placed on the mastheads before the masts are stepped, to steady them when stepped until the runners and tackles are got up and steadied taut.

The Gantline blocks are lashed on either side of the masthead above the trestletrees; the top tackle falls are generally used as gantlines, a pair of man ropes are clove hitched on the bight round the masthead above the upper hoop, for the men to steady themselves with while working aloft, and placing the tops. *See* sketch.

Q. How do you get the lower crosstrees in place?

A. Supposing the foremost crosstree to be on the starboard side of the deck, the starboard gantline is bent to it amidships, on its upper side, and stopped to the port-arm three parts out.

When the arm is well over the trestletree, cut the stop and sway across. The after one is crossed in a similar way.

Q. How do you get a top over?

A. There is no rule for getting a top over either before or after the lower rigging, but it is much better to do it before, as it gives the men placing the eyes of the rigging a sure footing, more room to work, and less chance in letting things fall on deck.

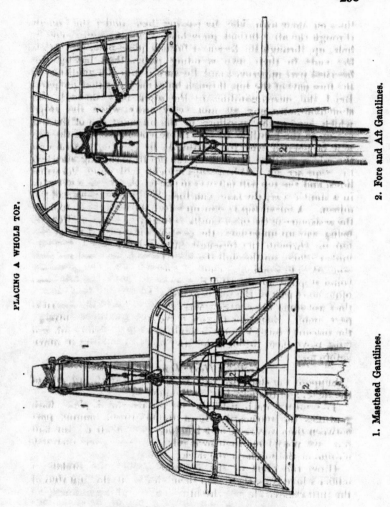

PLACING A WHOLE TOP.

2. Fore and Aft Gantlines.

1. Masthead Gantlines.

Sending a whole Top aloft—Main.

Stand the top abaft the mast on its after-edge, lower side facing forward, overhaul the gantlines down abaft all, the hauling parts being between the crosstrees, bend the gantlines on their own sides by passing them under the top, up through the after futtock plate-hole, down through lubber's-hole, up, through the foremost futtock plate-hole, and hitch the ends to their own standing parts, thus having the heaviest part uppermost and forward; stop the gantlines to the fore part of the top, through holes made for that purpose. Bend the mizen-gantline to the after part through the stanchion-holes, guy aft and sway away, when the stops which confine the gantlines to the foremost rim of the top are up to the gantline blocks, the foremost edge of the top will be pointed over the masthead; by keeping a strain on the mizen-gantline it will keep the top from canting aft when the stops are cut. When stops are cut pull up on the gantlines, and the top will fall over in place. A foretop is got over in a similar way, the main gantlines being used instead of the mizen. A mizen-top is sent up before the mast, so as to have the assistance of the main-gantlines to guy it clear, the after rim being sent up uppermost, the gantlines are passed under the top up through the foremost futtock-hole, down through lubber's-hole, up through the after futtock-hole, and the ends secured as in sending a main or fore top aloft, the gantlines being stopped to the after rim, so as to have the after and uppermost part of the top heaviest. In sending tops down, they are slung the contrary way, so as to have the heaviest part under; therefore if you reeve the gantlines through the foremost futtock-holes in sending a top up before all, you must reeve them through the after holes in sending it down before all.

Getting Half-Tops Over.

Suppose the starboard half to be on the starboard side of the deck, and the port-half on the port side.

To send the starboard-half over the masthead, place both gantlines the starboard side of the masthead, hauling part between the crosstrees, and bending parts abaft it; the half tops are placed on their own sides, foremast ends forward, bottom of the top next the deck.

Hitch the ends of the gantlines round the middle of lubber's-hole trap, then stop them down to the top rim, at the futtock-hole abreast the hitch; bend the mizen gantlines to the after part of the top through one of the stanchion-holes. Sway away, taking care to guy aft with the mizen gantlines clear of the after crosstree. When the half-top is above the crosstrees, it is easily placed in its proper position.

Placing Rigging over the Mast Head and Setting up.

Q. What are bolster-cloths?

A. Six parts of canvas, the length and breadth of the bolster, dipped in Stockholm tar and nailed on the bolster for the eyes of the pendants and rigging to rest on.

Q. How are shrouds numbered?

A. By knots in a rope yarn made fast to the crown of the eye, the first pair the starboard side has one knot; the first pair the port side has two knots, and so on, thus all the odd numbers will be the starboard shrouds, and all the even numbers the port shrouds. If the dead eyes are turned in, the starboard shrouds would easily be known from the port, and *vice versâ* by the seizings being aft, and the ends being inside and aft on both sides.

Q. How do you send the lower rigging over the masthead?

A. The gantlines are shifted to the after part of the trestletrees. A large toggle is seized on the end of each gantline to which a rounding line is bent. The starboard lower pendant is first sent up, a good temporary seizing is put on about three feet down the long or after leg, and instead of bending the gantline, the toggle is inserted under the seizing, and the upper part of the eye is stopped to the gantline. When the eye of the pendant is triced up to the gantline-block, the stop is cut, and the pendant is placed over the masthead, the seizing is cast off, and the gantline is rounded down by the rounding line, the port pendant is then sent up, then the first or foremost pair of shrouds the starboard side, then the first or foremost pair the port side, and so on, until all the rigging is over the masthead; in sending the shrouds up, the temporary seizing under which the toggle of the gantline is inserted, is placed about one-third down the shroud, and the gantline is stopped to the crown of the eye in a similar way to the lower pendants.

In large ships where the mastheads are very long, it is necessary to have a short gantline to assist the eye of the rigging over; which is lashed as high as possible up the lower masthead, and worked from the top, the hauling part of the gantline being dipped through the eyes of the rigging as soon as it is over the masthead.

When the lower pendants are in place, the runners should be triced up and lashed to the long or after legs, and the up and down tackles to the short or foremost legs, so as to get a good up and down pull to settle the pendants down in place, and make a foundation for the lower rigging; each pair of shrouds should be set up when placed over the masthead; in ships with nine shrouds of a side the single or after shroud is usually put on first; by so doing it gives more spread for the other shrouds, and the seizings lie clear of each other. There is also more certainty of placing the mast in the position you wish, if the after-swifters are put on the first thing after the pendants; and the mast placed by them and the runners. Before sending the lower pendants or shrouds aloft, open the eyes, which is done by lashing one side of the eyes to an eye-bolt, or any convenient place, and clapping a jigger on the other side, and haul the eyes sufficiently open to go over the masthead; by attending to this, it saves much time when the rigging goes aloft, as the men at the masthead have neither the means nor space to do it. After having got an up and down pull of the runners, pass a lashing across abaft the mast, from the after leg of one pendant, to the after leg of the other, carry the runners forward, and steady them hand taut.

Placing lower Stays over the Mast Head.

If for a foremast or mainmast, which have always two stays, send them up together by placing the upper one, which is always the starboard stay, upon top of the lower one, bend your gantlines to the fork of the stays, having first placed them fair with each other, and seize the two forks of the stays together, also put a good seizing on each side of the collars, about half way up (this applies to topmast stays also : for large ships, two seizings are put on each side of the collars), then put two seizings to the gantlines on each half-collar; when high enough, cut the seizings on the collar, lash the stays abaft the mast; they sometimes go over the foremast crosstree, so as to give more room for the lower yards to brace up. A mizenstay is sent up in a similar way.

' Q. For what reason are the lower and topmast stays put over the mastheads after the shrouds?

A. The lower the shrouds are placed, the sharper the yards will brace up. If the stays were placed over the masthead first, the eyes of the rigging would chafe the lashing of the eyes of the stays through, and the rigging would not lay snug.

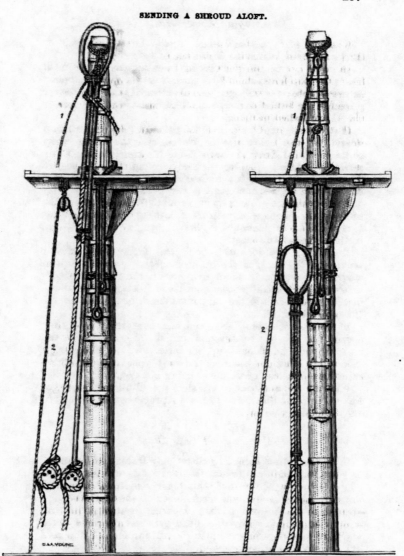

SENDING A SHROUD ALOFT.

1. Upper Gantline. 2. Lower Gantline.

Staying Lower Masts.

Runners and tackles lashed to the lower pendants or strops are used in staying lower masts.

In order not to run the risk of buckling the lower mast heads the purchases should be applied as far down the mast as practicable; for this purpose the long legs of the lower pendants are lashed together abaft the masts and the runner blocks are lashed to them.

If strops are used in lieu of the pendants, the upper strop should be just below the necklaces, and the lower strop about one third down the mast from the trestletrees. Care should be taken in placing the strops round the mast to put the after bight through the foremost on, this prevents the strops being nipped more in one part than another.

The advantage of using strops round the lower masts for securing the runners to, instead of lashing them to the long legs of the lower pendants, is, that it brings the strain more in the centre of the mast.

In staying the foremast, hook the single block of the tackle and the end of the runner to the bowsprit cap, in staying the mainmast to an eye bolt in the foremast head, or a strop round the foremast head, and in staying the mizen mast to an eye bolt in the mainmast head, or a strop round the mainmast head.

The purchases being in place and everything ready for staying the masts, the shrouds and all the gear abaft the masts should be slacked up, the after swifters being kept moderately taut, and eased as the mast goes forward, otherwise there is a risk of the mast being buckled.

The runners and tackles are then pulled up, the mast got forward into its place, and the stays properly secured before the shrouds are set up.

Turning in Lower Stays.

They are either turned in cutter-stay fashion, or on end.

When turned in cutter-stay fashion, hearts are used instead of dead-eyes; when on end, thimbles; sometimes the main-stays are passed round the cross-piece of the fore bitts, and secured to their own parts. Hearts are turned in and secured in a similar way that dead-eyes are in shrouds—the starboard stay the same as a starboard shroud, and the port stay the same as a port shroud.

Q. How are lanyards of lower stays rove?

A. Generally on the bight, and set up on both ends; sometimes they are only set up on one end, in which case the standing part of the lanyard is secured with a running eye round the underneath part of the lower heart.

When the hearts for the forestays are turned in on the bowsprit, with what is termed a long collar, the standing part of the lanyard of the stay is spliced in the lower heart. It is then rove in a similar way that a lanyard for lower rigging is, the hauling part of the lanyard on the standing part of the stay, each turn being placed in the notch or score in the heart. In large hearts there are four scores, and in small ones three, every turn is hauled well taut and is racked. After the riding turns are passed, the end is seized to its own part; three good spunyarn seizings are passed round the lanyard, at equal distances, to keep all parts in place.

Setting up Lower Stays.

When setting up with lanyards rove on the end, the same purchase is used as for setting up lower rigging, viz., up and down and luff; a boatswain's toggle is also used. Both stays should be set up at the same time, the luff being applied to a stay in a similar way that it is to a shroud, the single block well up the stay, hooked to a salvagee-strop, and the double block to the strop of the boatswain's toggle—the up and down to the fall of the luff.

The mast having been placed in the required position by the runners and tackles, the stays are set up until they have the strain of the mast.

When the lanyard is rove on the bight, top-Burton's, on luffs, are sufficient purchase. Great care must be taken to keep the eyes and lashing clear of each other at the mast-head; and the fork of the stays exactly middled. Men are stationed each side of the lubber's-hole with a strand, to keep the stays close to the crosstrees while setting up. If the seizings are well secured that are put on the forks of the stays before they are sent aloft, there is little fear of the stays getting out of place at the masthead when setting up; seizings thus put on have been known to last an entire commission, and not taken off until stripping the mast again.

Q. What size is a lanyard of lower stays in proportion to the stay?

A. Half an inch less than half the size of the stay.

Q. How many turns are there rove through a heart for securing lower stays?

A. Four lower turns, and three riding turns; should there be any end left after these turns are rove, it is expended in riding turns, if there is sufficient room left in the heart; the four lower and three riding turns generally fill the heart up.

Q. How are lanyards of lower stays rove?

A. Generally on the bight, and set up on both ends; sometimes they are only set up on one end, in which case the standing part of the lanyard is secured with a running eye round the underneath part of the lower heart.

When the hearts for the forestays are turned in on the bowsprit, with what is termed a long collar, the standing part of the lanyard of the stay is spliced in the lower heart. It is then rove in a similar way that a lanyard for lower rigging is, the hauling part of the lanyard on the standing part of the stay, each turn being placed in the notch or score in the heart. In large hearts there are four scores, and in small ones three, every turn is hauled well taut and is racked. After the riding turns are passed, the end is seized to its own part; three good spunyarn seizings are passed round the lanyard, at equal distances, to keep all parts in place.

SECURING THE LANYARD OF A FORE STAY.

Q. How do you send a lower cap up?

A. It is sometimes sent up before the lower rigging is put over the masthead, if after the lower mast is rigged; before the rigging is set up, so as to allow ample room for it to go through the lubber's hole; when one gantline only is used for sending the lower cap up, it is doubled by being rove through another block, the standing part being made fast to the masthead ; or both gantlines are shifted to the side of the mast you intend sending it up; there is sufficient room for it to lay in the fore part of the top, without in any way interfering with the rigging of the lower mast.

TO PUT A LOWER CAP ON.

(A Topmast is always used for this purpose.)

The cap is swayed out of the top, and hung above the eyes of the lower rigging with the top-Burton tackles fair for the topmast to enter, taking care the after part of the topmast is the same side as the top block is lashed ; hook the two up and down tackles to a strop round the heel of the topmast, to assist the hawser in swaying it up, put a small spar in the fid-hole, with a rope fast to it, so as to slew the mast as required. When the topmast is about 3 ft. through the fid-hole, slew it one square forward, then lash the cap to it with two pieces of rope, clove-hitched round the topmast-head, and through the eye-bolts in the cap, one forward and one aft each side, for the cap to go up square. When ready, bring the hawser to the capstan, heave round, and walk the up and downs up by hand at the same time. When the cap is above the lower masthead, slew the mast till the cap is fair for going on, then lower the mast, and the cap will go into its place, beat it well down with commanders, then make the end of the hawser fast to the foremost eye-bolt in the cap, keeping the weight of the mast in the tackles, unlash the top-block, and hook it to the after eye-bolt, in the cap on the opposite side to which the hawser is secured, take the lashing off the topmast-head and lower cap, and the up and down tackles off the heel, and the racking off the two parts of the hawser, put a gantline on the after-part of the topmast-head, ready for sending the topmast crosstree up ; sway the topmast for this purpose one-fourth up.

NOTE.—It is customary to fid the spare topmast first.

Q. How do you set up lower rigging ?

A. With an up and down and luff. The double block of the up and down is lashed to the short or foremost leg of the lower pendants, the single block is overhauled down ready to hook to the fall of the luff. The single block of

the luff is hooked to a salvagee-strop, which is put on the
shroud that is to be set up, about 10 ft. above the netting, a
strip of canvas having previously been placed round the
shroud to take the chafe of the salvagee-strop.

PLACING A LOWER CAP.

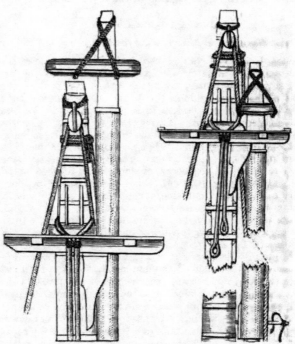

Bringing to a Lanyard.

If setting up with what is termed a boatswain's toggle,
the double block of the luff is hooked to a strop which goes
round both parts of the lanyard under the toggle.

A boatswain's toggle is simply a piece of hard round
wood; it is used by taking a round turn round it with the
lanyard; and then by taking two round turns round both
the parts of the lanyard, under the toggle, with a salvagee-
strop, taking care to have both parts of the strop on the
same side of the toggle.

This plan is much approved of by riggers, as the lanyard never jambs, nor do you run a chance of bursting the yarns of the lanyard.

Another plan, for setting lower rigging up, is by making a cat's-paw in the end of the lanyard, and hooking the double block of the luff to it, this plan is most objectionable, as the lanyard invariably jambs, and in many cases you burst the outside yarns of the lanyards; therefore, in all cases, a boatswain's toggle should be used.

Futtock Rigging

Is composed of iron rod and chain, the foremost shroud only being of chain, the remainder iron rods. The upper ends of the shrouds are fitted with legs to bolt to the futtock-plates, the lower ends are shackled to the necklace round the lower masthead, they are parcelled and served over with spunyarn; an iron Scotchman is seized to the shrouds of the lower rigging, in the wake of the futtock-rigging, to prevent it chafing.

When the futtock-plates are sent up, and rove down through their respective holes in the top rim, send the futtock-shrouds up one at a time and shackle them on in place.

Q. How do you send topmast crosstrees in place?

A. Gantlines are placed on the topmast-head for this purpose.

Send the end of the gantline down abaft the top, make it fast to the centre forepart of the crosstrees, bend an after-gantline to keep it clear of the top and lower cap, sway the crosstrees above the cap, slack the after-gantline, let the fore part rest against the mast, and the after part on the cap, make a rope fast to the after part of the crosstrees, and reeve it through the eye-bolt in the cap each side, and a man in the top to attend them to prevent them slipping off, lower the topmast, take the gantlines off the topmast-head. As the topmast goes down, the crosstrees will gradually come down on the lower cap in the right position to go over the topmast-head when the mast is again swayed up. The spare topmast is generally used for this purpose, and after the crosstrees are in place, the mast is swayed up, and fidded, to ascertain all is right; they are then sent down, and stowed in the booms or chains. The heel of the fore-topmast being taken aft, and the main and mizen forward.

SETTING UP RIGGING.

Topgallant and   Topmast   Lower Rigging.   Rattling Down.
Royal Breast   Backstay.
Backstay Purchase.

Q. How do you rig a topmast ?

A. Sway the mast up, so as to have the crosstrees about 4 ft. above the lower cap, and put the gantline or gantlines on for sending the topmast rigging up. There are two plans for sending topmast rigging over the topmast-head, either by putting a gantline and two man-ropes on the after part of the topmast-head, or by placing two gantlines on the after part of the tressletrees, and the man-ropes on opposite sides of the topmast-head.

Shackle the tye-blocks to the foremost legs of both the necklaces, and the jib halyard-block to the after-leg the starboard side, and topmast-staysail halyard or jibstay-block to the after-leg the port side of the fore-topmast necklace.

The jib and staysail halyard blocks are sometimes shackled to eye-bolts, driven up through the fore-part of the topmast tressletrees and crosstrees, and clenched above, which forms a much better lead ; it saves time to get the hanging-blocks in place, before sending or setting the topmast rigging up.

The iron binding of the blocks should be smoothed down at the edges, and the ends of the pins covered with leather, to prevent them cutting into the masts.

Nail the bolster cloths in place, the same as for the lower rigging, put the sail-tackle pendant round the topmast below the crosstrees.

The topmast rigging is fitted in the eyes, and the dead-eyes turned in the same as the lower rigging, the top-Burton pendant has only one leg of a side to hook the top-Burton to.

The topmast rigging is placed over the masthead the same as the lower rigging, after the Burton pendant is placed, the first pair of shrouds the starboard side, then the first pair the port side, so on until all the shrouds are in place ; then the first pair of backstays the starboard side, then the first pair of backstays the port side. Then the third and last pair of backstays, which is fitted with a single leg of a side and a horseshoe-eye, so the backstays shall lay fair on the quarter of the mast.

NOTE.—Single backstays, fitted with a horseshoe splice, are always put over the masthead first, after the shrouds, in Portsmouth Dock-yard, therefore they become the quarter backstays.

R 3498.   U

PLACING TOPMAST CROSSTREES.

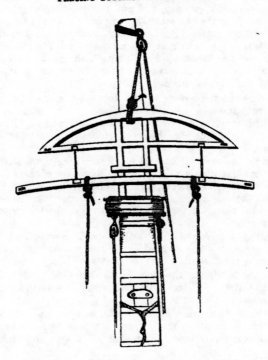

All backstays are now turned in alike, and set up with dead-eyes the same as the rigging, as quarter backstays.

There are always three of a side down to second class frigates, below that, only one pair of a side.

Breast or shifting backstays are done away with in the Navy, but if they should ever be used, after the topmast shrouds are placed, send the breast backstays up, which are one on each side; they are spliced together to form the eye.

Bend the gantline, on 3 ft. below the eye, the port side, and stop it along the starboard-leg, sway it up, and cut the stops as they come to the block, sending the starboard breast backstays down its own side; they are set up with a runner and tackle, instead of being set up, like the others, with dead-eyes.

In French ships of war the topmast breast-backstays are used instead of yard-tackle pendants and whips, having fiddle blocks seized in them for reeving the falls.

When required for hoisting boats in or out they are run out to the yard-arms, to the required distance, by a single whip, and secured round the yard-arm by a strop and toggle, thus doing away with the lumber on the main and foreyards of yard-tackle pendants and whips, leaving them much clearer for working studdingsails.

NOTE.—The "London," and "Princess Royal," when commanded by Captain (now Admiral) Sir Lewis Tobias Jones, in the Black Sea, had their topmast breast backstays fitted in this way.

When not in use as yard-tackle pendants and whips, the single blocks are hooked in the chains, the hauling part of the falls are hitched round the ass of the lower block, and coiled down, the standing part of the fall, which is secured by being hitched round the backstay above the fiddle-block, is cast off, rove through the pipe in the ship-side inboard, and used as a temporary hauling-part to set the backstay up, thus doing away with the necessity of having the whole length of the fall on the upper deck.

All backstays are usually served with sennit in the wake of the braces, so as to do away with the use of mats.

To send the Topmast-Shrouds over the Topmast-Head.

Bend the gantline 3 ft. below the eye-seizing, and stop it to the eye, pull up on the gantlines when the first seizing is up to the gantline-block, cut it, pull up again on the gantlines, and place the shrouds over the masthead.

The quarter backstays are then set up in the usual way, one pair of a side and set up with dead-eyes.

If you are sending the topmast rigging up by a single gantline on the after-part of the topmast-head, you must hang the shroud by the man-ropes, cast off the gantlines, unreeve it, dip it clear of the eye of the shroud, reeve it the reverse way, and pay it down for the next pair.

If you are sending the shrouds up by gantlines placed on the after tressletree, as soon as the second seizing is up to the gantline-block, reeve, if the starboard shroud, the port man-rope, which is placed on the topmast-head through the eye, and bouse it down in place; this latter plan, for small vessels, is much to be preferred, and in ships where the top-mast-heads are not too long, much time is saved in working the two gantlines.

In large ships, where the topmast rigging is very heavy, the single gantline on the after-part of the topmast-head is the best and easiest plan.

Funnels are used in small ships for the topmast rigging, the same as for topgallant rigging, only they are square instead of round.

Q. How are the lower dead-eyes for the topmast rigging fitted?

A. The lower dead-eyes of the topmast rigging are iron stropt, and, like the lower ones, swivel; they are connected to the necklace of the lower mast by the futtock shrouds.

It requires great care in placing the lower rigging, so the futtock rigging will lead clear between the lower shrouds without chafing them; but if the lower shrouds ride, there will be great difficulty in reeving them, and constant chafing afterwards.

Iron Scotchmen are placed on the lower rigging, so as to prevent chafing the lower shrouds.

Q. What is the difference in the fitting of the topmast shrouds?

A. The first or foremost pair of shrouds each side, has a sister-block seized in them for the topsail lifts and reef-tackles, and the foremost shroud on each side is wormed, parcelled, and served all the way down.

Q. How do you send up and place the topmast stays, fore, main, and mizen over the topmast-head, and how are they set up?

A. *For the Fore or Main.*—The stays are placed one on top of the other, seized together in the crutch, and two seizings are put on each side of the collar; if the jib-stay is fitted to secure at the masthead and set up on the forecastle, all three stays can be sent up together, the jib-stay upper-most; the gantlines are sent down before all, and bent to the crutch of the stays and stopped to the collars, swayed up, and when the seizing on the collars are up to the gant-line-blocks they are cut, and the eyes are lashed abaft the topmast rigging with a rose-seizing.

The legs of the collar of the jib-stay are passed down through the collars of the fore-topmast stays, and lashed in a similar way to the topmast stay abaft all, and below them. It takes it more clear of the foot of the fore top-gallant sail, and brings less strain on the topmast-head.

In large ships, where the stays are heavy, it is the best plan to send them up by a top-Burton, which is hooked to a strop round the fork of the stays.

The starboard stay is always the upper stay.

The fore-topmast stays are rove through the sheaves in the bees of the bowsprit, through holes in the spritsail gaff, and set up in the head, the port or inner stay having previously been rove through hanks for the topmast-staysail.

Main Topmast-stays.

In all screw ships they both lead through iron-bound clump blocks, shackled to the bolts at the foremast-head above the rigging, high enough to clear the peak of the gaff-foresail, and are set up to iron-bound hearts in the deck. Paddlewheel steamers have but one stay that reeves through the fore cap, and sets up to a collar under the third pair of shrouds.

The mizen topmast stays set up to a thimble, stropped round the eyes of the main shrouds ; in screw ships there is an iron-bound clump-block above the rigging, similar to the main topmast-stays.

In sailing ships, the upper main topmast-stay leads over a chock between the fore tressletrees ; the lower one leads through a clump-block bolted through the foremast, under the top ; both are set up to iron-bound hearts in the deck.

Q. How do you set up topmast rigging?

A. A top-Burton and runner are used for this purpose. The double block of the Burton is hooked to the Burton-pendant, and the single block to a thimble in the end of the runner ; the other end of the runner is secured round the shroud that is to be set up, about 10 ft. above the top, or as high up as the length of the runner will allow with two round turns, and the end is dogged round with the lay of the rope and stopped.

The end of the lanyard is rove through the thimble, in the crown of the runner-block.

A sheet-bend is formed round the neck of the strop, in which a belaying pin, or any round piece of wood is inserted, to prevent it from jambing.

The end of the Burton fall is led on deck, where it is worked.

If a hook were substituted in the crown of the runner-block, instead of the thimble, a boatswain's toggle could be used for setting up topmast rigging, the same as lower rigging, by which much time would be saved.

Q. How are topmast-stays turned in?

A. On end, with the end parts in amidships. Hearts are generally used by the dockyard riggers in large ships, and in small vessels, thimbles. For neatness in large ships, deadeyes are frequently substituted for hearts.

Q. How are the lanyards for topmast-stays rove?

A. If dead-eyes are used in a similar way to lower or topmast rigging, the end is secured by a Matthew Walker knot in the upper dead-eyes. If hearts are used, the standing part of the lanyard is spliced in the bolt in the deck, to which the lower heart is secured. If thimbles, the standing-part of the lanyard is spliced in the timble in the stay.

Q. What purchases are used for setting topmast-stays up, and how are they applied?

A. Luff upon luff.

Q. How do you rig a topgallant and royalmast?

A. Topgallant rigging is placed over a funnel, which is made of copper to fit above the hounds of the topgallant-mast; being of a smooth surface, it does not chafe the eyes of the rigging.

To rig a Fore Topgallant Funnel.

Send the gantlines down before all, and make it fast to the stays, about 6 ft. below the funnel, stop it to the funnel; pull up on the gantline, and place the funnel over the hole in the topmast cap, in readiness to receive the topgallant-mast, stop the stays to the crosstrees; send the gantlines down abaft the top for the starboard pair of shrouds, place them over the funnel, then send the port pair of shrouds up and place them; then the starboard pair of backstays, then the port pair of backstays and place them.

The main and mizen topgallant-masts are rigged in a similar way, with the omission of a flying jibstay.

Main and mizen royalstays are now rove through sheaves in the after-part of the fore and main topmast crosstrees. Iron jacks, or arms, are also fitted to the lower rim of topgallant funnels. The fore has six; the main five, and the mizen two. On the fore the blocks for the flying-jib halyards, fore topgallant-buntlines, and the topgallant studding-sail-halyard, are shackled to the four foremost ones, Jacob's ladder being shackled to the two after ones. On the three foremost lugs of the main, the main topgallant-buntlines, and topgallant studdingsail halyard-blocks, are shackled, Jacob's ladder to the two after ones. The mizen Jacob's ladder is shackled to the two lugs which are on the after part of the funnel.

Royal Funnels.

A royal funnel is made of copper, and similar in shape to a topgallant funnel.

A false royal masthead is fitted to go far enough down the funnel to be secured by screws; it is in every way the shape of the royal masthead, fitted with the lightning conductor, and a hole for the spindle.

Place the royalstays and backstays on the funnel, reeve the signal halyards and put the truck on. Send it up, and place it over the topgallant funnel, ready to ship on the head of the mast.

Sway on the mast-rope, when the head of the mast is through the topgallant funnel, place the royal funnel and truck, and reeve the royal halyards ; when the mast is high enough, settle the topgallant funnel down in its place, and when the sheave is above the cap, reeve the topgallant yard-rope : shackle the span-blocks for topgallant studding-sail halyards and Jacob's ladder, abaft all to the jacks attached to the funnel. The spindle goes with a screw into the false masthead.

N.B.—In most cases the flying-jib halyards block-strop is worked round the chafing grommet when the funnel is not fitted with jacks.

A fore topgallant stay is rove through the dumb-sheave in the jib-boom end, through the dolphin-striker, and set up to one of the knight-heads.

The main and mizen are led through a hole in the lower caps, and set up, the mizen in the main, and the main in the fore top.

The fore royalstay is rove through the dumb-sheave in the flying jib-boom end, through the lower part of the dolphin-striker, and like the topgallant stay, is set up to one of the knight-heads.

The main and mizen are rove through a sheave in the after part of the main and fore-topmast crosstrees, and set up to a thimble secured to the eyes of the lower rigging, the mizen in the main, and the main in the foretop.

The rope to be used for the ratlines should be well stretched. Before commencing to rattle-down, put two swifters on each side, and slightly frap the shrouds together in a fore and aft line, mark the foremost shroud all the way up 15 ins. apart for the foremast eye of each rattling, then place spars about 5 ft. apart, parallel with the sheer pole, all the spare ends of spars should be aft, otherwise they will interfere with lower yards and sails going up; the two lower ratlines are of larger rope than the others, and sufficiently strong to bear the weight of the number of men who crowd there at the order "man the rigging," waiting for orders to go aloft; great care should be taken that the marline-spikes in use for rattling-down should be fitted with lanyards, and either worn round the neck of the man at work, or hitched round the shroud. In sparring and rattling the rigging, commence from below, thus insuring both being placed horizontally; ratlines are clove-hitched on the intervening shrouds, and seized to the foremost and after one but one. Every fifth ratline is taken to the after-shroud, which is called a catch ratline.

To Rattle-Down.

Splice a small eye in one end, hitch your rattling stuff round the third shroud from aft, then round each shroud in succession, taking care the hitches are all formed the same way; lower part of hitch aft, seize the eye to the foremost shroud with two-yarn nettle-stuff, with about 3 in. drift, after the hitches are all hove taut round the shrouds, splice an eye in the other end, and seize it, in a similar way to the fore, to the after shroud but one; if a catch ratline, to the after shroud: every man should be furnished with a thin batten, 14½ ins. long, to measure between the ratlines, that they may be all square with the sheer pole; the batten should be held perpendicularly between the ratlines, and not with a rake, the same as the after shroud, which are four or five feet longer than the foremost shrouds ; when all the ratlines are in place, ease up the frapping.

Securing Spars for Sparring Down.

Light spars are lashed in the rigging about 5 ft. apart and flush the foremost end with the foremast shroud.

In a well ordered ship, a special set of spars are kept for this purpose, being cut to the proper length ; those for the fore being white, the main, red, and the mizen, blue.

Commander.

A large wooden mallet kept in the top.

LIFE BUOYS, AND THEIR USE.

There are two descriptions of life buoys supplied to Her Majesty's ships.

Kisbie's Life Buoy

Is a small circular buoy, fitted with beckets round it, to hang on by when there is more than one person floating by it.

These buoys are distributed round the upper deck of a ship, hung in conspicuous places, ready for use at the shortest notice.

At the alarm being given of a man overboard, one of these buoys is immediately thrown to his relief.

Care should be taken not to throw it at random, or in a wild way, merely for the sake of pitching it overboard, without any regard to the position of the man in the water.

First ascertain where the man is, and then throw it as near him as possible. If he has fallen from forward, by running aft you will, in all probability, be able to throw it in advance of the man in the water, and be the means of saving him.

The best position for one man to keep himself afloat by a Kisbie's life buoy, is to slip it over his head, and rest his arms over it on either side ; in this position, by keeping himself perfectly steady, he will float for any length of time until a boat can be sent to pick him up.

The Service Life Buoy

Is floated by two large copper balls, and is supposed to be capable of keeping four men afloat.

It is attached to a ship's stern by means of a slip, which is disconnected by pulling a trigger, when the buoy is immediately freed, and falls into the water, clear.

At night the same trigger fires a friction tube, which ignites a fuse that exhibits a blue light, and burns from fifteen to twenty minutes, thus marking the position of the buoy.

The buoy is primed every night at sunset, the tube being removed again at sunrise.

Great coolness and caution is required to float on this buoy. As soon as you get hold of the buoy, place your feet on the balancing plate, grasping the buoy above the balls with your left hand, and the up and down rod above again with your right hand, to keep it from striking you on your head by the quick motion the sea invariably gives one of these buoys.

In this position you will float with your head well out of the water.

Some men get frightened, and endeavour to raise themselves higher up the buoy, which is certain to overbalance it, and throw them headlong into the water again.

A sentry is constantly stationed by this buoy at sea.

LOG LINE.—LOG SHIP.

Q. Describe a log line ?

A. The first part of the line is called stray line; a piece of buntin marks the end of the stray line; the marking of the line commences from the piece of buntin, and is equally divided into parts, called knots and half-knots, and is marked thus :—47 ft. 3 ins. from the buntin which terminates the stray line, a piece of leather is put, which denotes the first knot or mile; thus at every 47 ft. 3 ins., knots are put to denote the number of miles or knots, from two knots up to the required number, the line being marked according to the highest rate of speed the ship is expected to go; between every knot there is what is termed a half-knot, which is a single knot.

Q. How does the log line so marked denote the speed of a ship?

A. Two log glasses are used in conjunction with the log line, called the long and short log glasses. The long glass is a 28-sec. and the short one a 14-sec. glass.

The long glass is used when the ship is supposed to be going less than five knots through the water, and the short glass when her speed is greater.

The division of knots on the log line bears the same proportion to a nautical mile as the log glasses do to an hour.

For example—If the long glass is being used, and three knots run out, the ship is going at the rate of three knots an hour; if the short glass is being used, she is going six knots an hour; if the one knot between the three and four knots with the short glass, it will denote that the ship is going seven knots; if the long glass, three and a half knots.

Q. What is the use of stray line, and what length ought it to be?

A. It takes the log ship out of the influence of the eddy water in the ship's wake, and also allows it to get a good hold of the water, before the whole of the stray line is out, and the marking of the ship's way through the water is begun.

The length of the line should be rather more than the length of the ship.

Q. How is a log ship attached to a log line?

A. By three pieces of line called legs, two being spliced into the log line, the end of the log line forming the third. There are three holes in the log ship; one in the upper or pointed part, the other two at the opposite extremes of the log ship, just above the circular part; through one of these, and the hole in the upper part, two of the legs are rove and knotted to keep them in place, the other leg has a peg of hard wood or bone spliced in it, and when the log ship is in use, it is put into the remaining hole of the log ship. When the log ship is thrown into the water, being slung in this way, it swims in an upright position, the lower, or arc part, being weighted, catches the water and remains stationary, and as the ship moves ahead away from it, the line which is kept on a reel runs out, the reel being held in a position to facilitate its movements.

A knot is divided into ten parts, but not so marked on the line, the person heaving the log judging according to the length of line out. For instance, a ship is said to be going 4 and 2, 4 and 6, 4 and 8, according to the length of line run out between the knot and half-knot.

Q. How is the log hove?

A. The person that heaves the log stands as near the lee quarter as possible, inserts the peg in the hole of the log ship, takes several fakes of the line in one hand, to insure sufficient slack line to allow the log ship to fall clear into the water, holding the log ship in the other, sees the reel is held in a good position, and then asks the question, " Is the glass clear ? " which is answered by the person holding the glass (which is generally the quartermaster of the watch), " a clear glass."

The log ship is then dropped into the water and floats astern, care being taken that the line is not checked; when the piece of bunting marking the stray line passes through the hand of the person heaving the log, or over the quarter, he calls out " turn," which is answered by the person holding the glass saying " turn," attending the line that it runs out freely, occasionally assisting it by a slight tug.

The person holding the glass, when all the sand has run out, calls out " stop," when the line is instantly checked, and the nearest knot is looked for, which denotes the rate the ship is going.

Directly a strain is brought on the line, the peg slips out, and the log ship floats on its flat in the water, in which position it offers no resistance, and is easily hauled in.

Should the peg stick fast in the hole, it is very difficult to haul the log ship in, and it often carries the line away ; therefore care should be taken not to jamb the peg in too tightly.

Q. Who heaves the log ?

A. The midshipman of the watch.

Q. How often is it hove ?

A. Every hour, and the result noted in the log book.

Q. What difference is there between a nautical and a land mile ?

A. A nautical mile contains 2027 yards, whereas a land mile is only 1760 yards.

Q. What is the cause of this difference ?

A. A land mile is measured without any reference to the size of the earth.

A nautical mile is the number of yards contained in the circumference of the earth at the equator, divided by 21·600 (360° × 60), the number of minutes in a circle, or the sixtieth part of a degree on the equator.

Patent Log.

Q. Is there any other mode of finding out the speed of a ship, or the distance run by her in any given time ?

A. Yes; Massey's patent log, which is considered the most accurate way of measuring the distance run by a ship.

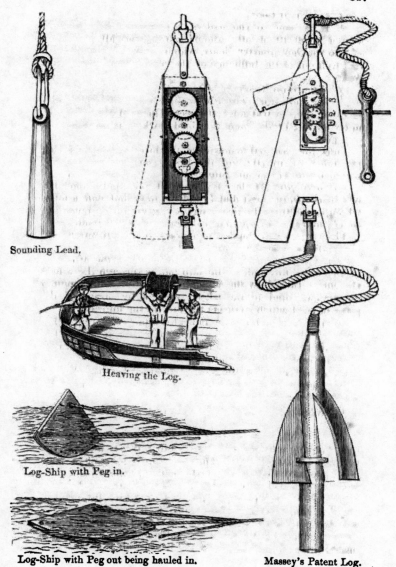

Sounding Lead.

Heaving the Log.

Log-Ship with Peg in.

Log-Ship with Peg out being hauled in.

Massey's Patent Log.

Q. How is it used?

A. It is bent to the end of a deep-sea lead line, and veered about 40 or 50 fathoms astern, generally from one of the weather quarter boats, which takes it to windward, and well out of the influence of the eddy water in the ship's wake.

Q. What does it consist of?

A. An indicator, with three dials, one marked in divisions of 10 up to 100 miles, the second marked in divisions of miles up to 10 miles, and the third marked in four quarters of a mile.

Thus the last dial denotes the quarters: the second dial, the miles up to 10; and the first shows the 10; that is, whether it is 47½ or 56¾ miles.

For example—If the ship has run 47½ miles, one dial will mark 40, the next dial 7, and the next dial half a mile, which, by adding the three together, gives the distance run as 47½ miles, so on up to any distance under 110 miles.

The log is usually hauled in at the end of each watch, and the result registered in the ship's log book.

A fan is attached by a piece of cord to the after end of the indicator, and, as the ship moves through the water, the fan is turned by the action of the water, which motion is communicated to the wheel, worked by means of the piece of cord which connects the face to the indicator.

On the fore end of the indicator a piece of iron rod is attached also by means of a piece of cord; just abaft the hole for the cord are two iron studs through the iron rod, crossing each other at right angles.

In the after end of the rod is a hole for bending the end of the deep-sea lead line to, which is bent in a similar way that it is bent to the becket of a lead.

Q. What advantage has the patent log over the common log?

A. Very often the wind is uncertain: at one part of the hour blowing a fresh breeze, at another nearly a calm; the common log merely shows what the ship is going at the time it is hove, and the officer of the watch judges what in his opinion the ship has really made, which of course is liable to error, whereas the patent log shows the exact distance the ship has run, whether it has blown fresh one part, and the ship has gone at the rate of ten knots, and at another part of the watch it has been nearly a calm, and she has scarcely moved through the water, still the true result is shown.

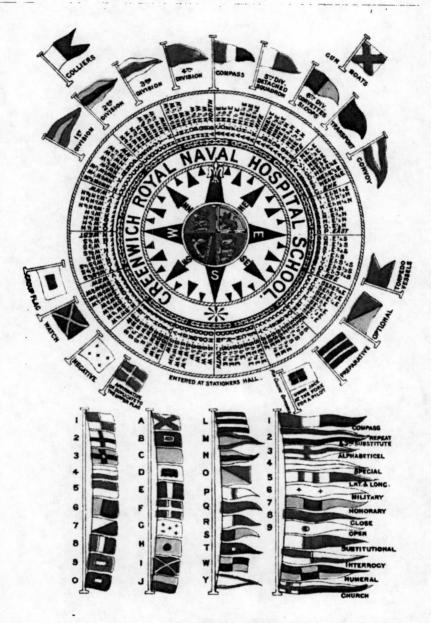

DANGERFIELD, LITH. 22, BEDFORD S! COVENT GARDEN

FLAGS OF THE COMMERCIAL CODE OF SIGNALS (Universal Series)

EXAMPLES.

Two Flag Signals, having,

Three Flag Signals are General.

Four Flag Signals having.

DISTINGUISHING JACKS, NATIONAL FLAGS, &c.

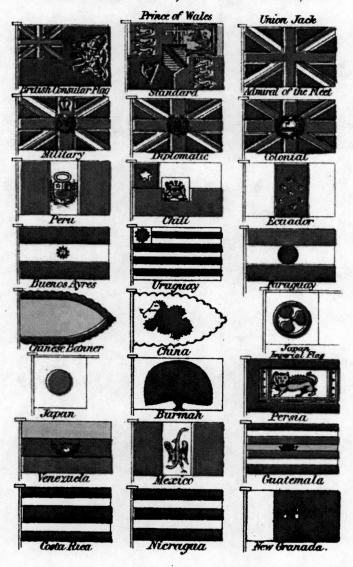

Prince of Wales
Union Jack
British Consular Flag
Standard
Admiral of the Fleet
Military
Diplomatic
Colonial
Peru
Chili
Ecuador
Buenos Ayres
Uraguay
Paraguay
Chinese Banner
China
Japan Imperial Flag
Japan
Burmah
Persia
Venezuela
Mexico
Guatemala
Costa Rica
Nicragua
New Granada.

DANGERFIELD. LITH. 22, BEDFORD S.ᵗ COVENT GARDEN

FLAGS
OF THE
PRINCIPAL MARITIME NATIONS.

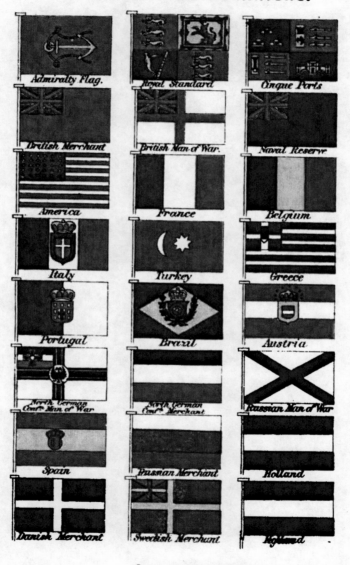

DANGERFIELD. LITH 22. BEDFORD S? COVENT GARDEN

COLOMB'S FLASHING SIGNALS.

COMPASS TABLE.

When a Compass Signal is made by itself it signifies that the Admiral intends to steer that course.

11.	N. by E.	27.	S. by W.
12.	N.N.E.	28.	S.S.W.
13.	N.E. by N.	29.	S.W. by S.
14.	N.E.	30.	S.W.
15.	N.E. by E.	31.	S.W. by W.
16.	E.N.E.	32.	W.S.W.
17.	E. by N.	33.	W. by S.
18.	East.	34.	West.
19.	E. by S.	35.	W. by N.
20.	E.S.E.	36.	W.N.W.
21.	S.E. by E.	37.	N.W. by W.
22.	S.E.	38.	N.W.
23.	S.E. by S.	39.	N.W. by N.
24.	S.S.E.	40.	N.N.W.
25.	S. by E.	41.	N. by W.
26.	South.	42.	North.

Quarter points are denoted by the figures 1, 2, and 3.
Thus "Comp." 232 = S.E. by S. ½ S.

HORARY TABLE.

11.	1 P.M.	23.	1 A.M.
12.	2 "	24.	2 "
13.	3 "	25.	3 "
14.	4 "	26.	4 "
15.	5 "	27.	5 "
16.	6 "	28.	6 "
17.	7 "	29.	7 "
18.	8 "	30.	8 "
19.	9 "	31.	9 "
20.	10 "	32.	10 "
21.	11 "	33.	11 "
22.	12 Midnight.	34.	12 Noon.

Minutes are denoted by their proper figures.

Thus " Hor." 2135 = 35 minutes past 11, P.M.

Seconds must be made separately.

COLOMB'S FLASHING SIGNALS.

To be answered and repeated the same as Flag Signals by day unless ordered to the contrary.

All Signals made to a single Ship, Division, or Squadron, to commence and *end* with their Pendants.

Care to be taken in trimming the lamps, not to spread the wicks.

The "Distant Signals" of Ships to be used with the "List of the Navy" Pendant.

"Starboard Division" is denoted by "Pendants" 1.

"Port Division" by "Pendants" 2.

TABLE OF FLASHES FOR ALL SIGNAL BOOKS.

1   6
2   7
3   8
4   9
5   0   &c.

Preparative &c.
Finish or Stop &c.
General Answer

NOTE.—Two descriptions of flashes are used, the short and the long, the former being about half a second in duration, and the latter about a second and a half.

NAVAL SIGNAL BOOKS.	FLASHES.	ALPHABET,					
Compass · · ·		A 5					
Pendants · · ·		B 6	C 7	D 8	E 9	F 10	
Numeral · · ·		G 11	H 12	I 13	J 14	K 15	
Geographical ·		L 16	M 17	N 18	O 19	P 20	
Horary · · ·		Q 21	R 22	S 23	T 24	U 25	
Interrogative ·		V 26	W 27	X 28	Y 29	Z 30	
Negative · · ·							
List of Navy · ·							
Alphabet · · ·							

DISTANT SIGNALS.

The Distant Signals are made with Square Flags, Triangular Flags, and Pendants, without any regard to their colour, and may be used as substitutes for the Numeral Flags when the distance is too great to make them out. Care is to be taken that all other Flags and Ensigns are hauled down when the Distant Signals are used.

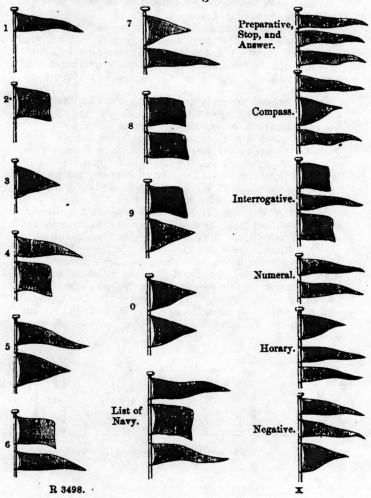

R 3498.

The distinctive mark of a Distant Signal is three Pendants hoisted together, which is used as a " Preparative," " Stop," and " Answer."

Three Pendants at the Main Truck denotes that the Distant Signals will be used by the Ship which hoist them; when hoisted after any of the Symbols have been shown, they denote that the number of the Signal terminates there.

When hoisted in reply to a Distant Signal, it is an affirmative answer to that Signal.

Two Pendants over a Triangular Flag is the negative answer, and also annuls the accompanying Signal, a Signal just previously made, or one which will immediately follow.

A Pendant between two Square Flags is interrogative of the accompanying Signal, or one which is to follow immediately.

When hoisted in reply to an ordinary Flag Signal, it signifies that the Flags cannot be made out, and that the purport must be communicated by Distant Signal.

. If a Distant Signal consists of two hoists (at the same Masthead) between the displays of the three Pendants, the first hoist represents Tens, and the second Units.

If the Signal consists of three hoists between the displays of three Pendants, the first hoist represents Hundreds, the second Tens, and the third Units.

If the Signal consists of four hoists between the displays of the Pendants, the first will represent Thousands, the second Hundreds, the third Tens, and the fourth Units.

When these Signals are made from the same Masthead, each figure must of course be expressed by a separate and distinct hoisting of the Symbols; but when it may be possible to show the numbers of a Signal together, by hoisting them at different places, they are to be displayed and read in the usual order, as given in Art. XII. of the " Instructions Relating to Signals," as in the following example :—

Means 123.   Means also 123.   Means 61.   Means also 61.

A Ship using the Distant Signals should endeavour to place herself broadside to the point addressed, and should, if possible, hoist the whole of the Signal at once at the different Mastheads.

If this is not practicable, the Signalling must commence with the display of three Pendants as a preparative, and when answered the rest of the Signal is to follow in order.

If a particular Ship is addressed, the Compass Signal, denoting her bearing from the Ship making the Signal, must first be displayed.

As Signal Flags can only be depended upon when their colours are distinctly visible, an important opportunity of communicating at sea is often lost because distance or haze prevents the Signal from being made out.

A Code of Distant Signals has therefore been introduced into the Commercial Code Signal Book, with the view of supplying what is obviously a defect in existing Codes.

The practice of making Distant Signals, with the combination of a Ball with Flags, is of very old date, and the plan may be found in obsolete Signal Books as well as in the Admiralty Codes.

Whilst, therefore, there is nothing new in the method now introduced, as regards the Symbols employed, the design has been to adapt in the simplest way the use of these Symbols to the Commercial Code of Signals, adhering, at the same time, as nearly as possible to the principles originally laid down by the Signal Committee of 1855.

Hence the characteristic of the Distant Signal is the Ball; one Ball at least appearing in every hoist of the Distant Code. With respect to the two other Symbols, they may be Pendants or Flags of any colour; that is to say, any of the Code Pendants or Code Flags may be employed irrespective of their colour. It will be seen from the Plate of Distant Signals, that the Code has been so arranged as to give the least possible trouble in finding the combination required; thus—

The first column contains all the combinations having the Ball or Balls first or uppermost in the hoist.

The second column contains all the combinations having the Ball or Balls second or separated in the hoist.

The third column contains all the combinations having the Ball or Balls last or lowermost in the hoist.

x 2

SIGNIFICATIONS OF THE DISTANT SIGNALS WHEN MADE SINGLY, WHICH WILL BE INDICATED BY "STOP" FOLLOWING EACH HOIST.

B. Asks name of Ship or Signal Station in sight.
C. Yes.
D. No.
F. Repeat Signal, or hoist it in a more conspicuous place.
G. Cannot distinguish your Flags, come nearer or make Distant Signals.
H. You may communicate by the Semaphore, if you please.
J. Stop, or bring to. Something important to communicate.
K. Have you any Telegrams or Dispatches for me.
L. Want a Pilot ; can I have one ?
M. Want a Tug ; can I have one ?
N. What is the Meteorological Weather Forecast ?
P. Calls attention of Signal Station in sight.
Q. Vessels asks for orders by Telegraph from Owner, Mr. ——, at ——.
R. Report me by Telegraph to my Owner, Mr. ——, at ——.
S. Send the following message by Telegraph.
T. Send the following message, by the Signal Letters, through the Telegraph.
V. ———————————————.
W. ———————————————

The following table shows the Morse Alphabet arranged for instruction :—

MORSE ALPHABET.

E	T	
I	M	
S	O	
	H	
A	N	
U	D	
V	B	
W	G	
	C	

R ▪ ━ ▪ ▪
L ▪ ━ ▪ ▪
F ▪ ▪ ━ ▪
P ▪ ━ ━ ▪

K ━ ▪ ━
Y ━ ▪ ━ ━
Q ━ ━ ▪ ━
X ━ ▪ ▪ ━

J ▪ ━ ━ ━
Z ━ ━ ▪ ▪

A ▪ ━
B ━ ▪ ▪ ▪
C ━ ▪ ━ ▪
D ━ ▪ ▪
E ▪
F ▪ ▪ ━ ▪
G ━ ━ ▪
H ▪ ▪ ▪ ▪
I ▪ ▪
J ▪ ━ ━ ━
K ━ ▪ ━
L ▪ ━ ▪ ▪
M ━ ━

N ━ ▪
O ━ ━ ━
P ▪ ━ ━ ▪
Q ━ ━ ▪ ━
R ▪ ━ ▪
S ▪ ▪ ▪
T ━
U ▪ ▪ ━
V ▪ ▪ ▪ ━
W ▪ ━ ━
X ━ ▪ ▪ ━
Y ━ ▪ ━ ━
Z ━ ━ ▪ ▪

MARKS OF PUNCTUATION.

Comma (,), ▪ ━ ▪ ━ ▪ ━   A A A
Full stop (.), ▪ ▪ ▪ ▪ ▪ ▪   I I I

MISCELLANEOUS SIGNALS.

Preparative and erasure, ▪ ▪ ▪ ▪ ▪ ▪ ▪ ▪ ▪ ▪, &c.
(A continued succession of dots.)
Stop, ━ ━ ━ ━ ━ ━ ━, &c.
(A continued succession of dashes.)
General answer, ━ ━ ━ ━, &c.
(A continued succession of prolonged dashes.)
Station sign, ▪ ━ ━ ▪ ▪   P
Repeat, ▪ ▪ ━ ━ ▪ ▪
Right, ▪ ━ ▪ ━   R T
Cipher, ━ ▪ ━ ▪ ▪ ▪ ━ ▪ ━   C C
Numerical sign, ━ ━ ▪ ▪ ━   Z
Signaller's indicator, ▪ ━ ▪ ━
Obliterator, ▪ ━ ━ ▪ ━ ▪ ▪ ━ ▪

EXPLANATION OF MISCELLANEOUS SIGNALS.

■■■■■■■■■■■■, &c. The PREPARATIVE SIGN is used
when communicating with two or more stations in sight to call
their attention before sending a message. It is also used to call
the attention of an unknown station. To acknowledge this sign
the receiving station should give, instead of the " General Answer," its distinguishing letter or letters (without the prefix P),
and repeat this till the next signal is begun.

This sign is also the ERASURE SIGNAL. It is used to erase a
word or group that has been wrongly sent. It should in this case
be answered by the ERASURE.

▬▬ ▬▬ ▬▬ ▬▬ ▬▬ ▬▬ ▬▬, &c. The STOP denotes the
end of a message when sending to two or more stations and no
distinguishing signal has commenced it.

▬▬ ▬▬ ▬▬ ▬▬, &c. The GENERAL ANSWER is the
acknowledgment that a word or group is seen and understood.
This series of prolonged dashes is to be continued until the first
letter of the next word or group is called out by the man reading.

P .
▬ ▬▬ ▬▬ ■. The STATION SIGN followed by a letter is the
DISTINGUISHING SIGNAL or CALL SIGNAL of the station.

SEMAPHORES.

The Semaphores, or Signal Stations, established on the
coast of France, have, wherever practicable, the means of
intercommunication by Electro-Telegraphic Wires with each
other, and with the chief Metropolitan, Provincial, and
Foreign Telegraph Stations.

By the method hereafter described, passing vessels will
be able to exchange communication with these Semaphores,
and their messages will be received, and, if required, forwarded to their destination according to the established
Tariff of Rates.

Although at present there are no similar facilities of communication placed at the Service of Shipping frequenting
the coast of the United Kingdom, it is believed that should
Signal Stations be hereafter established, the French system
affords the simplest means of Signalling by Semaphore
between the shore and Ships in the offing, at a distance
whence the colours of Flags would not be distinguish-
able.

At a moderate distance the Signal Flags of the Code can,
of course, be used by both Ships and Signal Stations, but

the Distant Signals should on all occasions be employed by Ships when it is found that. the Code Flags cannot be made out.

The Semaphores are furnished with three Arms. When at rest the Arms are not visible. When at work the position of the Arms in the three directions, indicated in the Plate, represents respectively the three Symbols used in the Distant Signal Code.

The Semaphore Signals will consequently be always read off as Distant Signals, the position or direction of the Arms indicating respectively the Pendant, the Ball or the Flag.

ADAPTATION OF THE FRENCH SEMAPHORIC SYSTEM TO THE COMMERCIAL CODE FOR MAKING DISTANT SIGNALS.

N.B.—*The Disc at the top of the mast remains in the position indicated below whilst Signals are being made by this Code.*

The Arm pointing downwards represents a Pendant.

The Arm in the horizontal position represents a Ball.

The Arm pointing upwards represents a Square Flag.

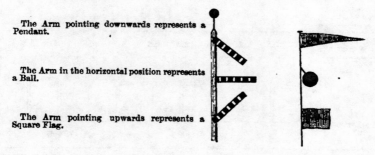

EXAMPLES.

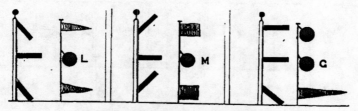

L.M.G.   Bar or Entrance is Dangerous.

SEMAPHORIC SIGNS,

APPLIED TO THE CHARACTERS OF THE SIGNAL FLAGS IN THE VOCABULARY.

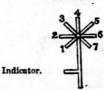

Indicator.

Positions of the Arms.	1	2	3	4	5	6	7	1.2	1.3	1.4	1.5
Application to the Vocabulary.	A	B	C	D	E	F	G	H	I & J	K	L
Numerical Application.	1	2	3	4	5	6	7		9	0	

Positions of the Arms.	1.6	1.7	2.3	2.4	2.5	2.6	2.7	3.4	3.5	3.6
Application to the Vocabulary.	M	N	O	P	Q & X	R	S & Z	T	U V W	Y

Positions of the Arms.	3.7	4.5	4.6	4.7	5.6	5.7	6.7	Indicator.
	Annul.	Numeral.	Alphabet.	Special.		Ships' Names.		Preparative, and when taken in denotes the Finish.

ALPHABET FOR SEMAPHORE SIGNALS.

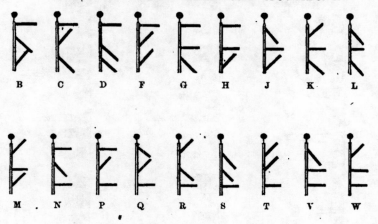

B   C   D   F   G   H   J   K   L

M   N   P   Q   R   S   T   V   W

ALPHABET FOR COMPOSING DISTANT SIGNALS USED IN CONNEXION WITH THE COMMERCIAL CODE OF SIGNALS BY MERCHANT SHIPS.

In addition to the examples on previous page, the following Distant Signals composed of two Symbols have the special signification indicated beneath.

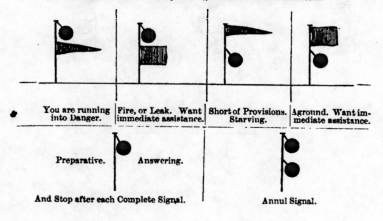

| You are running into Danger. | Fire, or Leak. Want immediate assistance. | Short of Provisions. Starving. | Aground. Want immediate assistance. |

Preparative.   Answering.

And Stop after each Complete Signal.   Annul Signal.

WEIGHTS AND MEASURES.
Division of the Circle.

60 Seconds	1	Minute.
60 Minutes	1	Degree.
360 Degrees	1	Circumference.
4 Minutes of Time	= 1	Degree of Longitude.
15 Degrees	= 1	Hour.

Time.

60 Seconds	1	Minute.
60 Minutes	1	Hour.
24 Hours	1	Mean Solar Day.
7 Days	1	Week.
28 Days	1	Lunar Month.
12 Calendar Months (365 Days)	1	Civil Year.
365 Days, 5 Hours, 48 Minutes, 47·6352 Seconds	1	Solar Year.

Money.

4 Farthings... 1 Penny.	20 Shillings .... 1 Pound.
12 Pence...... 1 Shilling.	21 Shillings .... 1 Guinea.

NOTE.—

		dwts.	grs.	
A Sovereign	weighs	5	$3\frac{171}{623}$	Troy.
A Half-Sovereign	—	2	$13\frac{397}{623}$	—
A Crown	—	18	$4\frac{4}{11}$	—
A Half-Crown	—	9	$2\frac{2}{11}$	—
A Shilling	—	3	$15\frac{3}{11}$	—
A Sixpence	—	1	$19\frac{7}{11}$	—
A Fourpenny Piece	—	1	$5\frac{1}{11}$	—
A Threepenny Piece	—	0	$21\frac{9}{11}$	—

WEIGHTS.
*Troy.**

24 Grains	1	Pennyweight.
20 Pennyweights	1	Ounce.
12 Ounces	1	Pound.

* Used for the precious metals and in Philosophical experiments. Diamonds and other precious stones are weighed by carats of $3\frac{1}{6}$ grs. $151\frac{1}{2}$ carats are equal to an ounce Troy.

NOTE.—By an Act of Parliament (5 George IV., c. 74). it was enjoined that the standard of weight for the Kingdom should henceforward be the Imperial pound Troy of 5760 grs., and that in case the standard should be lost or injured, it might be recovered from the knowledge of the fact that a cubic inch of distilled water, at a temperature of 62° Fahrenheit, and when the barometer is at 30 in., weighs 252·458 of these grains.

Avoirdupois.*

27·34375 Troy Grains...............	1 Drachm.
16 Drachms......................	1 Ounce.
16 Ounces	1 Pound.
14 Pounds	1 Stone.
28 Pounds	1 Quarter.
4 Quarters	1 Hundredweight.
20 Hundredweight	1 Ton.

* Used for all ordinary Goods.

NOTE.—By the before-mentioned Act it is provided that the Pound Avoirdupois shall consist of 7000 Grains Troy.

Apothecaries.

20 Grains	1 Scruple.
3 Scruples............................	1 Drachm.
8 Drachms	1 Ounce.
12 Ounces.............................	1 Pound.

By this Weight only, Apothecaries compound their Medicines; but Drugs are bought and sold by Avoirdupois Weight.

NOTE.—The Grain, Ounce, and Pound are the same as in Troy Weight.

480 Minims, or Drops	= 1 Fluid Ounce.
20 Ounces...............	= 1 Pint.
8 Pints ι...............	= 1 Gallon.
8760 Grains of Distilled Water	= 1 Imperial Pint.
437·5 Ditto Ditto	= 1 Imperial Fluid Ounce.

MEASURES.

Wine Measure.

4 Gills	1 Pint.
2 Pints.............................	1 Quart.
4 Quarts	1 Gallon.
10 Gallons..........................	1 Anker.
18 Gallons..........................	1 Runlet.
42 Gallons..........................	1 Tierce.
63 Gallons..........................	1 Hogshead.
84 Gallons..........................	1 Puncheon.
126 Gallons..........................	1 Pipe.
252 Gallons	1 Tun.

Ale Measure.

4	Gills	1 Pint.
2	Pints	1 Quart.
4	Quarts	1 Gallon.
9	Gallons	1 Firkin.
18	Gallons	1 Kilderkin.
36	Gallons	1 Barrel.
54	Gallons	1 Hogshead.
72	Gallons	1 Puncheon.
108	Gallons	1 Butt.

Dry Measure.

2	Imperial Gallons	1 Peck.
4	Pecks	1 Bushel.
8	Bushels	1 Quarter.
32	Bushels	1 Chaldron.
40	Bushels	1 Wey, or Load.
8	Bushels	1 Last.

Measure of Solidity, or Cubic Measure.

1728	Cubic Inches	⎫
2200	Cylindrical Inches (nearly)	⎬ 1 Cubic Foot.
3300	Spherical Inches (nearly)	
6600	Conical Inches (nearly)	⎭
27	Cubic Feet	1 Cubic Yard.
1357·17	Cubic Inches	1 Cylindrical Foot.
904·78	Cubic Inches	1 Spherical Foot.
459·39	Cubic Inches	1 Conical Foot.

NOTE.—A Cubic Inch is a cube 1 in. square; a Cylindrical Inch is a cylinder 1 in. long and 1 in. in diameter; a Spherical Inch is a sphere 1 in. in diameter; and a Conical Inch is a cone 1 in. in length, and 1 in. in diameter at the base.

Measure of Surface, or Square Measure.

144	Square Inches	1 Square Foot.
9	Square Feet	1 Square Yard.
30¼	Square Yards	1 Square Pole.
40	Square Poles	1 Square Rood.
4	Roods (4840 Sq. Yards)	1 Statute Acre.
640	Acres	1 Square Mile.
6084	Square Yards	1 Scotch Acre.
7840	Square Yards	1 Irish or Plantation Acre.
113·0972	Square Inches	1 Circular Foot.
183·346	Circular Inches	1 Square Foot.

NOTE.—A Circular Foot is a circle whose diameter is One Foot.

Superficial Measure for Land.

62·7264	Square Inches	1 Square Link.
10000	Square Links.............	1 Square Chain.
10	Square Chains............	1 Acre.

Measure of Length.

12	Lines	1 Inch.
12	Inches	1 Foot.
3	Feet	1 Yard.
5½	Yards	1 Pole, Rod, or Perch.
40	Poles	1 Furlong.
8	Furlongs (1760 Yards) ...	1 Mile.
2240	Yards	1 Irish Mile.
14	English Miles	11 Irish Miles.
3	Miles	1 League.

Miscellaneous.

3	Inches	1 Palm.
4	Inches	1 Hand.
9	Inches	1 Span.
18	Inches	1 Cubit.
5	Feet	1 Pace.
6	Feet	1 Fathom.
120	Fathoms (strictly 126¼ fathoms)	1 Cable's Length.
8	Cables' Lengths	1 Nautical Mile.
600	Square Feet of Inch Boards....	1 Load.
40	Cubic Feet of Round Timber ...	} 1 Ton, or Load.
50	Cubic Feet of Hewn Timber ...	
1000	Billets, or	}
8	Cubic Feet, or	} 1 Cord of Wood.
10	Hundredweight	}
108	Cubic Feet.................	1 Stack of Wood.
630	Pounds, or	} 1 Fathom of Wood.
6 ft. × 6 ft. × 2 ft.		}
84	Pounds	1 Bushel of Coals.
2	Hundredweight..............	1 Sack of Coals.
10	Sacks (42 ins. × 30 ins.)	1 Ton of Coals.
53	Hundredweight..............	{ 1 Chaldron of Coal (Newcastle).
112	Pounds....................	1 Sack.
40	Cubic Feet	1 Ton of Shipping.
8	Pounds of Meat or Fish.......	1 Stone.
56	Pounds of Butter	1 Firkin.

250 Pounds of Hops, Kentish...... } 1 Pocket.
112 Pounds of Hops, Surrey & Sussex }
236 Gallons of Sweet Oil .... } 1 Ton.
252 Gallons of Fish .... }

---

1 Acre Scotch, 1·271 Acres English, or 6084 Square Yards.
1 Acre Irish, 1·638 Acres English, or 7840 Square Yards.
1 Barrel, Imperial Measure .... 9981·86 Cubic Inches.
1 Barrel of Soap .... 256 Pounds.
1 Bushel, Imperial Measure.... 2218·19 Cubic Inches.
1 Bushel, Winchester .... 2150·42 Cubic Inches.
1 Bushel of Barley .... 50 Pounds.
1 Bushel of Coal .... 88 Pounds.
1 Bushel of Flour or Salt ...... 56 Pounds.
1 Bushel of Oats .... 40 Pounds.
1 Bushel of Wheat .... 60 Pounds.
1 Chain .... 100 Links.
1 Clove of Wool .... 7 Pounds.
1 Fodder of Lead—Stockton ... 22 Hundredweight.
1 Fodder of Lead—Newcastle .. 21 Hundredweight.
1 Fodder of Lead—London .... 19½ Hundredweight.
1 Gallon, Imperial Measure.... 227·27 Cubic Inches.
1 Gallon of Distilled Water, 60° 10 Pounds.
1 Gallon of Proof Spirit or Oil . 9·3 Pounds.
1 Gallon, former Wine Measure 231 Cubic Inches.
1 Gallon, former Ale Measure .. 283 Cubic Inches.
1 Gallon, Irish Measure .... 217·6 Cubic Inches.
1 League .... 3 Miles.
1 Geographical Mile .... 1·15 English Miles.
1 Geographical Degree .... 69·12 English Miles.
1 Nautical Mile (mean) .... 6075·5 Feet.
1 Gross..................... 12 Dozen.
1 Great Gross .... 12 Gross.
1 Hand...................... 4 Inches.
1 Hundred of Deals........... 120 In Number.
1 Hundred of Nails........... 120 In Number.
1 Hundred of Salt............. 7 Lasts.
1 Last of Salt................. 18 Barrels.
1 Last of Gunpowder .... 24 Barrels.
1 Last of Potash, Soap, Pitch, or
  Tar .... 12 Barrels.
1 Last of Flax or Feathers ..... 17 Hundredweight.
1 Link .... 7·92 Inches.
1 Line .... 1/12th of an Inch.
1 Load of Bricks .... 500 In Number.

1 Cord of Wood..............	128	Cubic Feet.
1 Load of Corn	40	Bushels.
1 Load of Hay or Straw.......	36	Trusses.
1 Load of Lime	32	Bushels.
1 Load of Planks (2-inch)	300	Square Feet.
1 Load of Sand	36	Bushels.
1 Load of Timber (Squared) ...	50	Cubic Feet.
1 Load of Timber (Unhewed) ..	40	Cubic Feet.
1 Mile......................	80	Chains.
1 Pack of Wool	240	Pounds.
1 Palm.....................	3	Inches.
1 Pole—Woodland	18	Feet.
1 Pole—Plantation	21	Feet.
1 Pole—Cheshire.............	24	Feet.
1 Sack of Wool	364	Pounds.
1 Seam of Glass..............	124	Pounds.
1 Cubit.....................	18	Inches.
1 Span	9	Inches.
1 Military Pace..............	5	Feet.

Cloth Measure.

2¼ Inches...........................	1 Nail.
4 Nails	1 Quarter.
4 Quarters	1 Yard.
3 Quarters	1 Flemish Ell.
5 Quarters	1 English Ell.
6 Quarters	1 French Ell.

RELATIVE VALUE OF BRITISH AND FOREIGN WEIGHTS AND MEASURES.

Weights.

French		British.
Gramme..........	15·434	Grains.
Décigramme	1·5434	Grains.
Centigramme.:....	0·15434	Grains.
Milligramme	0·015434	Grains.
Décagramme	154·34	Grains.
Hectogramme	{ 3·527	Ounces Avoirdupois, or
	3·2154	Ounces Troy.
Kilogramme	{ 2·6795	Pounds Troy, or
	2·2048	Pounds Avoirdupois.
Myriagramme	{ 26·795	Pounds Troy, or
	22·048	Pounds Avoirdupois.
Quintal..........	1 Cwt. 3 qrs. 24½ lbs.	
Millier, or Bar ...:	9 Tons 16 cwt. 3 qrs. 12 lbs.	

Measures of Capacity.

Litre*	{ 61·028	Cubic Inches, or
	{ 1·761	Imperial Pints.
Décilitre	6·1928	Cubic Inches.
Centilitre	0·6103	Cubic Inches.
Millilitre.................	0·0610	Cubic Inches.
Décalitre	{ 610·28	Cubic Inches, or
	{ 2·2	Imperial Gallons.
Hectolitre...............	{ 3·5317	Cubic Feet, or
	{ 2·75	Imperial Bushels.
Kilolitre.................	35·317	Cubic Feet.
Myrialitre...............	353·17	Cubic Feet.

* The Litre = a Cubic Décimètre.

Measures of Length.

Mètre	39·371	Inches.
Décimètre	3·9371	Inches.
Centimètre....................	0·39371	Inches.
Millimètre	0·039371	Inches.
Décamètre	32·809	Feet.
Hectomètre	328·09	Feet.
Kilomètre.....................	1093·6	Yards.
Myriamètre	6·2138	Miles.

Measure of Superficies.

Are†	119·60	Square Yards.
Déciare	11·960	Square Yards.
Centiare	10·764	Square Feet.
Milliare....................	155·00	Square Inches.
Décare.....................	1196·0	Square Yards.
Hectare....................	2·4712	Acres.

† The Are = a Square Décimètre.

Measures of Solidity.

Stère‡	35·317	Cubic Feet.
Décistère....................	3·5317	Cubic Feet.
Centistère...................	610·28	Cubic Inches.
Millistère...................	61·028	Cubic Inches.
Décastère	13·080	Cubic Yards.
Hectostère..................	130·80	Cubic Yards.

‡ The Stère = a Cubic Mètre.

NOTE.—The Décimètre, Centimètre, and Millimètre are respectively formed by dividing the Mètre by 10, 100, and 1,000; and the Décamètre, Hectomètre, Kilomètre, and Myriamètre, by multiplying the Mètre by 10, 100, 1,000, and 10,000. The other Measures and Weights of the Decimal System are formed in a like manner from their respective Units.

DATE.		£	s.	d.

DATE.		£	s.	d.

DATE.		£	s.	d.

CPSIA information can be obtained at www.ICGtesting.com
Printed in the USA
LVOW06*1448101213

364711LV00005B/111/P